WHAT'S HAPPENING TO INDIA?

WHAT'S HAPPENING TO INDIA?

Punjab, Ethnic Conflict, and the Test for Federalism

Second Edition

Robin Jeffrey

MACMILLAN

First edition 1986
Second edition 1994

Published by
THE MACMILLAN PRESS LTD
Houndmills, Basingstoke, Hampshire RG21 2XS
and London
Companies and representatives throughout the world

ISBN 0–333–59443–6 hardcover
ISBN 0–333–59444–4 paperback

A catalogue record of this book is available
from the British Library

Printed in Hong Kong

To L. J.
without whom . . .

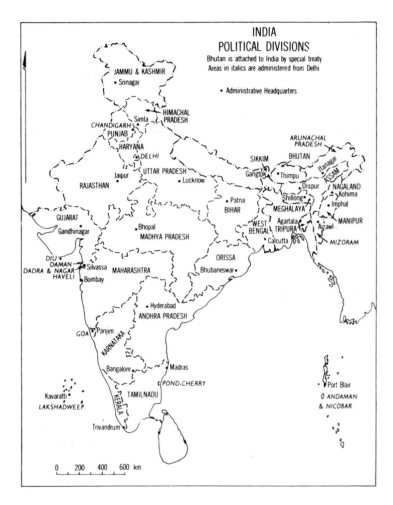

**INDIA
POLITICAL DIVISIONS**

Bhutan is attached to India by special treaty
Areas in italics are administered from Delhi

• Administrative Headquarters

JAMMU & KASHMIR
• Srinagar

HIMACHAL
PRADESH
CHANDIGARH Simla
PUNJAB
HARYANA
DELHI
Jaipur UTTAR PRADESH
RAJASTHAN • Lucknow

ARUNACHAL
PRADESH
SIKKIM BHUTAN Itanagar
Gangtok • Thimpu ASSAM
Dispur NAGALAND
• Patna Shillong • Kohima
BIHAR MEGHALAYA • Imphal
WEST Agartala MANIPUR
BENGAL TRIPURA Aizawl
• Calcutta MIZORAM

GUJARAT
Gandhinagar
• Bhopal
MADHYA PRADESH

ORISSA
• Bhubaneswar

DIU
DAMAN Silvassa
DADRA & NAGAR MAHARASHTRA
HAVELI Bombay

• Hyderabad
ANDHRA PRADESH

GOA Panjim
KARNATAKA
Bangalore • Madras
POND.CHERRY
Kavaratti TAMILNADU
LAKSHADWEEP KERALA

Trivandrum

Port Blair
0 ANDAMAN
& NICOBAR

0 200 400 600 km

MAP 1.1   *India, political divisions, 1985*

Contents

List of Tables and Maps

TABLES

MAPS

Abbreviations

AISSF	All-India Sikh Students' Federation
BJP	Bharatiya Janarta Party
BSF	Border Security Force
CM	Chief Minister
CPI(M)	Communist Party of India (Marxist)
CRP	Central Reserve Police
IPS	India Police Service
LTTE	Liberation Tigers of Tamil Eelam
MLA	Member of the Legislative Assembly
MP	Member of Parliament, the national legislature
OBC	Other Backward Castes
PEPSU	Patiala and East Punjab States' Union, the state, which existed from 1948 to 1956, made up of territories ruled by Indian princes during British times
RSS	Rashtriya Swayamsevak Sangh (Hindu revivalist organisation)
SGPC	Shiromani Gurdwara, Parbandhak Committee, the election committee established in 1925, which oversees Sikh temples.
UP	Uttar Pradesh (northern province); under the British, the United Provinces (same territory in both cases)

Preface to the Second Edition

I am grateful to Ian Dawes for his help in assembling materials to allow me to write the new introduction for this edition and to the School of Social Sciences at La Trobe University for a grant to pay for such research assistance. Dipesh Chakrabarty, John Miller, Talis Polis and Peter Reeves generously read and commented on versions of the new manuscript.

Melbourne
December 1992

ROBIN JEFFERY

Preface to the First Edition

Intended for general readers, but sufficiently well-documented, I hope, to satisfy specialists, this book is an essay in the strict sense – an attempt to work out and explain a problem. In November 1984, in the days after Mrs Gandhi's assassination, I heard the question, 'What's happening to India?', at least half a dozen times. Whenever I tried to answer it, I found myself beginning with an explanation of the past twenty years in Punjab. I heard myself dwelling on its amazing agricultural development and notable prosperity and telling anyone who would listen how Punjab was often invoked as the model that other regions of India must try to emulate. But if Punjab were a model, did it necessarily entail violence and secessionism? I found that I needed to explain the unique aspects of Punjab: its location on the frontier, its violent history and its place at the centre of the Sikh religion. I found myself then trying to explain how modernisation – vastly improved communications, government activity, commercial agriculture, etc. – reacted with Punjabi culture; and how greedy political decisions, aiming for short-term gains, ignited this volatile mixture to produce the explosions of the 1980s. Finally, as people shook their heads, I found myself parrying questions like 'What hope can there be for India?' by emphasising the enormous creative energies that have also been unleashed in the past twenty years. I tried to say that though such energies could lead to cruel ethnic violence, they have also generated powerful grass-roots organisations working for, and achieving, genuine, humanitarian change. The need to write the book grew out of attempts to tell this story, as I understood it.

Chandigarh, the common capital of Punjab and Haryana, was my first home in India. I taught English in a government high school there between 1967 and 1969. The fascination with Punjab particularly, and India generally, gripped me then and has never let go. Although academic research later led me to

Kerala in south India, I continued to write to old students and other friends in Chandigarh, Punjab and Haryana. I still enjoy the opportunity to visit Chandigarh when I go to India. As the torments of Punjab grew in 1983 and 1984, I felt more and more driven to try to explain to myself what was happening there and, by extension, throughout India.

An amiable librarian at the university where I work inadvertently prodded me forward. In April 1984, with news from Punjab becoming more bloody each day, he called me to his office and presented me with two brightly coloured booklets. 'Did you order these?'

'I don't think so', I said. Then I looked at the covers and the titles: *Supreme Sacrifice of Young Souls* and *The Immortal Story of Chamkaur Sahib*, tales of the martyrdoms of the sons of Guru Gobind Singh, the tenth and last preceptor of the Sikhs. 'I could have done,' I admitted, 'I ask you to order most things about the Sikhs'.

'I don't think comic books are worth cataloguing,' he said. 'You may as well take them.'

Later, as I perused the well-produced, colourful booklets (available in English, Hindi and Punjabi), their combination of old and new haunted me. (See the section entitled 'History-Making' in Chapter 4 of this book.) The stories were as old as the last Guru himself (he was assassinated in 1708) and are known to every Sikh. But the format owed much to Walt Disney. The first booklet was published in 1977, just right to come into the hands of children born after the mid-1960s, a time when many of their parents began to prosper from the 'green revolution'. Children were less needed in the fields and household, and parents saw an advantage in sending them to school to learn about the new agricultural technology. More Punjabi children than ever before acquired the opportunity to study and the leisure to read.[1] How did such innovations fit into the grisly puzzle that Punjab had become by the mid-1980s?

The sources on which this book is largely based are also in a sense part of the book's argument. The book relies heavily on Indian newspapers and periodicals. The flourishing of Indian journalism since the end of the 'emergency' in 1977 is one indication of the changes overtaking the country. The total circulation of all periodicals, which stood at 34 million in 1976, was more than 50 million by 1982. The circulation of daily newspapers more than doubled from 6.6 million copies a day in 1968 to 14.5 million in 1980.[2] Though some Indians criticise what they see as 'an obedient press',[3] subservient to the government, the fact remains that there are journals for every shade of opinion, and most versions of an event ultimately get aired. Indeed, to the Indian establishment the 'reports of wretched journalists' are a constant nuisance.[4] To me, the vigour of recent Indian journalism represents one of the country's strengths. Few nations, for example, can have a publication so scholarly and hard-hitting as the *Economic and Political Weekly* of Bombay or a provincial daily so comprehensive as the *Tribune* of Chandigarh. The debts to other journals, journalists and scholars will be evident from a glance at the notes at the end of the book.

I am grateful to the School of Social Sciences, La Trobe University, Melbourne, for a grant to pay for research assistance, without which I would not have been able to write the book during a busy teaching year. I am also grateful to Jon Bader, Victoria Holmes and Sherinda Kaur for providing that assistance at various times and for their never-failing good humour and conscientiousness.

I am deeply indebted to Hew McLeod of the University of Otago and to Talis Polis, chairman of the Department of Politics, La Trobe University, for encouraging me at an early stage to push on with this project and for invaluable comment on each of the draft chapters.

I am similarly indebted to Jon Bader, Dipesh Chakrabarty and Peter Reeves for reading and commenting on the entire manuscript.

Basil Johnson has kindly given me permission to use four maps from his *India: Resources and Development*, 2nd edition (Heinemann, 1983). Gary Swinton, Department of Geography, Monash University, has drawn three new maps for this book.

I am also very grateful to Tim Colebatch, Leon Glezer, John Miller, Prem Mohindra, Avinash Mookhy, Joyce Pettigrew and J. M. Sharma for reading and commenting on portions of the manuscript. Mr Mohindra was also a great help in locating difficult-to-find references, as were Daya Singh Dhaliwal, Joginder Singh, Anil Mehta, Chris Tomlins and Tom Weber.

The National Library of Australia, by providing a steady

flow of the *Tribune* of Chandigarh on microfilm, and the splendid people and collection of the Borchardt Library at La Trobe University, made it possible to consult a wide and deep range of sources in the space of about six months.

Marilu Espacio, Louise Gigliotti, Maree Nemeth and Mary Zaccari typed the manuscript, carried out countless revisions and always seemed one jump ahead of me. I am grateful to them for the care and interest they have taken.

Finally, I must emphasise even more than is customary that none of the above people is responsible for the errors or interpretations in this book. Because it deals with burning issues, the book is unlikely to please all readers. Those who fault it should remember that the responsibility for all its defects lies entirely with me and not with those who have helped me.

Melbourne   Robin Jeffrey
April 1985

Glossary

Akali Dal	the army of the faithful (political party)
Congress (I)	Congress (Indira); the Congress party that Mrs Gandhi drew around her in 1978–9
granthi	the reader in charge of scriptures in a *gurdwara*; often inaccurately described as 'a priest'
gurdwara	a Sikh temple; literally the 'door of the Guru'
Gurmukhi	the alphabet in which the *Guru Granth Sahib* is written and which is now commonly used to write the Punjabi language
guru	a preceptor, religious teacher (spelled with a capital G, one of the 'ten Gurus' – the founders of Sikhism)
Guru Granth Sahib	the Sikh scriptures
kesh-dhari	a Sikh who keeps his hair long and observes the other symbols of the *Khalsa* (the 'five Ks')
Khalsa	the Sikh order or brotherhood, begun by Guru Gobind Singh in 1699; 'the company of the pure'
mahant	the chief of a religious institution
Mazhbis	Sikh Untouchables
misl	eighteenth-century Sikh military bands
panth	the usual word to describe the Sikh religious community

xvii

panj piyare   the beloved five; the first five Sikhs
                            initiated into the Khalsa by Guru
                            Gobind Singh

Punjabi Suba   a state (suba) in which speakers of
                            the Punjabi language would be a
                            majority

sahaj-dhari   a Sikh who believes in the teaching
                            of the Gurus but does not wear the
                            symbols of the Khalsa

sant   a title given to a holy man or reli-
                            gious leader

Sant Nirankari Mission   a sect, dating from the 1930s, which
                            employs some Sikh symbols, but
                            whose members clashed with
                            orthodox Sikhs from the 1970s

Scheduled Castes   the official name applied to people
                            formerly called 'Untouchables'

What Happened to India, 1985–92?

Introduction to the Second Edition

The first edition of this book, completed in 1985, described an India undergoing profound change, in which the state of Punjab was the vanguard. I argued that India generally, and Punjab especially, were experiencing a 'modernising ferment that penetrates even remote corners' (p. 205) and that India was 'talking to itself as never before and forming a new "itself" in the process' (p. 11). The outcomes were not predetermined: they could be 'religious revival, ethnic conflict and secession' or transformation of states to make them work for the benefit of even their poorest citizens (p. 205). In both India and elsewhere, the experience of 1985 to 1992 has been too often of the destructive kind.

By 1992, peoples of central and eastern Europe found themselves struggling with processes with which independent India has contended for more than forty years – free communication, competition and contestation with the state. Emerging from the deep-freeze of authoritarian rule into which they were plunged in 1919 or 1945–9, various European 'peoples' discover and seek to shape themselves – with manifestos, assemblies and constitutions and with guns, armies and concentration camps. The apparatus of the modern state both creates these dilemmas of identity and is called on to solve them. Though these processes and their attendant crises pervade India in the 1990s, its democratic federation has so far coped better than the regimes of the erstwhile Yugoslavia or Soviet Union. The crises nevertheless are undeniable, each one seemingly more threatening than the last to India's post-independence polity.

Simultaneously, changes in the international environment since 1989 have forced policies on India that were almost unthinkable when Mrs Gandhi died in 1984. Then, old certainties remained: a Congress Party, led by a member of the Nehru

family, governed the country; economic policy was based on
'socialism'; the ideal of the Indian state was 'secularism'; and
foreign policy was 'non-aligned', located between two great
power blocs.

By 1992 none of these certainties survived. Rajiv Gandhi was
dead, assassinated in May 1991 as a result of complex adven-
tures in Indian foreign and domestic policy involving Tamils
and Sri Lanka. The Congress (I) ('I' for 'Indira') Party, having
lost an election in 1989 and then barely won one in 1991, struggled to rouse itself from the anaesthetic Mrs Gandhi and her
family had administered for twenty years. 'Socialism' was being
thrown out of the window, yet the apparatus of India's cen-
tralised, 'planned' economy, constructed over forty years, was
so ponderous that it proved hard to find a window big enough.
If it was necessary to knock out a wall, what would be the effect
on the building? The Soviet Union had dissolved, and with it, a
long-depended-on source of weapons and diplomatic support. In
a one-super-power world, with whom was a country to be non-
aligned? Most strikingly, 'secularism' – the doctrine proclaimed
since 1947 that the state must be neutral in sectarian or religious
affairs – was relentlessly challenged.

Results of the three national elections between 1984 and 1991
dramatise this challenge. In the elections of December 1984, the
Bharatiya Janata Party (BJP), whose senior leaders for forty
years have claimed to speak for 'the Hindus' (more than 80 per
cent of India's population), won only two seats out of 229 it
contested and 7.4 per cent of the total vote. In November 1989,
their tally grew to 85 seats and 11.4 per cent. And in the elections of May–June 1991, the BJP felt bold enough to contest
more seats than ever before (456), won 117 and took 20 per cent
of the total vote.[1]

The parliamentary results represented a formal, measurable
outcome of processes which the earlier edition of this book pos-
tulated as fundamental to an understanding of the crisis in
Punjab and suggested would become increasingly evident
throughout India:

> the innovations of the past twenty years . . . reacting with a
> proud, violent culture . . . [then] a series of unwise political
> decisions, aimed at short-term gains, set off the explosions
> . . . (below, p.205).

TABLE *Lok Sabha election results, 1989 and 1991*

	1989 Seats	*1989* % of vote	*1991* Seats	*1991* % of vote
Congress	197	39.5	226	36.0
Janata Dal	143	17.8	56	11.3
BJP	85	11.4	117	20.0
CPM	33	6.5	35	6.2
CPI	12	2.6	13	2.4
State parties	24	5.7	24	–
Others	23	9.8	31	24.1
Independents	12	5.2	–	–
TOTAL	529	98.5	502	100.0

SOURCE Butler *et al.*, *India Decides*, 2nd edn, pp. 90–1. Walter K. Andersen, 'India's 1991 Elections', *Asian Survey*, Vol. 31, no. 10 (October 1991), p. 980.

Similar developments led to the unprecedented mob-destruction of the Babari Mosque at Ayodhya in Uttar Pradesh on 6 December 1992. Electronic communications flash messages and images into remote corners and carry those corners' reactions back across the country to other localities which simultaneously do the same (see below, pp. 12–13). People can be informed, aroused and organised as never before. For anyone previously in doubt, the destruction of the mosque at Ayodhya made chillingly clear that a struggle has begun to control the body and capture the soul of the Indian state.

This new introduction discusses the way in which some of these themes unfolded in the seven years after 1985. It tries to explain the dissolution of cherished certainties of independent India – 'secularism', 'socialism' and 'non-alignment' – and to explore the territory into which the processes of change, seen so vividly earlier in Punjab, may lead.

SECULARISM: WHAT SORT OF STATE?

Among the statements made by shocked leaders after Hindu zealots tore down the Babari Masjid at Ayodhya on 6 December 1992, that of the Vice-President of India stood out. The attack on the mosque was, he said, the greatest political tragedy since the assassination of Mahatma Gandhi in 1948.[2] Though he was a

Congress politician and associate of Indira Gandhi, the destruction of the mosque appeared to him so grave a threat to the India
of which he was a leader that he ignored the assassinations of
Mrs Gandhi and her son Rajiv.

The Vice-President, K. R. Narayanan (b. 1921), embodied
many characteristics of the national elite that shaped India from
the time of Jawaharlal Nehru. An 'untouchable' by caste, a
Keralan from the south in origin, Narayanan married a woman
from Burma and became ambassador to China, vice-chancellor
of the national university that bears Nehru's name, a Congress
member of parliament and vice-president of the country in
1992. His biography symbolises the liberal, open, outward-look-
ing India that many hoped was being established after independence.

'Secularism' continues to have loud defenders, and the word
itself survives to shape debate. Even its opponents, for example,
advocate not the creation of a religious or sectarian state but
'positive secularism', in which governments would do justice
even-handedly to majorities (i.e. Hindus) and not pander to
minorities.[3] Formally, such a statement is forty years old: as old
as the Jana Sangh's, and its descendant, the Bharatiya Janata
Party's advocacy of the supreme rights of 'Hindus'. But for
nearly thirty years such advocacy made little impact except
among twice-born (higher-status) castes in urban north India.
The BJP's two seats and 7.4 per cent of the vote in the 1984
national elections were slightly worse than the Jana Sangh's
three seats and 3 per cent of the vote in the first general elections of 1951–2 (when the party had contested only half as
many seats).[4] By 1991, however, the BJP held close to 120
seats, was the second largest party in India and governed the
country's largest state, Uttar Pradesh and three others.[5]

The BJP has succeeded in recent elections because it has
found new support in north Indian society. The character of
India's politically active groups is changing: the English-speaking, lawyer-led old elite that shaped the Indian state after 1947
is being overtaken and absorbed by a broader, consumer-orient-
ed middle class intent on proclaiming both its religious convic-
tions and material success. Such people, though often divided
by language or caste, share certain aspirations and levels of
prosperity. How – and whether – such people find expression
within the present political system represents a problem which

politicians seek to solve. Since 1989, the BJP has shown increasing success in riding these waves, though the destruction of the mosque in Ayodhya suggests that the party also runs the risk of being capsized and drowned.

The story of Indian television exposes some of the processes at work. In the 1980s, television overwhelmed India for the first time. In 1981, there were only 18 transmitters and fewer than 2 million television sets; by 1990 there were more than 520 transmitters covering 80 per cent of the country and more than 30 million sets.[6] A media annual wrote – doubtless in exaggeration – of 'the 500 million people who watch TV every evening'.[7] A more sober estimate put the number of regular viewers in the late 1980s at 200 million.[8] As the medium gushes into distant corners, it is changing practices, attitudes and possibilities. For a growing consumer class, it sets standards of behaviour and aspiration. In a hut or a tea-shop, wistful consumers and the poor can experience dreams and escapes once possible only in the cinema.[9]

One of the paradoxes of the nation-state system since the collapse of the Eastern bloc is the way in which people are ostentatiously both very international and very parochial. In the former Yugoslavia, for example, men wearing American blue jeans, carrying Russian rifles and talking into Japanese portable phones fight for the future of Bosnia. In outward forms they are globalised; in themselves, they are prepared to die for identities as local as a Balkan valley was to its inhabitants in the nineteenth century.

India has proved similar. Television seduced it in the 1980s, but it was not foreign television. Indeed, the content of the medium responds to its audience at least as much as the audience is bewitched by the medium.[10] Indian television generated programmes that captured Indian audiences,[11] and nowhere was this more dramatically seen than in the religious epic. From 1987 to 1990, much of the country stopped for 45 minutes on Sunday mornings for episodes first of the *Ramayana* (78 parts) and later the *Mahabharat*, the Hindu epics.[12] Video-cassettes of particular episodes became popular as gifts, and surveys reported an 'extremely high . . . level of identification with various characters'. Indeed, it was suggested that 'the average Indian has treated both epics as a mix of fact and fiction, *more of the former*'.[13]

In the past, local variations of these great tales were the accepted version. 'In my place', people in effect said, 'we tell the story this way'. Now, all of India is acquiring a common telling, based on the conventions of the popular religious films and complete with appropriate costumes and gilt headgear. Various groups protested at their version or their people being left out or treated disrespectfully, but the popularity of the series was unquestionable.[14]

This transformation of local variations into homogenised all-India tales or products opened up possibilities that no politician could overlook. Rajiv Gandhi, with his love of gadgetry and personal computers, had given notoriety to such possibilities during the election campaign of 1984. One estimate suggested that 5000 prints of a video-cassette about Mrs Gandhi were used all over India by Congress Party campaigners.[15]

Paradoxically, the 'modern' technology appears to have been of most use to those who see themselves as carrying an 'old' message – politicians of the Hindu right. In August 1990, the month after the last episode of the *Mahabharat* was shown on television, a sequence of events began that eventually brought down a government and catapulted the BJP into the position of India's second most important political party.

On 8 August V. P. Singh (b. 1931), Prime Minister of the Janta Dal-led minority government, announced that 27 per cent of all jobs in central-government undertakings would henceforth be set aside for people from the 'Other Backward Castes' or OBCs.[16] This category is a creation of bureaucrats and census-takers, a lumping together of hundreds of castes (*jati*) who rank above 'Untouchables' or Scheduled Castes but below the so-called twice-born or 'forward' castes like Brahmins and Rajputs. Together, these *jati* probably constitute more than half the population of India. But accurate figures do not exist: caste has not been enumerated in Indian censuses since 1931.[17]

In making the announcement, Singh asserted that he was simply implementing the recommendations of a report commisioned by government in 1979 and presented by its chairman, B. P. Mandal (1918–82), an OBC politician from Bihar.[18] Since roughly 22 per cent of posts in government institutions are already reserved for Scheduled Castes and Scheduled Tribes, the effect of Singh's announcement was to set aside half the jobs in the central government on the basis of caste or tribal origin.

Judgements about voting strengths and new social identities were behind Singh's announcement. He was locked in a struggle within his own party against a wily rustic, Devi Lal (b. 1914), a Jat from Haryana. Jats, though not a 'twice-born' caste, have prospered as wealthy peasants and farmers in north India in the past thirty years and are not included among the Other Backward Castes. Indeed, there is little that is backward about Jats (see pp. 48–52 below). Devi Lal thus claimed to represent one of the most influential groups in the north Indian countryside – where more than a hundred seats in the central parliament are decided. Moreover, Devi Lal had played the kingmaker in December 1989 when his carefully-planned deceit had allowed Singh to become Prime Minister.[19] By July 1990, Devi Lal was threatening Singh's leadership. To thwart him, Singh appears to have calculated that the so-called OBCs could be united into a reliable voting bloc by implementing the recommendations about job reservation contained in the Mandal Report. With close to half the population of north India wooed and won by this symbolic gesture, a Singh-led Janata Dal party could face Devi Lal, the Congress or the higher-caste Hindu chauvinists of the BJP.

Singh miscalculated, though this is not to say he will ultimately be proved wrong.[20] It is conceivable that OBCs of north India might be persuaded at a future election that they have sufficient in common to vote for a party claiming to represent them. In the state of Bihar, the government formed in 1990 has survived on something like this recipe.[21] But the outcome of Singh's announcement was not what he could have hoped for. The 'forward' or 'twice-born' castes who predominate in the government services and places of influence in north India's towns and cities reacted in frenzy. They attacked Singh's proposal as an unjust betrayal of merit, upper-caste students took to the streets and before the fall of the government in November an estimated 100 adolescents[22] had killed themselves, often setting themselves on fire, in symbolic protest.[23]

Television and the video-cassette played a notable role in dignifying these protests. In perhaps the most notorious example, *Newstrack*, the monthly video-cassette news programme, produced by Living Media India, the owners of *India Today*, devoted virtually all of its October 1990 edition to a bitter attack on

the proposal to introduce reservation for OBCs. The print magazine *India Today* had been outraged at the proposal,[24] and the
video-cassette attacked V. P. Singh for 'mouth[ing] infuriating
inanities'; it compared the upper-caste student protests in New
Delhi to the Tiananmen Square protest in Beijing in 1989.[25] A
key sequence took the camera into a Delhi hospital where a 13-
year-old boy, suffering severe burns after having tried to immo-
late himself, was encouraged to tell the Prime Minister that
'either he should resign or run this country sensibly'.[26] The
video-cassette reported that the boy later died. The passion that
50 000 government jobs could evoke was time-honoured and
understandable,[27] but the rapidity and intensity with which the
passion spread were new.

In August 1990, it was by no means obvious that the
stratagem of uniting Other Backward Castes as a voting bloc
would fail. Indeed, that so shrewd a politician as the Prime
Minister would try it suggested that it had a good chance of
succeeding – that the next national election, which would obviously come long before the due date in 1994, could be won by a
party proclaiming such a programme. For the Congress (I) Party
of Rajiv Gandhi, then in opposition, the dilemma was almost
insoluble. To support the Mandal recommendations would simply sustain the government and alienate the Congress's upper-
caste supporters in north India. But to oppose the recommendations meant further alienation of the various groups that made
up the OBC category. The Congress was held to have already
lost ground dramatically among such people in the mammoth
states of Uttar Pradesh (85 seats in the national parliament) and
Bihar (54 seats). Rajiv Gandhi and the Congress could only
equivocate and hold out the possibility of directing benefits
towards poor people regardless of caste: 'socially and economi-
cally backward *classes* are not backward *castes*. We must broad-
en the definition to include the groups who are not defined by
caste'.[28]

The bold counterstroke of the Bharatiya Janata Party, however, has had far wider consequences. The ability of new media
to popularise homogenised versions of the epics changed the
boundaries for politicians striving to create 'the Hindus' as a
single social entity.[29] The BJP attempted to exploit this potential. If V. P. Singh's electoral goal was to unite OBCs as a voting
bloc, the BJP had long aimed to create a sense of a common

'Hindu-ness' that would lead to the election of BJP governments. Television – particularly the two epic serials – spread a
message that it was previously almost impossible to take seriously: that there was a 'Hindu community' with shared ideals
and a single, unvarying version of its great religious stories.
After all, had the authorised version not been seen on TV? The
division of Hindus into hundreds of *jati* with strong local customs and prohibitions seemed surmountable. The creation of a
'Hindu community' – or at least a single body of Hindu sentiment sufficient to win first-past-the-post elections – became a
possibility for the first time.[30] The technology, which Rajiv
Gandhi and others expected to 'modernise' and 'secularise'
India, could just as well create broader identities based on religious residues. Such developments had shown up in Punjab ten
years before (see below, pp. 73–97).

In the mid-1980s, the patience of older BJP politicians like L.
K. Advani (b. 1927) and A. B. Vajpayee (b. 1926) had seemed
ill-rewarded, especially after the crushing defeat in the 1984
general elections. They had been working for the cause since
the early 1950s, yet the party had few strongholds beyond the
original base among upper-caste Hindus in towns in northern
India.[31] Scholars have argued that the failures of the 1960s
stemmed from a lack of openness, democracy and moderation in
the old Jana Sangh, the forerunner of the BJP. It was too much
influenced by its zealous patron, the Rastriya Swayamsevak
Sangh (RSS).[32] Yet the recipe of the late 1980s added even more
RSS militance. And this is the important point: the Bharatiya
Janata Party and the RSS have not changed. What has changed
are the perceptions of new generations of north Indian Hindus,
aspiring to improve their circumstances, disenchanted with
state-proclaimed 'secularism' and ready to believe that 'Hindus'
have common interests that a political party can serve.

The events surrounding the destruction of the Babari Masjid
in Ayodhya, 150 kilometres east of Lucknow, on 6 December
1992 emphasise the power that such appeals now exercise.[33] In
Ayodhya a dispute festered over a mosque, said to stand on the
site that many Hindus believe was the birthplace of Lord Ram
of the *Ramayana* epic. Though the courts closed the premises to
all worshippers in 1949 to prevent clashes, the demand to build
a Hindu temple on the site gained new life in 1986 after a court
ordered removal of the locks on the gates of the precinct. The

sudden decision of the court after 37 years of inaction appeared to result from covert efforts of Congress (I) politicians, meddling once again in local issues to try to further their own national goals (see below, pp. 19, 135–7, 189–90). Their aim, it appears, was to placate Hindus angry at legislation proposing to remove Muslims from the purview of the civil code in matters of divorce and alimony.[34] Once the order to remove the locks at the disputed site was issued, the BJP and its allies proclaimed their intention to build a splendid temple to Lord Ram on the very spot to restore 'national honour'.[35] The mosque, it was implied, would be torn down.

A comparison of the confrontations at Ayodhya in 1990 and December 1992 illustrates the growth in influence of the BJP, the social tendencies it represents and the challenge to the principles on which the Indian state was founded in 1947. In September 1990, Advani, the party president, announced that he would undertake a round-India *rath yatra* or 'chariot journey' to culminate at Ayodhya where construction of a Ram temple would begin. Here was a counter to V. P. Singh's 'Mandal stratagem' of trying to consolidate lower-caste people into a bloc. Instead, the BJP aimed to unite *all* Hindus to assert their dignity; caste did not matter; what mattered was the humiliation of a non-Hindu place of worship standing on the site of Ram's birth.[36] The *rath yatra* was to provide a means of 'obliterating the casteist animosities' that divided Hindus.[37] The *rath yatra* and the Ram temple would unite them all.

The outcome signalled an advantage to the BJP's struggle to unite all Hindus. Advani's *rath* or chariot left Somnath, a holy city in Gujarat on the west coast of India, on 25 September 1990.[38] The 'chariot' was a specially modified Toyota van, designed in florid colours and bits of tin to look like the chariots from the *Ramayana* and *Mahabharat* television series. Taking three weeks to weave its way towards Ayodhya through parts of north and central India carefully chosen for the sympathy of their populations, the procession entered the expectant state of Bihar, ruled by an anti-BJP government, on 20 October.[39] On 23 October, the Bihar government arrested Advani, but the march on the mosque in Ayodhya went ahead on 30 October. Dozens were killed when the police and paramilitary forces opened fire, but some demonstrators were able to enter the mosque and put flags on the dome. Outraged at the arrest of Advani and the central and Uttar Pradesh governments' use of the police against the demonstrators, the BJP withdrew its support to V. P. Singh in the national parliament. Simultaneously he was deserted by a group from his own party, led by Chandra Shekhar (b. 1927), whom Singh had double-crossed to become Prime Minister less than a year before. Singh's government fell on 6 November when it lost a vote of confidence in the lower house. Rioting in various parts of India went on for a month; hundreds were killed.[40]

The major contrast between the confrontations of 1990 and 1992 lies in the fact that by 1992 a BJP government had come to power in Uttar Pradesh. In 1990, the Janata Dal government of UP did what it could to prevent volunteers from reaching Ayodhya, and police opened fire to disperse crowds.[41] In contrast, in 1992 the central government pleaded that the constitution prevented it from using its forces: law and order was a matter for the state government. The state government did nothing. When youths began to overrun the barricades, the police simply melted away, 'one terrified officer push[ing] through his platoon determined to be the first to get out'. By dusk on Sunday, 6 December, the mob had destroyed the mosque.[42]

The lead-up to the confrontation in Ayodhya was much shorter in 1992 than 1990. The notoriety generated in the previous two years and the tacit approval of BJP state governments in Uttar Pradesh and Madhya Pradesh meant that huge crowds could confidently be expected. Advani, now leader of the opposition in parliament, and the BJP president, Murli Manohar Joshi (b. 1934), undertook six-day tours through selected areas of UP before reaching an Ayodhya bulging with volunteers whose travel had been aided rather than discouraged by the state government. Advani appears to have believed that peaceful ceremonies could be held to signal a symbolic beginning to the building of a Ram temple that would slowly grow up around the mosque. In fact, however, many leaders in Ayodhya on 6 December did not want to control the crowd. When it began to surge over the fences and enter the mosque, 'a holy woman' in the party of senior leaders 'took over the microphone and screamed encouragement to the frenzied Hindus. . . . According to one reporter who was with Advani and his colleagues throughout the day, he alone was downcast' at the turn of events.[43]

The composition of the crowd that destroyed the mosque will tantalise analysts for years to come. We shall probably never know with any exactitude the sorts of people who were there; but in film clips and photographs it is notable that so many of the young men wear trousers and sports shoes. Even today, these are not clothes generally worn by village people, which suggests that the youths at Ayodhya were from towns and that they were aspirants, at least, for a place in India's much-discussed 'growing middle class'.[44] In addition, however, a journalist following Advani through the poorer districts of eastern UP asserted that 'the rural poor, including lower castes are, quite inexplicably, responding to the [BJ] party'.[45] Such a combination – the disenchanted, would-be middle class of the towns and the lower-caste rural poor – can provide muscle on the streets and victory at the polls. As the screaming denunciations of Muslims and the attacks in Ayodhya on journalists indicate, such people have little interest in retaining 'secularism' and liberalism as central tenets of their state.

The rapid turnover of unstable national governments since 1989 further undermines the legitimacy of the present state and what it stands for.[46] In November 1990, Chandra Shekhar, outfoxed prime-ministerial aspirant in December 1989, became Prime Minister of a farcical minority government, based on his following of 56 Janata Dal MPs whom he had led out of the party. His ministry survived on Congress support until 6 March 1991 when he resigned and new elections were called for May.

Rajiv Gandhi died in the course of that campaign, on the night of 21 May 1991, his killing related only indirectly either to the struggle in Punjab or the attempt to implant a new 'Hindu' ideal for the Indian state. Yet the fact that he was campaigning in Tamilnad when he was murdered stemmed from the Congress Party's concern to win seats in south India because they expected to do poorly in the north. And his apparent killers, the Liberation Tigers of Tamil Eelam (LTTE), the major secessionist organisation of Sri Lankan Tamils, dated their anger against him from his use of the Indian army against them in 1987. Such a motive – anger at the use of the Indian army against armed secessionists – had much in common with that of Mrs Gandhi's killers in 1984.

The results of the 1991 elections emphasised the intensifying contest about the principles on which the Indian state should be founded. Of the 225 seats in Hindi-speaking north India,[47] the BJP won 81 and the Congress only 58. In Bihar, neither party did well: the Janata Dal, championing Other Backward Castes, won 27 seats out of 54. Tele-versions of the Hindu epics and politicians dressed to look like tele-gods punctuated the BJP campaign. The spoken message was clear: the so-called secularism that Nehru foisted on India after 1947 was false, pernicious and humiliating.[48]

In south India, Congress won 86 seats out of 129, including all 28 it contested in Tamilnad; the BJP won five seats, its best-ever performance.[49] The apparent success of the Congress was less an endorsement of 'secularism' than a reflection of a different social structure and fear that a BJP national government might try to impose the Hindi language. The BJP, and its forerunner, the Jana Sangh, have long championed Hindi, a north Indian language, as the sole national language of India. Moreover, in the north, the 'forward caste' constituency, made up of 'twice-born' wearers of the sacred thread, is the core of Hindu chauvinism; but in the south, such people represent a far smaller proportion of the population.[50] Battles against a tiny elite of Brahmins – similar to the recent struggles revolving around the 'OBC' category in the north – were won in the south by the 1960s.

There is an added difficulty for the BJP. To make the need for 'Hindu unity' convincing requires a significant 'non-Hindu' presence. But a credible adversary is missing in all the south Indian states except Kerala, where Muslims and Christians each comprise about 20 per cent of the population. It is conceivable that the persistent efforts of Hindu-chauvinist groups in Kerala will eventually pay off in election victories; but to date they represent a weak third force in the state – caught between strong alliances led by Congress and the Communist Party of India (Marxist).[51]

Such differences between north and south appear at first glance to emphasise yet another fault-line along which the Indian state could fracture. Yet the very fact that there seem to be so many lines suggests that the metaphor may be misguided: we are seeing, not cracks in porcelain, but filaments of a web. Single 'fragments' are not so large or discrete that they will easily break off. The national elite is genuinely national and intertwined: a south Indian Brahmin is Prime Minister; a north

Indian Brahmin, President; a south Indian 'untouchable', Vice-President; an Anglo-Indian, chief of the army. As well, a national economy is increasingly (as we shall see below) controlled by companies and capitalists who seek smooth-running nationwide markets. Powerful interests hold India together. By no means, however, do they guarantee that the 'secularism' proclaimed since 1947 is assured of survival. In 1992, the struggle for India's soul was just beginning.

PUNJAB: WHAT SORT OF FEDERALISM?

Where does Punjab fit into these contests about how the Indian state is to define itself in the future? Secessionist movements, like those in Punjab and Jammu and Kashmir,[52] challenge India's state apparatus and practices in two ways. First, they pose an overt, obvious threat: an area wants to break away. If that should occur, the present state structure and the people who operate it would consider themselves diminished. Second, however, the fact that the challenge seems intractable allows advocates of 'positive secularism' and a 'genuine' – that is, Hindu – nationalism to point to the failings of the present system. 'Give us the chance', they say, 'and we will deal with these anti-Indian, anti-Hindu activities and restore the nation's greatness.'

Punjab proved to be the death of Mrs Gandhi; for her son, Rajiv, it marked his proving – and failing – ground. In July 1985, he reached perhaps his peak of popularity when he concluded the so-called Punjab Accord with Harchand Singh Longowal. Though Longowal was murdered within a month, the Punjab elections went ahead in September, and Rajiv expressed almost satisfaction when the Akali Dal, not the Congress, won (see pp. 206–10 below). With a popular Sikh-dominated government in power in Punjab, a durable settlement seemed possible. Rajiv's naiveté, the fight-to-the-death quality of Punjab politics and the influence of political forces external to Punjab destroyed such a prospect by January 1986. The destruction also revealed the limitations of Rajiv Gandhi.

When he became Chief Minister of the Akali Dal government in September 1985, Surjit Singh Barnala suffered from three drawbacks. First, the mass leader, Longowal, was dead. Second,

Barnala himself had no such wide following. His urbanity and national connections made it predictable (p. 208 below) that he would light few fires in the hearts of young Sikhs. Third, he was unable to entice into his government the hurt, jealous Parkash Singh Badal, whose dismissal from the Chief Ministership in 1980 provided the spark for much of the subsequent agony (pp. 190 and 198 below). Badal remained outside the government to snipe and wait. To survive, and to win the confidence of Sikhs, Barnala needed a symbolic triumph.

Since the 1950s, the most obvious symbol in Punjab has been the city of Chandigarh. A new city, designed by the French architect Le Corbusier to compensate for the loss of Lahore to Pakistan, Chandigarh symbolises a switched-on, sanitised India. When Punjab was divided into Punjab, Haryana and Himachal Pradesh in 1966, Chandigarh became a Union Territory of the central government and the joint capital of Punjab and Haryana. For politicians of both states, it glittered. Mrs Gandhi had promised its transfer to Punjab in 1970 – with territorial compensation for Haryana. That promise was never redeemed, but it was reiterated in the Rajiv–Longowal agreement in July 1985: Chandigarh was to become the capital of Punjab from 26 January 1986, India's Republic Day. A commission under a retired Supreme Court judge with a long record of loyalty to Indira Gandhi was appointed to work out the details.[53]

But in December 1985 and January 1986, pressure grew in neighbouring Haryana, Congress-governed and due for an election within 18 months, to prevent the loss of Chandigarh. Haryana's influence in Indian politics is out of proportion to its size. The state contains less than 2 per cent of India's population and sends only 10 members of parliament to a lower house of 542 members in Delhi. Haryana, however, encircles the Union Territory of Delhi on the north, south and west; Haryana's lax labour laws have made it a haven for new industries; Haryana provides the crowds for Delhi demonstrations. Indeed, Haryana can perform as a tourniquet bandage to tighten pressure on the politicians and officials of the national capital, who tend to treat it as a litmus paper for the whole of north India.

On 26 January 1986, Chandigarh was not transferred to Punjab. The wily judge fudged his award. Called on to identify Hindi-speaking areas of Punjab to transfer to Haryana as compensation for the loss of Chandigarh, he refused and told the central government to appoint a new commission to identify such areas.[54] Two further commissions were appointed to determine the territory to be transferred,[55] but by mid-1986 the transfer of Chandigarh was as dead as Longowal. By November 1986, the Punjab Accord was dismissed as 'virtually unimplementable'.[56]

In January 1986, Rajiv Gandhi could have forced through a decision, but he chose to heed the pressures and advice coming from Haryana and its protagonists, even though the consequence undermined his brightest achievement – the Punjab agreement. This indecision foreshadowed the crumbling of his authority and government over the next two years.

The lack of decision on Chandigarh also marked the beginning of the end for Barnala. Always susceptible to portrayal as a creature of the central government, he desperately needed the symbolic victory of Chandigarh. Once this was denied, he quickly became what his foes had claimed he was all along: a tool of the central government. Secessionist devotees took control of the Golden Temple in January 1986 and demolished the just-reconstructed Akal Takht to rebuild it with the labour, not of Indian-government lackeys (as they saw them), but devout Sikhs.[57] As the initiative passed from governments in New Delhi and Punjab, killings increased. More people were murdered in March 1986 than in the first four months of Barnala's ministry.[58] Rajiv Gandhi's government reacted by trying to exert the authority of the centre: it sent a prominent police officer, Julio Ribeiro (b. 1929), to Punjab as Director-General of Police on 28 March and a new Governor, Siddhartha Shankar Ray (b. 1920), on 1 April.[59] The appointment of Ray carried grim implications: he had been Chief Minister of West Bengal in 1972 when the Naxalite movement of Maoist-inspired revolutionaries had been ruthlessly crushed.

In July, the Akali Dal formally split, the breakaway group electing Badal as its leader.[60] Barnala's government, now in a minority and surviving in the assembly with the support of the Congress and the BJP, staggered on until May 1987. Then, with elections in Haryana due in the following month, the central government imposed President's Rule in Punjab. It made no difference: Congress was wiped out in the June 1987 elections in Haryana.

Punjab remained under central rule for nearly five years. In the period between May 1987 and the Punjab elections of February 1992, more than 15 000 people were killed in violence that official sources linked to terrorists.[61] At the same time, tens of thousands of central-government paramilitary police and soldiers of the Indian army were deployed in Punjab. The state had five different Governors, and the Akali Dal – and the secessionists themselves – divided into a dozen or more groups or factions.[62]

The technology of violence produced new and particularly intractable circumstances. In the past, as this book argues, violence has been common in Punjab and rural India; but such violence was often hand-to-hand. In the 1980s, as weapons from the war in Afghanistan flooded across Pakistan and north India, a few could quickly murder many, without ever having to look a victim in the eye. The list of the dead included the commander of the Indian army at the time of the battle at the Golden Temple in June 1984, murdered in retirement in Pune in 1986. Barnala's Finance Minister and chief manipulator, Balwant Singh, was gunned down in a car in Chandigarh in July 1990.[63] Even Ribeiro, the police chief from 1986 to 1988, though made ambassador to Rumania in an attempt to protect him, was seriously wounded by would-be assassins in Bucharest in August 1991[64] (and see below, pp. 183, 213).

Rajiv Gandhi's government after the middle of 1986 brought no new ideas to Punjab, though it attempted halting initiatives to bring various Sikh groups into political negotiations.[65] But the government did not prosecute people accused of murder and riot in the grim days in Delhi after Mrs Gandhi's murder in 1984 when thousands of Sikhs were killed.[66] Sikhs could legitimately complain that the government had no interest in justice. Indeed, the evidence suggests that Punjab interested members of the government mostly as a weapon in calculations about electoral politics. In December 1989, the new Prime Minister V. P. Singh made an emotional visit to Amritsar and the Golden Temple, but the enthusiasm of that visit quickly passed. Because Singh led a minority government, even if he had been inclined to order elections in Punjab, his essential supporters – especially the Bharatiya Janata Party – may have prevented him.

It was as if the view from New Delhi invariably made India appear as a giant chess board on which Punjab was a capital piece, important to be sure, but not to be analysed and consid-

ered in its own right but moved about to satisfy the larger game.
Evidence of such calculations extended well back into Mrs
Gandhi's lifetime (pp. 124–6 below). But they were not her
responsibility alone. India's constitution, much of it inherited
from colonial rule, and the thrust of Soviet-inspired economic
policy after independence, have excessively concentrated power
and initiative with the central government. From the comfortable vantage-point of New Delhi, the view of India too often
becomes distorted.

The question of elections in Punjab and in north India illustrates the proposition. The transfer of Chandigarh to Punjab –
the one symbol that might have sustained Barnala and his government – was put off because of fears of the effect on impending elections in Haryana, just as Barnala's government was
eventually dismissed just prior to Haryana elections in the desperate hope that such actions would influence the result. In
Punjab itself, elections were called for late June 1991 as part of
the national general elections. Virtually every political group in
Punjab threw itself into the campaign, and though more than a
dozen candidates were murdered,[67] electioneering went on
unabated and a good turnout of voters seemed likely. But only
days before Punjab's polling, once it became apparent that
Congress would form the new national government but lose in
the Punjab assembly, the Chief Election Commissioner 'postponed' the Punjab election. The official reason was that security
could not be guaranteed. The real reason, it appears, was the
fact that Congress would do poorly: the BJP would poll well in
Punjab's towns and various Akali Dal groups would win rural
seats. The Governor of Punjab, O. P. Malhotra (b. 1922), a former commander of the Indian army (1978–80), protested and
resigned.[68]

When elections were finally held in Punjab in February 1992,
it was after the entire state had been declared 'disturbed' and
the Indian army had been deployed on counter-insurgency duty
for more than two months.[69] Ultimately, only one of half-a-
dozen Akali Dal factions contested – the one associated with
Amarindar Singh, the erstwhile Maharaja of Patiala (see below,
pp. 42, 163) – and it was humiliated. The turnout was about 22
per cent; the turnout of Sikh voters was estimated to have been
10 per cent or less.[70] Congress won 12 out of 13 seats to the
national parliament – a valuable accretion for a minority gov-

ernment – and three-quarters of the 117 seats in the state assembly.[71] The new Chief Minister, Beant Singh (b. 1922), elderly and platitudinous, seemed the classic 'creature of the centre' against which Sikh militants had railed for years. Yet *any* elected government seems better than central rule. By the end of 1992, Beant Singh and security chiefs were claiming – and journalists were confirming – that rural Punjab was safer than it had been for two years.[72] Police killed leading secessionists, including prominent foreign-based men like Talwindar Singh Parmar of Vancouver, Canada. Parmar was often named in accounts of the bombing of the Air India jumbo-jet off the coast of Ireland in June 1985 that killed more than 300 people.[73] Police claimed that if such highly-placed leaders were forced to return to Punjab, the secessionists were on the run. To reinforce this impression, the Punjab government held successful local-government elections in rural areas in January 1993.

The politics of Punjab pose a challenge to the Indian state, yet they also suggest ways forward. In ten months under an elected government (even a dubiously-elected one) in 1992, Punjab seemed to move more noticeably towards relative peace than it had in nearly five years of central rule between 1987 and 1992. Genuine federalism remains India's best bet, though the odds are not short, nor the result certain. But outcomes for nations never are: 'quests for the political community of the future are never quite finished'. What is 'the nation'? 'The outcome', according to Gyan Pandey, 'of many different visions and the struggle between them'.[74] Punjab is likely to remain a cockpit for those struggles.

SOCIALISM: WHAT SORT OF ECONOMY?

'Socialism' and 'non-alignment' are themes scarcely touched on in the first edition of this book. When it was written, their intonation in India was a regular as sunrise. The fact that this is no longer so requires examination. Fundamental changes in economic and foreign policies have ramifications for the structure and survival of the Indian state.

Anyone who thinks about India's poor[75] must ask whether the dismantling of government controls, created in the name of 'socialism', also means abandonment of the belief that govern-

ment has a role to play in economic activity. The intention of
Jawaharlal Nehru when the Planning Commission was established in 1950 and the First Five-Year Plan inaugurated in 1951
was that the 'commanding heights of the economy', the heavy
industries and infrastructure, should be under the control of
government and 'the people'. The wealth generated by such
major investments would then be reinvested in projects that
would increasingly benefit the mass of the population.
'Socialism is not the spreading of poverty', he told parliament
in 1956. 'The essential thing is that there must be wealth and
production.'[76]

Economic regulation in India, however, has produced too few
beneficial results. The crisis of 1990 was many years in the
making. Though a few public enterprises, notably those with the
monopoly on petroleum products, returned profits, the majority
did not. By the late 1980s, it was estimated that 244 enterprises
conducted by the central government with US $40 billion worth
of capital invested in them brought a return of less than 4 per
cent on the investment. If the huge earnings of the petroleum
monopoly were deducted, the return was less than 1 per cent.[77]
The record of companies set up by India's 25 state governments
was worse. A 1989 survey of 843 state-government enterprises
found losses of US $800 million, and 'the bulk' of the compa-
nies surveyed were at least two years behind in completing their
annual accounts.[78] Even a publication like the famed *Seminar*,
founded by two Communist sympathisers in the 1960s, concluded in 1991 that 'nobody even claims that the present system
works . . . . The poor . . . eke out a living that is almost shame-
ful.'[79]

Attempts to find new economic vigour began with 'productivity year' in 1982 and gathered momentum in 1985 after Rajiv
Gandhi came to power. Members of his Planning Commission
argued that 'liberalisation is not inimical to the objectives of
true socialism, as opposed to the sham socialism practised in
this country'.[80] Restrictions on imports were relaxed; the old
policies of 'self-sufficiency' through 'import substitution' were
diluted; producers were mildly encouraged to *export* so that
India would earn more foreign exchange to pay its international
bills, especially for oil. Indian industry grew: by roughly 8 per
cent a year in the 1980s.[81]

The results, however, were troubling. To be sure, between

1985 and 1989, exports increased by 55 per cent to US $24 billion. But imports increased by 50 per cent to US $32 billion, and a large trade deficit remained. Total debt grew from US $40.8 billion in 1985 to US $62.5 billion in 1989 to US $75 billion in 1992.[82]

Until 1990 India had sufficient foreign exchange to pay its bills because of the flow of hard currency into the country from Non-Resident Indians (NRIs), both working people in menial jobs in the Gulf, Britain and Canada and wealthy professionals in countries like the USA and Australia. But the Iraqi invasion of Kuwait in August 1990, only days before V. P. Singh's announcement of the adoption of the Mandal Commission's recommendations, added financial crisis to domestic upheaval. Indians in Kuwait, whose monthly remittances hitherto provided a reliable source of foreign exchange, lost their livelihoods and became a foreign-exchange liability. The price of petroleum products, India's major foreign-exchange expense, rose – at one point from US $17 to US $42 a barrel for crude oil.[83] An Iraqi debt to India of US $800 million was frozen and looked unlikely to be repaid.[84] Once India's credit rating was lowered in October 1990,[85] Non-Resident Indians began to withdraw their deposits from India. Foreign exchange had to be found to honour such withdrawals, which hit a peak of US $56 million a week.[86] In January 1991, the minority government of Prime Minister Chandra Shekhar was forced to negotiate a US $1.8 billion loan from the World Bank and the International Monetary Fund,[87] and by the time P. V. Narasimha Rao's (b. 1921) newly-elected Congress government took office in July 1991, India had taken a reported US $2.4 billion in World Bank and IMF loans.[88] Within days, the new government devalued the rupee by 20 per cent, and began to remove economic controls.[89]

The ensuing restructuring of India's economy has been open to challenge in three major ways. First, the apparent capitulation to the IMF and the World Bank left Indian pride painfully exposed. 'Socialism' had been a broad codeword for 'Indian control' and 'self-sufficiency'. Critics argue that foreign capitalists were responsible the last time India lost its independence: to the English East India Company in the 1760s. Today, even those who might wish for fewer government controls can deplore 'the IMF–World Bank takeover of the Indian economy'.[90] Opponents of the economic changes claim to be both patriots and defenders of the poor.

Second, in the middle of 1992 India's biggest stock-market fraud disgraced banks, other financial institutions and the stock market. Involvement of foreign banks fostered fears that the capitalist economies of the West were leading India into a sinister economic trap. The corrupt dealings permitted profits of tens of millions of rupees to be made on the basis of promises of money that did not exist.[91] Opponents of economic change could argue for more, not fewer, government controls in the face of rampant free-enterprise corruption.[92]

Third, there was no certainty that an economy made free of government controls would produce more wealth or distribute it more widely. The best that defenders of liberalisation could claim was that forty years of 'socialism' had not done enough – an economic growth rate of 3.5 per cent a year between the 1950s and the 1970s, while population grew at 2.5 per cent. Such figures, they argued, made the need for change urgent. To be sure, government documents proclaimed the need 'to protect the poor during the adjustment process', but a close observer of the economic transformation concluded that government had not worked out systematically the way in which an unregulated, internationally-connected economy would affect the poor.[93] Can we afford, a critic asked, to 'worry about taking 15 per cent of our urban population and our industrial sector closer to the most advanced industrialised countries . . . at the risk of ignoring the social and economic development of the other 85 per cent who live in the rural and semi-urban areas?'[94] For many Indians, the economic changes lead into fog-shrouded, unknown territory.

NON-ALIGNMENT: WHAT SORT OF WORLD?

Foreign policy and economics are linked. Now the Soviet Union and communism in Eastern Europe are gone, India's communists and socialists find immense difficulty in defending a 'planned economy'. Internationally, the consequences are even more troubling: with whom is India 'non-aligned'? Moreover, a liberalised economy requires foreign investment which must come from the major capitalist countries – the USA, Germany, Japan, the United Kingdom.

To encourage such investment, Indian planners have targeted

wealthy Indians abroad (NRIs), particularly in the USA, who might either be induced to invest in India themselves or facilitate investment by nationals of their new countries. By the 1990s, close to a million Indians lived in the USA where they were held to be the best-educated ethnic group in the country.[95] Such considerations must now be part of Indian foreign policy.

The Gulf war of January 1991 emphasised the disquiet, disarray and 'near-paralysis'[96] of Indian foreign policy. India did not influence events in the Gulf. It had no plan to prevent the war and the slaughter of thousands of Iraqis. Nor did it support the war and move closer to the United States and the Western powers. And India was unable to ensure its oil supplies or the savings and futures of hundreds of thousands of Indians who had been working in the Gulf.[97] When the minority government of Chandra Shekhar permitted US planes to refuel in Bombay in January 1991, the government was denounced on all sides for abandoning non-alignment.[98] Yet none of the critics had suggestions about what India's positions on foreign affairs should be. When the government fell in March 1991, it was not on the issue of India's place in the world, but over the placing of parish-pump policemen: Haryana police had been used improperly to observe Rajiv Gandhi's house in New Delhi. According to one critic, the Minister of External Affairs admitted to parliament that 'New Delhi did not know what its policy on the Gulf was!'[99]

By the end of 1992, India had established full diplomatic relations with Israel,[100] and the Indian cricket team was playing test matches in South Africa where a 'cultural centre' with full visa facilities was to be opened. Formal diplomatic relations with Israel or South Africa were almost unthinkable when Mrs Gandhi died.

One interpretation of India's position in the transformed world of the 1990s holds that it must be ready to face an Islamic onslaught. The Muslim states of central Asia, including Afghanistan, have the potential to align with Pakistan and Iran to confront an India that is portrayed as oppressing a Muslim territory – Kashmir. The destruction of the mosque at Ayodhya can also be built into such an evaluation: a Muslim coalition could quickly involve itself in India's internal affairs. Even the most sober Indian foreign-policy analysts feel the need to note – albeit to discount as 'a trifle exaggerated' – the 'horrendous theory of an immediate threat from an Islamic fundamentalist movement of continental dimensions'.[101]

With 'non-alignment' no longer a meaningful concept, a recipe for an Indian foreign policy has to be devised from a complex list of ingredients. The new desire for foreign investment would support closer relations with the USA and Western capitalist countries; yet national pride and longstanding suspicion suggest that such a policy could be a liability in Indian elections. The disintegration of the Soviet Union and the end of the insurgency in Afghanistan pose the question of how to relate to new, militant Muslim states in central Asia, and the interest such states might show in the condition of India's 100 million Muslims. The loss of the Soviet Union as a reliable supplier of arms (for which payment did not have to be made in hard currency) means that foreign policy must ensure arms supplies and not assume positions that overstretch a vulnerable Indian military. India may be dominant in South Asia, but it was unable to enforce a settlement in Sri Lanka by using troops there in 1987–90. Nor has such dominance enabled easy suppression of insurgencies in Punjab, Kashmir and the northeast.

The domestic consequences of foreign policy are underlined in the assassination of Rajiv Gandhi in 1991. Campaigning in the national elections, he had returned to Tamilnad to reinforce the chances of his Congress (I) Party. He was murdered, the available evidence suggests, by Sri Lankan Tamil separatists, the LTTE, once clients of the Indian government. Their motive appears simple: revenge for the use of the Indian army against them in Sri Lanka in 1987–90 and fear that if Rajiv Gandhi were returned to office, he would be an implacable opponent.[102] The domestic consequences of his murder – as with that of his mother in 1984 – appear to have been a flow of sympathy and votes towards his party and revulsion against the LTTE among the people of Tamilnad. Similarly, the insurgency in Kashmir, the dispute at Ayodhya and the uprising in Punjab have threads that extend across international borders. While the map of Eastern Europe is being redrawn, and wolves in the guise of international bankers are at the door, defenders of the present Indian state have to contend with a host of interconnected, yet often unknown variables. They might well yearn for a time when Nehru could be applauded for saying 'we are in no camp and in no military alliances. The only camp we should like to be in is the camp of peace and goodwill.'[103] In the 1990s, a similar speech would be dismissed as simply naive.

THE POOR AND THE POLITY: WHAT SORT OF FUTURE?

In the programme of economic liberalisation, little is said of the effect on the poor, who constitute 30 per cent of the population even by the central government's rosy-spectacled calculations.[104] The first edition of this book ended with suggestions that 'action groups' or non-government organisations held the potential to force major changes in the distribution of power and wealth. Those suggestions remain to be fulfilled. Action groups have not diminished in number or in local influence since the mid-1980s. One estimate in 1988 identified 8800 individual groups attracting annual donations from abroad of roughly US $300 million. But voluntary associations have so far not fulfilled the hopes of those who saw them as vehicles for broad change in the Indian political system. Governments have attempted to co-opt them by incorporating them into the planning process.[105] Moreover, the groups themselves show few signs of being able to unite to work for wider goals.

The strength of such groups lies in their particular or local interests and their ability to wax and wane independently of government. Thus in the 1990s a group like the Narmada Bashao Andolan, founded to resist the huge dam-building programme planned for the Narmada River in Madhya Pradesh and Gujarat, rises to prominence,[106] while other groups disband or disappear. The social energy embodied in such voluntary associations remains impressive and full of hope, yet there is no sign that the groups themselves can become more than what they currently are: local responses to local concerns.

Nor have the parties of the Left been able to take up or take over the energy that drives the voluntary associations. Shared economic interests are not potent enough to act as an organisational principle or heart-stirring rallying cry. The energy nevertheless remains. More people read, discuss and organise than ever before. But to mobilise beyond the locality appears invariably to require appeals to religion or caste. The target for tens of thousands of impassioned people in December 1992 was a mosque in a small town in Uttar Pradesh, not the Reserve Bank of India in Bombay (see below, p. 212). The unresolved tensions of federalism may command more attention in the 1990s. In January 1992, Rasheeduddin Khan, who twenty years before had advocated redrawing the boundaries and increasing the number of India's states (see below, pp. 198–9) produced a new book on the same theme. *Federal India: a Design for Change* calls for more, smaller states to promote economic development and bring decision-making closer to the people.[107] Though such change is unlikely in the near future, politicians allude to the possibility of redrawing the federal map. In Uttar Pradesh, the BJP government declared its commitment to create a hill-state of Uttarakhand. The former Prime Minister, V. P. Singh, said he favours smaller states. And even the Home Minister in Narasimha Rao's government argued that a new state of Jharkhand ought to be established in southern Bihar.[108]

The Home Minister's intervention illustrates a recurring theme: the compulsion for central politicians to interfere in the politics of the states (see below, pp. 189–96). In the case of Jharkhand, the Home Minister, S. B. Chavan (b. 1920), could be portrayed as being on the side of the decentralising angels: let us have more states, he seemed to be saying. Yet his statement had more to do with discomfiting the non-Congress government of Bihar than with commitment to a revamped, more genuine federation. From New Delhi, to interfere in the states seems essential, whether to benefit friends and allies or to preserve the nation-state against some perceived threat.

However, evidence powerfully suggests that such interference seldom succeeds in achieving the aims of its instigators and often inflames powerful regional sentiment (see below, p. 196). In Punjab, five years of central rule between 1987 and 1992 resulted in little noticeable progress towards ending the secessionist movement. On the other hand, ten months of an elected government – even a dubiously-elected Congress government – appeared to bring a notable return of public confidence by the end of 1992.[109] Why then is it so difficult for governments in New Delhi to forswear interference in the states? First, central politicians genuinely fear that a state may go too far and either embroil India in the affairs of its neighbours (for example, with Tamil causes in Sri Lanka) or try to slip out of the federation altogether. Second, to survive at the centre one must have allies in the states, and such allies demand help when out of office. The nature of Indian society – there are few safety-nets to sustain out-of-office politicians – means that those cries come quickly and insistently.

The first edition of this book ended with the suggestion that 'contests to appropriate symbols and win mass sentiment' (p. 212), which a revolution in communications had fostered in Punjab from the 1970s, would become increasingly common throughout India. The destruction of the mosque at Ayodhya, struggles over the Mandal Report and the insurgency in Kashmir since 1989, are of that kind. Now, however, other areas of the world join India in similar quests and upheavals. In comparison with the erstwhile Yugoslavia or parts of the former Soviet Union, India's democratic federation has flexed, strained and bounced back relatively successfully in the years since 1985. Federalism and democracy will not guarantee survival, peace and economic well-being; but they seem to offer better long-term prospects than the alternative visions of religious or ethnic-based one-party states enforcing an arbitrary orthodoxy.

NOTES

Notes to subsequent chapters appear at the end of the book, preceding the Select Bibliography, where abbreviations are explained.

1. For an introduction to the BJP, Yogendra K. Malik and V. B. Singh, 'Bharatiya Janata Party: an Alternative to the Congress (I)?' *Asian Survey*, Vol. 32, no. 4 (April 1992), pp. 318–36.
2. All India Radio, General Overseas Service, 6 December 1992.
3. *IT*, 15 May 1991, p. 61.
4. David Butler, Ashok Lahiri, Prannoy Roy, *India Decides* (New Delhi: Living Media Books, 1991), p. 74.
5. *Statesman Weekly* [hereafter *SW*], 22 June 1991, p. 3. *Hindustan Times*, [hereafter *HT*], 21 June 1991, various pp.
6. *TofI*, 20 February 1987, p. 19. *India 1990. A Reference Annual* (New Delhi; Publications Division, 1990), pp. 277–9. Lloyd Rudolph, 'The Media and Cultural Politics,' *EPW*, 11 July 1992, p. 1489, accepts an estimate of 90 million viewers and 11 million television sets in 1988.

7. *Press and Advertisers Year Book 1990–1* (New Delhi: INFA Publications, 1991), p. 445c.

8. Manjunath Pendakur, 'Political Economy of Television: State, Class and Corporate Confluence in India', in Gerald Sussman and John A. Lent (eds), *Transnational Communications: Wiring the Third World* (Newbury Park; Sage, 1991), p. 246. See also Arvind Singhal and Everett Rogers, *India's Information Revolution* (New Delhi: Sage, 1989), p. 62, where the estimate is a still more modest 90 million.

9. Singhal and Rogers, *India's Information Revolution*, p. 85.

10. An Australian description of television is apposite: 'a mirror [that people] take for a window'. A. F. Davies and S. Encel, *Australian Society* (Melbourne: F. W. Cheshire, 1965), p. 229.

11. Singhal and Rogers, *India's Information Revolution*, p. 112.

12. *SW*, 6 August 1988, p. 3. *IT*, 31 October 1988, p. 118.

13. Mehendra Ved, 'Doordarshan's Epic Serial', *India Perspectives*, October 1990, pp. 24–5 (my emphasis).

14. Ibid., p. 28. See also Paula Richman (ed.), *Many Ramayanas: The Diversity of a Narrative Tradition in South Asia* (Berkeley: UCP, 1991).

15. Nicholas Nugent, *Rajiv Gandhi: Son of a Dynasty* (London: BBC Books, 1990), p. 67. Singhal and Rogers, *India's Information Revolution*, p. 144.

16. *ToII*, 9 August 1990, p. 1. The figure of 27 per cent results from the fact that roughly 22 per cent of positions were already reserved for Scheduled Castes (untouchables) and Scheduled Tribes (tribal people).

17. Previous judicial decisions made it unlikely that the courts would uphold reservations totalling more than 50 per cent of all jobs – thus the proposed figure of 27 per cent for OBCs. To make the system work, OBCs would at the time of entering government service have to prove their caste status.

18. *ToII*, 3 September 1990, p. 7, for profile of Mandal.

19. *IT*, 15 December 1989, pp. 10–16.

20. On 17 November 1992, the Supreme Court ruled that the recommendations of the Mandal Report were constitutional and could be implemented, but it laid down terms and conditions that would have to be met, including provision to take 'economic backwardness' into account. BBC World Service, 'South Asia Report', 17–18 November 1992.

21. See the calculations about the composition of the Bihar assembly in *Muslim India*, No. 89 (May 1990), p. 196.

22. Dharma Kumar, 'The Affirmative Action Debate in India', *Asian Survey*, Vol. 32, no. 3 (March 1992), p. 290.

23. *HIE*, 20 October 1990, p. 2.

24. *IT*, 31 October 1990, pp. 1, 5, for example. For a critique of the October 1990 edition of *Newstrack*, see *Manushi*, Nos 63–4 (March–June 1991), p. 54.

25. The *Times of India* did the same on 28 September 1990, p. 18 with a headline: 'India's version of Tiananmen Square'.

26. *Newstrack*, October 1990. One of the youths who attempted to kill himself in New Delhi was elected president of the Delhi University Students' Union a year later. *HT*, 15 September 1991, p. 1.

27. Estimate in *Business India* [hereafter *BI*], 3–16 September 1990, p. 10 and 15–28 October 1990, p. 56. Agitations about reservation of government jobs were part of political life in south India from the time of the First World War. For example, Robin Jeffrey, 'Travancore: Status, Class and the Growth of Radical Politics, 1860–1940', in Jeffrey (ed.), *People, Princes and Paramount Power* (New Delhi: Oxford University Press, 1978), p. 148.

28. *TofI*, 2 September 1990, p. 9. Interview with Rajiv Gandhi. Emphasis added.

29. The first edition of this book traced a similar strand of this story in Punjab in the 1970s. See Chapter 4 below, pp. 73–97.

30. For scholarly attempts to deal with caste, 'Hinduism' and the implications of electoral politics, see for example Lawrence A. Babb, *Redemptive Encounters: Three Modern Styles in the Hindu Tradition* (New Delhi: 1987), pp. 1–2 and Douglas E. Haynes, *Rhetoric and Ritual in Colonial India: the Shaping of a Public Culture in Surat City, 1852–1928* (Berkeley: 1991), p. 295.

31. B. D. Graham, *Hindu Nationalism and Indian Politics. The Origins and Development of the Bharatiya Jana Sangh* (1990), pp. 3–4, 253–8.

32. Ibid., p. 258.

33. For earlier developments at Ayodhya, see Peter van der Veer, '"God Must Be Liberated!" A Hindu Liberation Movement in Ayodhya', *MAS*, Vol. 21, no. 2 (1987), pp. 283–301.

34. This is the so-called Shah Bano case, in which an elderly Muslim woman was awarded alimony, but the outcry from Muslims was so great that the Congress (I) government legislated to exclude Muslims from the civil code. *TofI*, 5 February 1986, p. 12.

35. L. K. Advani, quoted in *TofI*, 26 September 1990, p. 1.

36. For examples, see Neeladri Bhattacharya, 'Myth, History and the Politics of Ramjanmabhumi', in S. Gopal (ed.), *Anatomy of a*

Confrontation. The Babri Masjid-Ramjanmabhumi Issue (New Delhi: 1991), p. 126.

37. Advani, quoted in *TofI*, 21 November 1990, p. 7.
38. *TofI*, 26 September 1990, p. 1. *IT*, 15 October 1990, p. 18.
39. *TofI*, 21 October 1990, p. 1.
40. *HIE*, 22 December 1990, pp. 2, 3
41. *TofI*, 31 October and 2 November, both p. 1.
42. Mark Tully, 'South Asia Report', BBC World Service, 13 December 1992.
43. Ibid.
44. These observations are based on videotapes of film screened on Australian television in the week of 7–13 December 1992. See also *IT*, 31 December 1992, pp. 18–29 and *Newstrack* video, December 1992.
45. Chandan Mitra in *HT*, 6 December 1992, p. 12.
46. India had four governments in twenty months between November 1989 and July 1991.
47. Bihar (54), Delhi (7), Haryana (10), Himachal Pradesh (4), Madhya Pradesh (40), Rajasthan (25), Uttar Pradesh (85).
48. *TofI*, 29 November 1990, p. 9.
49. Four in Karnataka and one in Andhra Pradesh. *Sunday Observer*, 23–29 June 1991, p. 7.
50. A rough piece of evidence: throughout south India, Brahmins were never estimated to constitute more than 3 per cent of the population. In Uttar Pradesh, on the other hand, they were estimated at 9.1 per cent in 1931.
51. K. Jayaprasad, *RSS and Hindu Nationalism. Inroads in a Leftist Stronghold* (New Delhi: Deep and Deep, 1991), especially pp. 336–50.
52. The insurgency in Kashmir exploded immediately after the election of the V. P. Singh government in December 1989. *Seminar*, No. 392 (April 1992), is devoted to the Kashmir struggle.
53. K. K. Mathew (1910–92). *Frontline*, 11 September 1992, p. 19. *HIE*, 9 May 1992, p. 16.
54. *IE* (Chandigarh), 28 January 1986, p. 6.
55. Headed by judges Venkataramiah and Desai.
56. *HIE*, 8 November 1986, p. 4.
57. *Statesman* (Delhi), 28 January 1986, p. 1. *IT*, 28 February 1986, p. 22.
58. Estimates were that 'more than 50' people had been murdered between September 1985 and mid-January 1986. *SMH*, 13 January 1985, quoting Press Trust of India. In March, more than 70 murders were recorded. *Age*, 29 March 1986, p. 11.
59. *Age*, 2 April 1986, p. 7.

60. *HIE*, 12 July 1986, p. 1.
61. *National Integration Council Meeting, 31 December 1991, Agenda* (New Delhi: Ministry of Home Affairs, 1991), Annexure 1, p. 11. I am grateful to Manoj Joshi of *Frontline* for these references.
62. For discussion of some of the factions and their motives, see Joyce Pettigrew, 'Martyrdom and Guerrilla Organisation in Punjab', *JCCP*, Vol. 30, no. 3 (November 1992), pp. 387–406.
63. *Frontline*, 21 July–3 August 1990, p. 16.
64. *SW*, 24 August 1991, p. 3. *HIE*, 31 August 1991, p. 4.
65. *IT*, 15 October 1988, p. 22 and 31 March 1989, p. 14.
66. Uma Chakravarti and Nandita Haksar, *Delhi Riots, Three Days in the Life of a Nation* (New Delhi: Lancer, 1987) has 650 pages of interviews with victims. Attempts to prosecute a Congress politician led to the police being mobbed and driven away by his retainers. *HIE*, 22 September 1990, p. 11.
67. *HT*, 16 June 1991, p. 1.
68. *HT*, 23 June 1991, p. 1.
69. *HIE*, 30 November 1991, p. 1.
70. *IT*, 15 March 1992, p. 20. *FEER*, 5 March 1992, p. 11. *HIE*, 29 February 1992, pp. 1, 13.
71. *SW*, 29 February 1992, p. 7.
72. *Frontline*, 20 November 1992, pp. 27–34.
73. *HIE*, 24 October 1992, p. 2 and 31 October 1992, p. 4. Salim Jiwa, *The Death of Air India Flight 182* (London: W. H. Allen, 1986), p. 76. Ian Mulgrew, *Unholy Terror: The Sikhs and International Terrorism* (Toronto: Key Porter Books, 1988), pp. 128–32, 179. Parmar was reported killed in a shoot-out with police in Jalandhar district on 15 October 1992; two Pakistani nationals died in the same fight.
74. Gyanendra Pandey, *The Construction of Communalism in Colonial North India* (New Delhi: 1990), pp. 22, 261.
75. The Government of India estimates 29 per cent of the population lives below a calorie-defined poverty line. *HIE*, 19 August 1989, pp. 8, 16. The World Bank in 1990 estimated 40 per cent of the population lives in poverty; an Indian market-research group estimated closer to 50 per cent. *HIE*, 28 July 1990, p. 12. *SW*, 15 December 1990, p. 3.
76. Jawaharlal Nehru, Lok Sabha, 23 May 1956, in K. T. Narasimha Char (ed.), *The Quintessence of Nehru* (London: George Allen and Unwin, 1961), p. 145.
77. *IT*, 30 April 1991, p. 55. Abid Hussain, *Indian Industry in the 1990s – Challenges Ahead*, 17th Frank Moraes Memorial Lecture (Madras: United Writers' Association and Southern

India Chamber of Commerce and Industry, 1989), pp. 10–12. *The Financial Times* (London), 16 September 1991, p. v. *FEER*, 8 August 1991, pp. 48–9. P. N. Agarwala, 'Restructuring the Public Sector,' in *The Hindu Survey of Indian Industry 1991* (Madras: Kasturi and Sons, 1992), p. 51.

78. *HT*, 30 April 1991, p. 55.
79. *Seminar*, No. 380 (April 1991), p. 12. Romesh and Raj Thapar, the magazine's founders, died in 1987.
80. Hussain, *Indian Industry*, p. 20.
81. Ibid., p. 2. *BI*, 11–24 December 1989, pp. 57–8.
82. *EPW*, 9 February 1991, p. 318. *BI*, 26 October–8 November 1992, p. 50. India's debt-service ratio in 1991–2 (repayment requirements as a proportion of total export earnings) was 26.2 per cent. India's foreign debt was three times greater than its total export earnings in 1991–2.
83. T. N. Anantharam Iyer, 'Towards a Viable BOP', *The Hindu Survey of Indian Industry 1991*, p. 35.
84. *HIE*, 29 September 1990, p. 2.
85. *IT*, 31 October 1990, p. 56.
86. S. L. Rao, Director-General, National Council for Applied Economic Research, seminar, Melbourne, 23 November 1992.
87. *HIE*, 29 December 1990, p. 12. *FEER*, 18 April 1991, p. 70.
88. *Australian Financial Review*, 31 July 1991, citing *New York Times*.
89. T. A. Seshan, 'Testing Time for Indian Economy', *The Hindu Review of Indian Industry 1991*, p. 13.
90. *Frontline*, 31 July 1992, p. 9.
91. *Frontline*, 19 June 1992, p. 27. *FEER*, 18 June 1992, p. 76.
92. *HIE*, 14 November 1992, p. 12.
93. *HT*, 20 July 1991, p. 12, quoting the pre-budget Economic Survey. S. L. Rao, Director-General, National Council for Applied Economic Research, seminar, Melbourne, Australia, 23 November 1992. See also P. V. Narasimha Rao, *Planning for the Poor and Market Mechanism for Competitive Efficiency Must Go Together* (New Delhi: Ministry of Information and Broadcasting, 1992), speech of 22 May 1992, especially p. 2.
94. T. Krishna Kumar, 'Forgetting to Remember', *EPW*, 17 October 1992, p. 2301.
95. *HIE*, 22 June 1991, p. 9. *FEER*, 23 May 1991, p. 34; 25 July 1991, p. 14. This was in striking contrast to the position of Indian immigrants in Britain or Canada where they often tended to be less qualified, working-class people.
96. Dileep Padgaonkar, 'Changing Times', *Seminar*, No. 381

(May 1991), p. 30.
97. *IT*, 31 March 1991, p. 34.
98. *Frontline*, 16 February–1 March 1991, p. 98.
99. Padgaonkar, 'Changing Times', p. 30.
100. *SMH*, 1 February 1992.
101. A. K. Damodaran, 'Reassessing Strategies,' *World Focus*, Nos 143–4 (November–December 1991), p. 5.
102. *HT Magazine*, 16 June 1991, p. 5; 25 August 1991, pp. 1, 5. *Frontline*, 22 May 1992, pp. 38ff; 5 June 1992, pp. 17ff; 19 June 1992, p. 18. Mohan Ram, *Sri Lanka: the Fractured Island* (New Delhi: Penguin, 1989) for detail on the period.
103. Nehru, speech at banquet for Bulganin and Khrushchev, New Delhi, 20 November 1955, in Narasimha Char (ed.), *Quintessence*, p. 196.
104. See D. P. Chaudhri and Ajit K. Dasgupta, *Agriculture and the Development Process: a Study of Punjab* (London: Croom Helm, 1985), Appendix D, pp. 188–91 for a discussion of definitions of the 'poverty line'.
105. *HT Magazine*, 18 October 1992, p. 15.
106. Ibid.
107. Rasheeduddin Khan, *Federal India* (New Delhi: Vikas, 1992), p. 46.
108. *HIE*, 31 August 1991, p. 7; 19 September 1992, p. 4. *IT*, 30 September 1992, pp. 22, 30. *SW*, 5 September 1992, p. 1.
109. Journalists toured Punjab freely in September and October 1992 and reported that 'Punjab is on the mend and no traveller who ventures into areas where silence and fear ruled at dusk last October can miss the lights, the people, the movement on the highways and an occasional marriage celebration [today].' Manoj Joshi in *Frontline*, 30 November 1990, p. 26. *IT*, 15 September 1992, p. 30.

1 Ethnicity

7 a.m. Melbourne, Australia. Friday, 2 November 1984. In much of the world it's still Thursday – early evening in western Europe, late afternoon on the east coast of North America. Already, however, the international communications satellites are transmitting pictures from India where Prime Minister Indira Gandhi was assassinated on the morning of 31 October. Via the USA, Australians see a report from New Delhi showing the effects of rioting against Sikhs, two of whom are said to have shot the prime minister. Palls of smoke. Burned-out buildings. Passive khaki-clad policemen. The American voice-over refers to India's poverty and the tragedy of 'communal violence' – conflict between different communities, in this case Hindus and Sikhs. Only economic development and education, it says, can eliminate this scourge.

In the days of riot and uncertainty following Mrs Gandhi's death, this was to be a common theme. 'Despite 37 years of modern democracy and industrialization', wrote an Indian journalist, 'India is slowly slipping backwards into religious anarchy.'[1] Pump wealth and education into a country as poor as India – this popular argument ran – and these old-fashioned 'communal' conflicts ought to be swept away.

Indeed, even the new Prime Minister, Rajiv Gandhi, seemed to reflect this belief. 'The real danger', he told an American interviewer after his victory in the December 1984 elections, 'is economic stagnation. Whenever we've had a problem with the minorities it's been when there has been an economic problem.'[2] Get the economy right, he seemed to say, and one could reasonably expect the conflict between ethnic groups to dissolve.

The assumption that illiteracy is also a cause of such conflict is equally widespread. Commenting on recent Hindu–Muslim riots in the city of Hyderabad, a writer concluded: 'To a very large extent the general situation is worsened by the high

1

illiteracy rate'. A review of the state elections in Tamilnad pointed out that a Hindu-revivalist candidate had won the seat of Kanyakumari on the southern tip of India where Hindus and Christians had rioted against each other in 1982. 'Communal politics taking root . . . in a district with 62 per cent literacy [i.e., very high for India] is a dangerous portent.'[3] Again, the writer implied that literacy ought to *decrease* such conflicts.

These apparently common-sense arguments, however, do not stand up to scrutiny. The evidence of the past thirty years or more from throughout the world suggests that 'modernisation' – economic development, government activity, schooling, satellite television, etc. – may harden ethnic identities and provoke, or intensify, conflict between ethnic groups. Indeed, such modernisation played a large part in shaping the Sikh unrest (represented in its extreme form in the demand for a sovereign state) which ultimately led to storming of the Golden Temple, Mrs Gandhi's death and the 'communal violence' that ripped cruelly through New Delhi and other north Indian cities in November 1984.

First, Sikhs do not fit the poor-and-illiterate picture. On the whole (with the possible exception of the Parsis of Bombay), they are the most prosperous religious group in India, as we shall see in Chapters 2 and 3. Punjab, the state in which they form more than half the population, has the country's highest per capita income. Nor is Punjab educationally backward. 'In or near every big village', a Punjabi journalist wrote in 1980, there is 'at least one degree college.' Twenty years before, 'it was difficult to come across a degree holder in rural areas, but now it [is] not easy to find a young Sikh who [has] not passed the matriculation examination'.[4] Punjab, he concluded, has experienced 'an "education explosion"'.

In the nineteenth century, Marx believed that industrialisation and the creation of an urban working class would erode and eventually destroy allegiances based on religion, language or race. In India today, some Marxists are surprised and dismayed that this has not happened. 'Against all expectations', wrote one in 1984 'it [communalism] has shown no sign of "withering away" with the passage of time and process of modernisation of our socio-economic structure. Even the great expansion in education . . . has not modernised the minds of the people . . . It is distressing, indeed!'[5] As India has 'modernised' – and Punjab, according to many of the statistics, is the most striking example – demands based on religion, language, region or caste seem to have increased, not diminished. The most dangerous crisis independent India has faced – the Punjab crisis of 1984 – has occurred in the country's most prosperous state and involved some of its most travelled, alert, diligent people.

ETHNICITY

In the past twenty years or more, many scholars have argued that aspects of modernisation in fact shape and intensify feelings based on religion, language, caste or similar characteristics. The blanket word applied to these characteristics is 'ethnic', and an 'ethnic group' is sometimes defined as one that perceives a common identity based on characteristics acquired either at birth (colour, for example) or through cultural experience (language, religion, caste, sense of regional identity, etc.).

Many scholars would agree on a basic check list of processes which, once triggered by economic change, seemingly ought to make people 'modern'. In fact, however, they seem rather to sharpen ethnic identities and make such identities more 'salient' for politics than before. The list would include:

* increased government activity
* expansion of communications
* spread of ideas of competition.

Economic change, it needs to be emphasised, invariably underlies all three processes. Without changes in the way wealth is produced and distributed and in the way some people earn their livings, it is difficult (though not impossible) to conceive of governments performing more tasks, of communications reaching ever-more remote areas or of ideas about the rightness of competition (and perhaps even equality) seeping into the minds of growing numbers of people. Each of the three processes needs to be spelled out in a little detail before we examine the anti-Sikh riots of November 1984 for evidence of the applicability of this argument.[6]

Government Activity and the Role of the State

Since the industrial revolution in nineteenth-century Britain, governments in most parts of the world have played an increasingly important role in people's lives. It was not simply in urban, industrial societies that this process occurred – not simply in so-called welfare states – but also in areas ruled by foreign imperialists. The old colonial governments attempted to extend their sway over the people they ruled. Three scholars have suggested that wherever 'the state was the major source of power and employment, ethnic nationalist movements arose that in form and development were similar to those of contemporary America and western Europe'.[7]

As an economy changes, whether as a result of government or independent activity (or both), the state is placed in a position where it is able – indeed, it has to – distribute resources. In short, it increasingly behaves as referee or Santa Claus. People perceive that economic changes are happening around them and that 'others' may be benefiting while 'we' are not. For people to get what they want from the state, they must organise, and one way of organising is the construction (or reconstruction) of ethnic groups. One person petitioning the state for a school, for example, may not receive much attention. An organisation demanding a school on behalf of 50 000 'backward castes' or Sikhs or Afro-Americans or Italo-Australians is far more likely to get a hearing. And a school.

Communications

This umbrella word relates to the innovations of the industrial revolution and to the growing technical ability of governments to exert greater influence over the lives of their subjects. One of the laments of the British civil service in India was that the telegraph reduced the 'man on the spot' to a postman. Instead of dealing with problems and people on his own common-sense initiative, he had simply to carry out orders from headquarters. Even the Government of India, once insulated from London by a sea voyage of several months, by the 1870s could receive telegraphic instructions in a matter of hours.

Communications involved not merely moving people –

steamships, trains, the Suez Canal, macadamised roads – but moving ideas (the telegraph, the printing press, cheap paper and later, the telephone, radio, films and television). These in turn concerned the state and led to the spread of formal, state-sponsored education. To help to make the industrial revolution happen, certain skills were needed among the mass of people. Basic literacy was one; discipline and obedience were others. Schools were expected to develop all three (though they seem never to have been as effective as those who have most to gain from them would like).

Schooling has unintended effects. Bringing children and youths together regularly heightens their awareness of similarities and contrasts. Teaching them to read allows them to discover a wider range of ideas than ever before. 'The progress of schools and universities measures that of nationalism', writes the English historian E. J. Hobsbawm, 'just as schools and especially universities become its most conspicuous champions.'[8] 'Ethnic identity' and 'nationalism' share many of the same characteristics. Where an 'ethnic group' ends and a 'nation' begins is one of the smouldering questions of the twentieth century, and in Punjab in the 1980s, it burns.

Schooling forces people to travel. If a child is to get a good education, it is likely that at some stage he or she will have to go regularly to a town or a city. A 'good education', moreover, often suggests intellectual movement: away from old ways or 'superstition'. Both kinds of mobility sharpen consciousness. Students meet people different from themselves, people about whom in the past they would have known nothing. Similarly, they meet ideas that would seem unnecessary or outlandish to their parents.

Industrialisation also makes people migrate to find work and to live. It is not an accident that Calcutta's first major communal riots in the 1890s were between Muslims from Bihar, drawn to the city to work in the jute mills, and Bengali Hindus. At this stage, Bengali Muslims, long part of the local fabric, were not involved. It was the outsiders – alone and seeking to soothe that loneliness by emotional performances of their village ceremonies – who collided with local Hindus angry at strange, offensive intrusions.[9]

Communications may both dilute and intensify identities. North India provides apt examples. In the past fifteen years or so, Sikh identity has undoubtedly hardened and sharpened, and the differences between Sikhs and Hindus have been rigorously spelled out and emphasised, as we shall see. At the same time, however, throughout the vast Hindi-speaking heartland of north India, from Rajasthan to Bihar, the 1984 national elections were fought with appeals to a broad 'Hindu' sentiment. This suggests the dilution – at least briefly for electoral purposes – of the scores of deep, caste divisions which separate people in daily life. Those divisions were overcome (if this argument is correct) because an idea of 'Hindus-in-danger' was successfully communicated to the voters.

Ideas of Competition

Few states in the modern world openly base themselves on the principle of inequality. South Africa was one, but most states loudly pledge themselves to the well-being of all citizens and the right of all citizens to compete on equal terms. In practice, of course, such avowals are often more honoured in the breach than the observance. Nevertheless, the principle is constantly affirmed. The idea of the rightness of equal opportunity – of the equal right to compete – has spread rapidly throughout the world in the past hundred years. In the 1850s, those in Britain who advocated government mass education ran 'the risk of being pelted ... as fanatical democrats'.[10] There was no unanimity that deeds in the name of 'the people' were necessarily worthy deeds. Today, however, even in totalitarian states, dictators talk constantly about the well-being of the masses. A hundred years ago, they would have found it less necessary to do so.

This emphasis on equality of opportunity, which has been preached as loudly in India as in any country in the world since 1947, is at odds with the inequalities which ordinary people see around them every day. Part of their dilemma lies in answering the question, 'Why do others have more than I have?'. One possible answer, of course, is that 'others' belong to the ruling class and have seized the fruits of the workers' labour. Yet class-consciousness does not arise as spontaneously as some Marxists believed it would.

Another way of answering the question involves ethnic

labels. 'Others' have more than 'we' do, because their ethnic group controls the good things and excludes 'us'. In Bombay, Bombay-born, Marathi-speakers may see all south Indian immigrants, whether from Tamilnad, Kerala, Karnataka or Andhra Pradesh, as a single group which has 'stolen' all the best jobs. Local Marathi-speakers, by this line of argument, are being discriminated against – that is, treated unequally.[11]

In Assam since 1979, a powerful movement of Assamese-speakers has sought the expulsion of non-Assamese, many of them Muslim, Bengali-speaking, illegal immigrants from Bangladesh. Assamese, according to this cry, face the threat of becoming a minority in their own birthplace. In Andhra Pradesh in 1983 and again in March 1985, the Telugu Desam Party defeated Indira Gandhi's Congress – 'Congress (I)' – on a promise of restoring the dignity of the Telugu people, winning a fair deal for them and ending their slavish subservience to New Delhi.[12]

In all these examples, people are objecting to 'unfair' or 'unequal' competition. 'Others' have got control of jobs and the machinery of government and are using their advantage to threaten 'our' self-respect, well-being and perhaps even existence. 'We' must unite, regardless of our social class or other attributes that might sometimes divide us, if we are to compete effectively with 'them'. Implicit in this process is an emphasis on certain symbols or attributes and the down-playing of others.

CHOICE

One strand of scholarly writing about ethnicity emphasises the importance of choice, once processes of modernisation have begun, in the shaping of ethnic groups. Ethnic characteristics, according to this argument, are not chiselled into people's character like letters into granite. Rather, certain characteristics float like vegetables in a bowl of soup: at the discretion of the diner, one may be spooned out and another ignored. Particular situations, government actions and economic conditions determine choices, and choices may change over time.[13] In Assam, for example, the current agitation in theory unites all speakers of the Assamese language, whether Hindus, Muslims or (presumably) tribal people. The threat comes not from another religion, but from another language and culture. It is easy to see, however, that in changed circumstances, religion could become the important line of division.

In Andhra Pradesh, too, we see the importance of choice. From 1969 to 1972, a powerful movement in the Telengana area (around the city of Hyderabad and once part of the princely state of that name) campaigned against discrimination suffered at the hands of people from coastal Andhra. Though everyone spoke the Telugu language, difference on this occasion was based on a sense of regional disadvantage.[14] By 1982, however, many millions of Telugus felt that their main identity now lay as Telugus, unjustly treated by governments in New Delhi. The victory of the Telugu Desam Party, and its film-star leader, N. T. Rama Rao, would seem to bear out the argument that a sense of 'Telugu-ness' is now the dominant characteristic among the state's 55 million people. Yet even as Rama Rao's party was recording its impressive victory in March 1985, a new regional movement from the poor, arid districts (known as Rayalseema) in the south of the state was seeking to make people there join in 'a struggle for the . . . existence of the Rayalseema people'.[15]

Since choice is so important, and since particular situations influence choices (for example, a Telengani in 1970, but a Telugu in 1985), politicians play a crucial role. The American political scientist, Paul Brass, a close student of Punjab, argues that politics and political organisation are central 'to the formation and channelling of group identities . . . They shape group consciousness'.[16] In other words, though modernisation makes it likely that ethnic identity will sharpen and that rivalry will result, such conflict need not end in assassination and secessionism. The choices politicians make – the ground rules they establish within states – can mitigate and channel ethnic conflict. But this requires skill, sensitivity and an awareness of the dangers of ethnic conflict dissolving into open war, as in the Nigerian civil war of 1967–70.

In Punjab from the late 1970s, however, politicians played a desperate game in which few holds were barred. They were, it seems, unaware of the fact that the once-contained factional rivalries, which were the essence of Punjab's politics in the past, were now adrift on a sea of mass politics. Masses of people were now able to hear and respond to appeals that

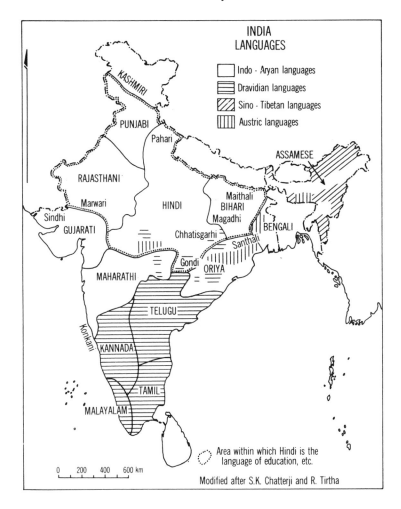

MAP 1.2 *India: major languages*

previously reached only the notables of a locality, who would
then reinterpret them to their underlings as they saw fit.

Now, however, a figure like Jarnail Singh Bhindranwale
(1947–84), scudding across Punjab's splendid new network of
village roads in the bus owned by his religious group, his
activities publicised by a steadily expanding vernacular press,
was able to become a celebrity in weeks. Within five months
of the gun-battle in Amritsar that brought him notoriety in

April 1978, he could claim to be powerful enough to bring down the state government, while journalists conceded that he had become a 'political eminence no less important ... than the four top men' of the governing Akali Dal party. Within five years, at the age of 36, he became 'the most formidable force in the Punjab'.[17] Within six years, he was dead, one of hundreds of casualties in the largest single battle the Indian Army had been asked to fight against other Indians since independence. The repercussions of the battle at the Golden Temple in Amritsar in June 1984 led first to Mrs Gandhi's murder, then to anti-Sikh riots and then to the country's greatest-ever electoral landslide in favour of her son.

The anti-Sikh riots in New Delhi and elsewhere in November 1984 after Mrs Gandhi's death illustrate how the profound changes overtaking India *may* lead to the cruellest ethnic violence. But part of the argument of this book is that they *need* not, if sensitive constitutional arrangements can be made and maintained. A middle way is possible between, on one hand, regional secessionism and communal violence, and on the other, the ill-judged 'remedy' of ever-increasing centralisation.

THE ANTI-SIKH RIOTS, NOVEMBER 1984

In the aftermath of Mrs Gandhi's assassination, gangs in towns throughout north India murdered thousands of Sikhs, most of them men, and attacked Sikh homes and property. In New Delhi alone, estimates of the number of murders range from the official figure of about 600 to the more plausible one of 2500.[18] All this occurred in the space of about four days – from the evening of 31 October, the day Mrs Gandhi was assassinated, until 4 November, the day after her cremation. In the sprawling state of Uttar Pradesh, the losses sustained by Sikh families and businesses have been estimated as high as US $55 million (Rs. 600 million).[19]

In New Delhi and elsewhere, many of the Sikhs who were killed had had little connection with Punjab and almost certainly none with the so-called 'Khalistan' campaign for a sovereign Sikh state. The victims were mostly non-Jats (though Jats form the largest, most influential caste among Sikhs, as we shall see). Many had never lived in Punjab, but were in fact refugees from an earlier pogrom: their families had come from Pakistan when India was partitioned in 1947.

The obvious explanation for the killing of Sikhs in November 1984 – and the one which the Indian government would like people to accept – is that the spontaneous anger of a grief-stricken people regrettably exploded in attacks on the most obvious target – members of the same religion as Mrs Gandhi's killers, Sikhs. Vengeance, this line of apology runs, is detestable, deplorable . . . but understandable. It is as old as human society. This explanation, however, leaves many questions unanswered. The riots, in fact, appear to have been organised and co-ordinated. They had far less to do with the ancient sin of vengeance than with the contemporary problems posed by ethnic politics. Indeed, the riots provide a way of exploring characteristics of 'ethnicity' as a political force in the modern world.

Most of the killings in New Delhi took place in lower middle-class or poorer areas of the city, where Sikhs were established in humble, yet still enviable homes. Usually, it appears, they were killed not by their neighbours but by gangs who came in buses and trucks from outlying areas. Sometimes, neighbours joined the attacks, but often, it seems, they took risks to help Sikhs who lived near them.

Mobility, literacy and large sections of other 'ethnic groups' were all involved. So too were the compulsions of electoral politics and the effects of television and international communications. Indeed, these killings were evidence not of something primitive, backward or ancient, but rather of how India changes, how 'modernity' sends its roots wider and wider.

Let us begin with communications, because a great deal of what follows in this book is based on the contention that more people in India today are exposed to more ideas than at any time in history. This volume of ideas, and the reactions they produce, are the most important aspect of change in modern India. If I had to answer in a single sentence the question, 'What's happening to India?', I would say that it is talking to itself as never before and forming a new 'itself' in the process. The nationalists of the 1930s stamped their mark on the country at independence in 1947 and for twenty years thereafter. But a bigger, more complex 'India' than they ever knew is coming into being, and to comprehend it and cope with it requires perspective and imagination. In the aftermath of the November riots, one of the many new voices, the battling feminist magazine *Manushi*, captured well the crucial importance of the revolution in communications for today's India: 'These riots have highlighted with great urgency the role that wrong, bad and dishonest information plays in breeding hatred, violence and injustice'.[20]

Non-official inquiries into the riots have mentioned a number of noteworthy features.[21] First, the importance of rumours. Rumours that the New Delhi water supply had been poisoned were said to have been broadcast from loudspeaker vans. They thereafter sped around New Delhi by telephone. There were rumours too that Sikhs had large caches of weapons stored in their *gurdwaras* (temples). They were also said to have distributed sweets to celebrate Mrs Gandhi's death and some were supposed to have danced the *bhangra*, a jubilant Punjabi dance associated with festivals. (In fact, this story seems to have begun when college students, who had been rehearsing for a month, were noticed rehearsing on the day Mrs Gandhi was killed.)[22]

Television also provided some of the essential ingredients of the riots. Television as a national medium has spread across India only since 1980. Indeed, at the end of 1984, the government claimed proudly that 70 per cent of the population was at last within range of a television signal. That signal is highly controlled. Most of the programming still emanates from New Delhi, another mark of the centralisation of the Indian state which Mrs Gandhi fostered. In the wake of her assassination, the national television and radio network repeatedly identified her killers as Sikhs. Television showed scenes of the crowds at the place where her body lay in state. Some people shouted slogans: 'Blood for blood!' Given that radio and television are normally closely controlled and obedient, it was surprising that this provocative segment should have been shown. On the other hand, it was not until early evening of the day Mrs Gandhi was killed that radio and television announced her death, though she was dead by 10 a.m. and foreign news agencies had broadcast the news before noon Indian time.

Such foreign reporting, quickly beamed back to India, was a fruitful source of rumour and incitement. The few foolish

Sikhs who popped champagne corks for cameras in Britain to celebrate Mrs Gandhi's death were soon the talk of New Delhi. It was said that airline travellers had brought video-cassettes of the provocative newsreel incident to India within hours or that it had been beamed into Punjab – and videotaped – from Pakistan television. The stories of champagne corks in foreign places blended all too easily with those of sweets, dancing, poisoned water supplies and arms caches in Sikh gurdwaras in New Delhi.

The video-cassette recorder (VCR) also symbolised the increasingly noticeable gap between rich and poor that accompanies economic change in India. Possession of an array of gadgets and consumer goods now separates the comfortable from the 40–50 per cent of the population who live below the government's own definition of the poverty line. When more prosperous Sikh homes were looted in November, the gangs quickly grabbed VCRs. By the end of the month, the stolen VCRs were 'finding their way to the market at a ridiculous price'.[23] Though the benefits of the 'green revolution' have not been evenly spread among all Sikhs (particularly not among the lower-middle and working classes of New Delhi), there is a vague notion throughout India that because Punjab is now known to be prosperous, all Sikhs are therefore well-off. They are sometimes mocked (behind their backs) but more often envied.

In some areas of New Delhi, Sikh homes, shops and businesses were interspersed with those of Muslims and Hindus. Yet the rioters seemed to aim with unerring accuracy for the Sikh premises, in spite of the fact that their owners were in hiding and did all they could to disguise the fact that Sikhs lived or worked there. In some instances, neighbours were probably advising the rioters. But where the neighbours did not co-operate, the gangs sometimes used the lists compiled by local ration shops. From the names, it was possible to guess fairly accurately which places were Sikh. Pre-literate, less-governed societies had the advantage of a certain anonymity. In recording information, governments change opportunities and possibilities.

A further activity of the state – closely connected to the ideas of competition which increasingly affect people even in 'caste-bound' India – also played a part in the New Delhi riots.

When the rioters were not armed with lists of ration-book holders, they had obtained voting lists compiled for the elections that are a regular feature of Indian life. Again, they could pick out Sikh houses and businesses from the names on the lists. The electoral lists were not the only part that elections and competitive politics played in the New Delhi riots. According to some accounts, the riots themselves were engineered for specific electoral needs. Indeed, the constraints of winning elections, as I shall try to show in Chapter 7, influenced both the central government's handling of affairs in Punjab and the rivalries between Punjab politicians.

Non-official inquiries into the riots have contended that they were 'well-organised' or 'masterminded and well organised' or 'well planned and well organised'.[24] According to Amiya Rao, writing in the outspoken *Economic and Political Weekly* of Bombay, the rioting was 'engineered for political reasons and because of the gnawing fear that the Congress (I) might lose in the coming elections'.[25] A sense of deep and widespread insecurity would enhance the appeal of the Congress (I) as the only party capable of maintaining national unity and stability. Certainly, once the election was called in mid-November, the Congress (I) did everything it could to project itself in this way. 'Judging from the alarmist Congress (I) advertisements', wrote the respected historian Dharma Kumar, 'they seem to believe that in our panic lies their strength.'[26]

The Government of India, though quickly setting up an inquiry into Mrs Gandhi's assassination, resisted calls for an investigation of the anti-Sikh riots until April 1985. Then, as part of a series of measures aiming to reconcile Sikhs, an inquiry under a Supreme Court judge was announced. All high-ranking detainees were released, and the ban on the All-India Sikh Students' Federation lifted.

Earlier, however, the Prime Minister, Rajiv Gandhi, had sounded adamant in his rejection of demands for an inquiry, which 'would not be in Sikhs' interests'. The central government also dismissed the reports of the two private-citizens' inquiries, one headed by S. M. Sikri, a former Chief Justice of India, the other by Rajni Kothari, an internationally known political scientist. Reporters were told that the government was 'not inclined to accept the findings of a politically oriented group of individuals . . . who have always been finding fault with the ruling party at the Centre'.[27] *Who Are the Guilty?*, the report with which Kothari was associated, named four Congress (I) Members of Parliament (in 1984) as having been involved in instigating or protecting the rioters.[28]

ELECTIONS, COMMUNICATIONS, ETHNICITY

The national elections of December 1984 returned the Congress (I) with the greatest majority in post-independence history: more than 400 seats out of 515 contested. Moreover, the turnout was the highest ever (62 per cent against a previous best of 61 per cent in 1967) and the winning party for the first time won 50 per cent of the votes cast (previous best: 48 per cent in 1957).[29] (See Table 1.1.)

It was a new style of campaign. Indeed, *India Today*, the country's slickest news magazine, itself (and its 325 000 fortnightly circulation) a reflection of the communications revolution, used a quotation from Marshall McLuhan, the late Canadian philosopher of the media, to lead a story on election publicity. Before the voting, the magazine suggested that the Congress (I)'s use of a public-relations firm to create a Western-style campaign might go over the heads of the voters. A writer in a business magazine, in fact, ridiculed the campaign as inept. 'One searches in vain' in the printed material 'for the stuff that sells parties, gets votes, wins elections and creates governments.'[30] Yet *India Today* itself used sophisticated polling and computer analysis to predict the result with remarkable accuracy.[31] The magazine, too, assumed that the nature of the Indian electorate has changed and that it can be questioned and analysed and appealed to in a way that would have seemed impossible in 1970.

Video-cassettes and posters were perhaps more effective in spreading the Congress (I)'s message than the ridiculed newspaper advertisements. But every method of advertisement hammered away at the theme of 'vote for Congress and save the country'. Garish posters of Mrs Gandhi, blood spurting from her body, appealed to voters: 'Indira's final wish – save the country with every drop of blood'.[32] Old styles of communication blended with new. For example, Congress (I)

TABLE 1.1 *Seats won in parliamentary elections, December 1984*

	Congress (I)	Major opponent		Countermanded or postponed
Andhra Pradesh (42)	6	TDP	28	c2
Assam (14)		No poll		
Bihar (54)	48	CPI	2	
Gujarat (26)	24	Janata	1	
		BJP	1	
Haryana (10)	10		0	
Himachal Pradesh (4)	3		0	p1
Jammu and Kashmir (6)	2	NC-F	3	p1
Karnataka (28)	24	Janata	4	
Kerala (20)	13	CPI(M)	*1	
Madhya Pradesh (40)	39		0	p1
Maharashtra (48)	43	Cong-S	2	
Manipur (2)	1		0	p1
Meghalaya (2)	2		0	
Nagaland (1)	1		0	
Orissa (21)	20	Janata	1	
Punjab (13)		No poll		
Rajasthan (25)	25		0	
Sikkim (1)	1		0	
Tamilnad (39)	25	DMK	*1	c1
Tripura (2)	0	CPI(M)	2	
Uttar Pradesh (85)	82	DMKP	2	p1
West Bengal (42)	16	CPI(M)	18	
Union Territories (17)	17		0	
Total (542)	402			
Total of all non-Congress (I)			105	

c countermanded
p postponed
* Parties allied with the Congress (I) won most of the remaining seats

ABBREVIATIONS BJP: Bharatiya Janata Party; Cong-S: Congress–Sharad Pawar group; CPI: Communist Party of India; CPI(M): Communist Party of India (Marxist); DMK: Dravida Munnetra Kazhagam; DMKP: Dalit Mazdoor Kisan Party; Janata: Janata Party; NC–F: National Conference–Farooq Abdullah group; TDP: Telugu Desam Party.

SOURCE *Asiaweek*, 11 January 1985, p. 10.

campaigners in Calcutta placed a garlanded portrait of Mrs Gandhi by the roadside, played tape-recordings of her speeches behind it and then placed a microphone in front of her picture. To be sure, the microphone was for effect – to augment the sense that this was a real speech and this was really she. There was, however, a bizarre quality to the suggestion that the sound was coming, not from a tape-recorder and loudspeaker, but from the picture itself. Passers-by, however, seemed to accept the scene as unremarkable.[33]

The compulsion of elections led politicians to try to create large, favourable blocks of voters. In north India, there could be nothing larger than 'Hindus' as a united category. It was to create this category, and derive votes from a large section of it, that the Congress (I) campaign aimed.

Indeed, one writer makes the extraordinary assertion that this strategy was decided before Mrs Gandhi's death and that riots 'would have burst forth even if Indira Gandhi had been alive'.[34] The writer presents no evidence. If the charge were true, it would constitute perhaps the most monstrous and vicious piece of mischief in post-independence history. Other writers, in conservative publications, however, have also asserted that 'the nature and the extent of the violence points to the fact that the riots were planned'.[35]

There seems little doubt that once Mrs Gandhi was dead, some members of the Congress (I) in New Delhi abetted the riots against Sikhs and that the party capitalised on the sense of national insecurity in its election campaign. To transcend hitherto unbridged gaps of caste and class, a powerful threat had to be created: national disintegration fuelled by the secessionist plots of the (purportedly) wealthy, powerful, internationally connected Sikhs. 'Give unity a hand', said the Congress (I) election slogans, playing on the fact that the party's symbol was the palm of an uplifted right hand. In Amethi in Uttar Pradesh, which Maneka Gandhi, widow of Mrs Gandhi's other son Sanjay, was contesting against Rajiv Gandhi, one of the slogans said to have been used against her was: 'She is the daughter of a Sikh [quite true] – a nation/community of traitors'.[36]

An obituary of Mrs Gandhi pinpointed this aspect well: 'Indira Gandhi consolidated the bulk of the Hindu community, after her death, in a manner in which it had rarely been consolidated. No other ideology has ever succeeded so much in the past in submerging the notorious sub-divisions of Hindu society'.[37] In the national elections, large sections of north Indian Hindus seem to have been swept along by a novel sense of Hindu-ness, of Hindu unity. Usually divided by caste and class, now briefly at least, a wider identification appears to have influenced them. 'Something peculiar and new has happened to the Hindus', concluded Rajni Kothari. 'The Hindu religion never [before] thought of itself as monolithic.'[38] This may well be only a single, remarkable example, but – if early impressions stand up to more rigorous analysis – the notion of a 'Hindu unity' throughout north India is merely further evidence of the way in which the revolution in communications makes possible the redefinition of social groups.

The revolution in communications has had one further effect. Just as it allowed the sense of threatening chaos and of young, clean, bereaved Rajiv Gandhi to reach millions of people, it also transmitted a negative picture: of a squabbling, shop-soiled, geriatric opposition. Opposition politicians were unable to agree on a common programme or even a rational sharing of seats to ensure two-party contests and prevent division of the anti-Congress vote. In fact, 1984 produced more candidates (more than 5000 for about 510 seats) than any of the eight general elections since independence. This image of opposition disarray also reached millions of voters.

THE CASE FOR FEDERALISM

So far, this may appear a gloomy story. However, the following narrative should emphatically not be read as some sort of proof for statements like 'modernisation makes things worse' or 'there's no way out for countries like India'. This book is a cautionary tale, not an argument for predestination.

The incipient conflicts of states containing a number of ethnic groups *can* be contained. Indeed, India's record since 1947 has not been disastrous: five major religions (Hindus, Muslims, Christians, Sikhs, Buddhists), fifteen official languages, thousands of castes, twenty-two states and dozens of sub-regions within those states. Yet in spite of its failures, the Indian state is still some way – though not as far as before June 1984 – from a Biafra or a Lebanon. The very complexity of India is in some ways an advantage, because it makes it difficult for a single group to dominate the state (as, for example, Muslim Punjabis came to dominate Pakistan).

However, to moderate the potential for ethnic conflict requires sagacity, caution and a willingness to abide by the federal system. These qualities are particularly necessary among national political leaders controlling the central government, for in India 'the centre', as it is called, has large financial and coercive powers.

For national politicians to encourage aggressive ethnic assertion – as the Congress (I) Party did in Punjab between 1978 and 1980 – simply to undermine political rivals is fraught with dangers. It ought to be regarded as the equivalent of poison gas in the Second World War or nuclear weapons (so far) today – too dangerous to risk.

However, in Punjab, as we shall see, desperate members of the Congress (I) looked to any weapons they could find in 1978–80 to try to pull down the coalition government of the Akali Dal and Janata parties. When Mrs Gandhi returned to power at the centre in January 1980, she used the President's Rule clause of the constitution to dismiss the Punjab government (along with nine other state governments). Though the government in Punjab appeared to be tottering, it had not been defeated in the legislature and still had two years of its term to run. It was dismissed because the Congress (I) Party saw (correctly) that elections would enhance its own chances of regaining power in Punjab. This short-sighted decision should carry a dazzling warning: the gravest dangers to the Indian state are posed by attempts to govern 730 million people directly from the Prime Minister's house in New Delhi.

Indeed, if the crisis in Punjab and Mrs Gandhi's assassination were not enough, the results of the national elections in December 1984 and the state elections in March 1985 (see Table 1.2) underline this point. The Congress (I) Party was rejected in regions where the interference from New Delhi could be portrayed as intolerable: in Andhra Pradesh, in Muslim areas of Kashmir, in Karnataka, in Sikkim. In the Punjab state elections in September 1985, the Congress (I) won only 32 out of 115 seats (see the 'Postscript'). Because the Congress (I) succeeded so stunningly in the

TABLE 1.2   *Seats won in ten state elections, March 1985*

	Congress (I)	Major opponent	
Andhra Pradesh (294)	48	TDP	202
Bihar (324)	190	DMKP	41
Gujarat (182)	149	Janata	14
Himachal Pradesh (68)	55	BJP	5
Karnataka (224)	66	Janata	139
Madhya Pradesh (320)	250	BJP	58
Maharashtra (288)	162	Cong–S	54
Orissa (147)	117	Janata	19
Rajasthan (200)	113	BJP	38
Sikkim (32)	1	SSP	30

ABBREVIATIONS   As for Table 1.1.
              SSP: Sikkim Sangram Parishad

SOURCE   *OHT*, 16 March 1985, p. 16 (a few results incomplete).

national elections, there is a danger that these lessons will not be understood. Indeed, the danger is still greater. The party's ability to evoke a pronounced 'unity' among Hindus in north India may tempt it towards greater centralisation and attempts to gratify the Hindu, Hindi-speaking heartland at the expense of the rest of the country.

However, the results of the elections in three of the ten states which went to the polls in March 1985, ought to emphasise the dangers of such a course. In Andhra Pradesh, Karnataka and Sikkim, the states in which the central leaders of the Congress (I) had instigated or connived at attempts to claw down rival governments in the previous two years, the Congress (I) was overwhelmingly defeated (see Table 1.2). In Andhra Pradesh, where the central government backed a comic-opera attempt to destroy the Telugu Desam ministry in August–September 1984, the Telugu Desam and its allies reduced the Congress (I) to fewer than fifty seats in a house of 294. In Karnataka, where continual efforts had been made to destroy the Janata-led coalition of Ramakrishna Hegde, voters returned Hegde's party with a majority in its own right. In Sikkim, where again a legitimate government had been overturned by central-backed interference in May 1984, voters returned the dismissed Chief Minister, Nar Bahadur Bhandari, with thirty seats in a legislature of thirty-two. It is likely, too, that were elections to be held in Jammu and Kashmir (where the Congress (I) staged a devious and successful coup in July 1984), the National Conference of Farooq Abdullah, the former Chief Minister, would win. His party won three of the five parliamentary seats in December.[39] Finally, in the Punjab state elections in September 1985, the Akali Dal won outright victory for the first time: 73 out of 115 seats contested and 38.5 per cent of the vote (see the 'Postscript'). Two messages seem implicit in these state elections. Both relate to the way in which ordinary Indians – 'the masses' or whatever term one cares to use – are in touch with ideas about politics and the nation. First, the results suggest sophistication. Voters know the difference between national and state elections, and they know how to punish. They may see the Congress (I) as the only viable national alternative, but in their own states, given genuine options, they will support those options. Even in Maharashtra, an opposition alliance, led by a popular local politician, Sharad Pawar, limited the Congress (I) to about 160 seats in an assembly of 288. Moreover, if a government in power, or a greedy party out of power, appears to act against the interests of 'us' (and here we return to ideas about ethnic groups) – then voters will turn on such a party as they did in Andhra Pradesh, Karnataka and Sikkim.

The second inference relates to the latter point. If voters are constantly frustrated – if central governments disregard local pride, aspirations and opinion – the possibility exists for secessionists to acquire popularity. Andhra Pradesh, for example, does not have the violent traditions of Punjab, nor is it the homeland of a distinct religion, as Punjab is for the Sikhs. Yet if the Telugu Desam Party were again to be cheated of a fair opportunity to govern the state, the ingredients exist for a Telugu separatist movement which would emphasise the impossibility of ever getting fair treatment from the centralising Indian state.

In attempting to explain why events in Punjab, the country's most prosperous state, erupted in the battle of the Golden Temple and Mrs Gandhi's assassination, this book examines processes going on throughout India. The 'biographies' of Punjab and of the Sikhs, contained in the next two chapters, could similarly be written about other states and religious or caste groups. Chapter 4 discusses the innovations which are penetrating every corner of India, though nowhere have they spread more swiftly than in Punjab. The account of politics in Chapter 5 examines the interaction of these innovations with the old forms of rivalry which have long characterised Punjab. Chapter 6 tries to show how factional networks, which are fundamental, I believe, to most peasant societies and are particularly deeply etched in Punjab, have been caught up and overwhelmed by the innovations accompanying the 'green revolution'. Chapter 7 outlines how the resulting mixture of innovation and old factional expectations produced a dizzying, uncontrollable political brew. Chapter 8 suggests that similar problems – now evident, for example, in Assam, Andhra Pradesh, Jammu and Kashmir and Sikkim – will increasingly confront central governments.

Further centralisation will not overcome them. What India requires is a more genuine federalism, a greater readiness of central governments to follow the spirit (indeed, even following the letter would be an improvement) of the present constitution. The Indian state is remarkably resilient. There are strong, structural reasons for its unity, on which I try to comment in Chapter 8. But no one can hold the reins of state as tightly as Mrs Gandhi tried to do. To do so is to increase the pulling and chafing and thereby the risk of snapped reins and bolting horses. Indeed, Punjab and its Sikh population in the 1980s are far from being quietly settled into the team.

2 Punjab

When I first went to Punjab in 1967, I worked for an institute of English whose task was to retrain secondary teachers in 'modern' methods of English instruction. Every four months or so, dozens of teachers from throughout Punjab and Haryana were ordered to Chandigarh, the common capital of both states, to undergo the course. It was not popular. People resented leaving their villages, families and subsidiary occupations. One day Dhoom Chand, a likeable, bulky man in his forties, who came from a fairly distant village in Punjab, looked particularly unhappy as he went about his practice rounds at the school where we worked.

'Is anything the matter?' I asked.

'I have had a letter from my wife', he replied. 'She has given birth to a third daughter, and our best milk buffalo has died'. He paused gloomily. 'Only two things are important to a Punjabi man: his sons and his buffaloes'.

Since then I have often thought of Punjab in terms of sons and buffaloes: a passion for agriculture combined with a culture that emphasises masculinity and hardiness. Indeed, other north Indians, who consider themselves more genteel, will tell you that 'the only culture Punjabis know is agriculture'. But they know it well. The buffalo is a good example. Punjab today is estimated to have more than 2 million buffaloes – huge, shiny black creatures with closely curled horns, each one looking twice the bulk of its longer-horned, hairier cousin farther south. Punjab accounts for more than a quarter of India's total daily milk production of close to 25 million litres.[1] Milk is a cult in Punjab. Punjabis consume an average of 500 grams of milk a day, nearly five times the national average – and twice as much as many nutritionists would recommend. 'Twice a day he drank milk', wrote a Punjabi judge of a particularly bad but robust character, 'five litres at a time. He liked it as it came from the

23

she-buffalo ... He would pick up the brass bucket ... and drain it in one long draught.'[2]

In a book of reminiscences, Prem Bhatia, diplomat and long-time editor of the *Tribune*, entitles a chapter 'Pure Milk' and tells the story of the senior railway official who demanded that his subordinates should provide 'pure milk' for him wherever he went. 'The slightest trace of impurity' was said to be enough to blight a career. A quick-witted junior solved the problem by bringing a cow to the station and having it milked before his chief's eyes. Bhatia recalls the chapati-eating competitions in the college hostels of his youth (they continue even now) where the winner was rewarded, after having consumed forty or fifty of these round, flat wheatcakes, with 'a king-sized glass of milk with cream on top'. His mother, he writes, 'even at the advanced age of 76 ... still eats more than I did at 20'.[3]

Punjabis take pride in eating well. To cook with plenty of ghee (clarified butter) and to force a steaming glass of hot creamy milk on a guest are matters of self-respect. Estimates of nutrition show the average rural Punjabi as the best-nourished person in India, getting 111 grams of protein and 3711 calories a day (national average: 76 grams and 2724 calories).[4] 'The natural diet of the Punjab', writes a long-time resident and scholar, 'with its wheat, its milk and its green vegetables, is one of the best the world can offer.'[5]

Punjabis themselves argue that a good diet is one of the things that has produced a vigorous, virile people. Indeed, people occasionally talk about Punjab as the 'Texas of India'. Everything is bigger, better, rougher, tougher. Punjabis, one of them writes, 'believe in hard work and ... would rather move their hands then merely wag their tongues'.[6]

In accounting for their energy, Punjabis often cite climate. It is extreme, and people must work hard at the right times to survive. In May and June, as the heat builds day by day and the earth seems on the verge of combustion, the temperature reaches 45° Celsius in the middle of the day and may fall no lower than 30°C at night. In winter, it drops at night to freezing and below. On 25 December 1984, for example, it was −3° Celsius in Amritsar. Such a range, writes Prakash Tandon, has 'made both farming and farmers hard'.[7]

Rural Punjabis value an aggressive masculinity. They love the tough guy, the 'he-man who defie[s] authority ... but prove[s] true to friendship.'[8] Violence for large sections of rural Punjabis has always been a part of life: ' "Death" ... was within the range of the immediately possible. It was a tragedy only for sisters and for mothers. But for men, young and old, death was excitement, drama, a proof of their daring'. Such feelings, as we shall see, are particularly prevalent among Sikh Jats, but they are not exclusive to them. 'Love and death to the Punjabi go together', writes Prakash Tandon in his beguiling autobiography, *Punjabi Century*. 'The Freudian death wish is common in [the] Punjabi [language]; in love, in disappointment, in culmination, in frustration, in triumph, in defeat.'[9]

Murder is more common in Punjab than in most places in India. In 1974, for example, Punjab had 659 *recorded* murders (and many go unreported) or about one murder for every 20 600 people. Only the state of Uttar Pradesh (UP) had a higher ratio (1:19 300), though Punjab had exceeded even the UP in 1970. By contrast, Canada in 1974 had 545 murders or one to every 39 600 people. Murder and violence are quite openly discussed in Punjab. A minister of the Punjab government admitted in 1979 that he had killed a Muslim during the partition riots; a former senior police official 'murdered a servant on his father's estate when he was 13½'; and 'the youngest brother' in a landlord family in the 1970s could claim 'with some pride' to have 'totally eradicated virginity among the daughters of his father's labour families'. Among some people, violence is almost considered a virtue.[10]

Punjab is a male-dominated society. Indeed, one scholar writes of the 'machismo world of Punjabi males – drinking, card-playing, boasting and quarrelling'. Though Jat women do more than their share of work in the household, daughters are still seen as a burden. Sons are an asset, both in daily work and, when necessary, in village conflicts. 'In these villages', a Sikh in his fifties told an inquirier, 'we have faction fights, and you win fights not with contraceptives but with men.'[11] A proverb says: 'A fireplace is never satisfied with the fuel it's given. A mother is never satisfied with the sons she has'.[12] Dhoom Chand was not unusual in his disappointment at the birth of a third daughter.

Girl babies are often less well cared-for than boys. The 'infant death rate among females' is 'much higher' than among males, and this shows up in the sex ratios for Punjab compiled at the decennial censuses.[13] In 1981, Punjab had only 886 females to every 1000 males. The all-India ratio of 935:1000 is one of the very few instances where statistics for the nation as a whole may be described as better than those for Punjab. It was not a coincidence that Punjab was the centre of a bitter controversy over the abortion of female babies in 1982. A clinic in Amritsar was doing a brisk trade by determining the sex of a foetus by amniocentesis (analysing a sample of the fluid in which the baby lives) for a charge of Rs. 500. Couples could then choose to abort a female foetus. Under pressure from women's groups, the Punjab government ordered that the clinic should stop offering the tests and the abortions; but the incident lent new poignancy to the Punjabi blessing: 'May you have seven sons!'[14]

SOME PEOPLE'S STATISTICS: THE MOST PROSPEROUS STATE

In March 1979, as the Janata government of Morarji Desai quarrelled its way to collapse, and inflation ran at 17.5 per cent, *India Today*, the country's leading news magazine, devoted a cover story to 'Punjab: Island of Prosperity ... An Affluent State'. The cover photograph nicely caught the sense that the writers sought to convey, a feeling that generated both envy and admiration in other Indians. Punjabis, particularly Sikhs, were prospering. The photograph showed a well-dressed Sikh family of eight, grouped around its tractor, a calf tethered behind it. The young wife wore a wrist-watch; the young boys, jogging shoes and socks. In the background, building stones stacked against a solid brick wall heightened the sense of dynamism. Here was a place where things were happening. The brick wall protected a field of vivid yellow mustard, and behind it, fields of sugar cane. It was, as the photographer intended it to be, everyone's picture of the go-ahead Punjabi and the fruits of his labour.

The writers confessed themselves 'staggered by the abundance of gadgets' in rural Punjab. A transistor radio was 'virtually ... a must in every Punjab farmhouse and TV is fast catching on'.[15] They described the family on the cover as representing 'a perfect picture of contentment and prosperity', living examples of the Punjab success story.

Refugees from Pakistan in 1947, they were resettled on 25 acres of unirrigated land, about a quarter less than they held in the rich canal colony of Lyallpur in Pakistan from which they had been driven. Within thirty years, however, they had sunk three tubewells to irrigate crops of wheat and sugar cane. As well as their tractor, they owned a thresher, a sugar-cane crusher, a *gobar* (methane) gas plant, two cows and three buffaloes. Even the daughter – as yet unmarried – had been to secondary school. 'Peace, prosperity and three decades of unfaltering progress', concluded *India Today*'s writers, both Punjabis, 'have transformed Punjab into India's boom state, a model of success.'

Yet five years later, Punjab was close to civil war, the army had fought its biggest battle against Indian citizens in free India's history and in the most dramatic consequence, Indira Gandhi lay dead in the garden of her own house, murdered by two of her own guards – Punjabis, Sikhs. Were these the fruits of affluence?

Statistics show Punjab to be India's most prosperous state, a model to which other regions, and indeed, other 'third world' countries, aspire. Punjab's estimated gross domestic product per person was Rs. 2528 (about US $250), nearly 20 per cent greater than its closest rival, Maharashtra, whose figures are inflated by the inclusion of Bombay, India's major industrial city. The average per capita GDP for the Indian states was Rs. 1334; that of Punjab was nearly twice as great.[16] The income of the 'average Punjabi' was 65 per cent greater than that of the 'average Indian'.[17]

According to the 1981 census, Punjab had a population of 16.7 million, just under 2.5 per cent of India's 684 million people.[18] It occupies an area of 50 400 square kilometres (19 460 square miles) or 1.5 per cent of India. It is about two-thirds the size of Scotland. Yet in recent years Punjab has produced more than 10 million tonnes of food-grain annually, roughly 7 per cent of the country's total production. Indeed, in 1984–5 it looked likely to produce 17 million tonnes, more than 10 per cent of the nation's total yield.[19]

By a number of material indicators, Punjab stands out as the state where a large proportion of the people have come to enjoy a reasonable standard of comfort. Punjab has 10 per cent of India's television sets and 17 per cent of its tractors. A

Punjabi is twice as likely as the 'average Indian' to own a radio and three times as likely to own some sort of motor vehicle. If he does have motor transport, he has three times more road per square kilometre on which to drive it. Since 1976 governments claim that every Punjab village has electricity (nationally: 40 per cent), and Punjabis use more than twice as much electricity per hour as the 'average Indian'. Punjabis put more than three times as much fertiliser on each hectare of their land, and of that land, more than 80 per cent is irrigated (national average: 28 per cent). The average Punjabi has twice as much money in the bank as the average Indian (Rs. 600 against Rs. 305), and he or she has twice as many bank branches per 100000 people in which to make deposits. The sum of the cold numbers reveals itself in one flesh-and-blood statistic: the average Punjabi has an estimated life expectancy of 65 years; the average Indian, 47 years.[20] What Indian would not be a Punjabi? What complaint could Punjabis have against the Indian state?

REVOLUTIONS: GREEN

Punjab's prosperity since the late 1960s flows overwhelmingly from agriculture. More than any other area of India – perhaps more than any other area in the world – Punjab has exploited the opportunities provided by the 'green revolution'. The phrase, of course, is the shorthand of journalists and the public-relations men who work for international agencies. It conveys to most people the idea of improved agriculture – more food grown on the same amount of land. However, to understand the complexity of the 'green revolution', one needs to think of a jigsaw puzzle, each piece of which is necessary if the picture is to be completed. To be sure, the 'green revolution' is based on the high-yielding varieties (HYV) of seed developed for wheat (in Mexico) and rice (in the Philippines) in the 1960s.[21] The new seeds, however, are hungry, thirsty and delicate. They demand large amounts of chemical fertiliser, pesticides to protect them from parasites and carefully timed irrigation. To acquire these, a cultivator needs finance; to apply them successfully, he needs intelligence. For planners and policy-makers, it was not enough simply to dump parcels of the new seed from the back of speeding lorries, like an evening newspaper drop in a big city. Governments had to promote the complete package skilfully. Credit had to be made available to allow farmers to pay for tubewells, pumps, diesel fuel, fertilisers and pesticides.

To induce cultivators to gamble on trying new seeds and taking loans, remunerative prices for agricultural produce had to be guaranteed. This was partly achieved until the early 1970s by substantial subsidies for inputs and high 'procurement prices' – the price at which the government guaranteed to buy the farmer's crops. Until the oil-price rises of 1973, the returns on wheat cultivation in Punjab were handsome: more than 27 per cent on investment in 1971–2, according to one survey.[22] Since 1973, however, subsidies have been reduced, the cost of agricultural inputs has risen and prices for crops have not kept pace. By 1977–8, cultivators complained that their return had fallen to less than 2 per cent of their investment.[23]

The champions of the 'green revolution' in Punjab claim that if the incentives are right, farmers will turn 'sand into gold'. And as an incentive, 'price support' – the government-guaranteed high price – 'is best'.[24] Supporters of this argument point to the amazing increases in production achieved in Punjab from the mid-1960s to the late 1970s. Between 1964–5 and 1977–8, Punjab trebled its output of food-grains – from 3.4 million tonnes to 10.3 million tonnes.[25] Punjab stands out as the state which has most successfully introduced the new agricultural techniques. More than 90 per cent of its area under wheat, and more than 85 per cent under rice, are planted with high-yielding varieties.[26]

Why have Punjabi cultivators proved so eager and able to exploit the new agricultural techniques? To be sure, both the central and Punjab governments have at various times instituted policies intended to encourage cultivators to adopt the new methods. But governments throughout India have made similar attempts. Why was success so striking in Punjab? An answer must take into account two sets of ingredients.

The first involves an elusive, slippery, yet recognisable area labelled 'qualities of the people' or 'culture'. Long ago British officials waxed eloquent about the abilities of Punjabi culti-vators. Malcolm Darling, one of the keenest and most sympath-etic of observers, described the Jats of Punjab quite simply as 'the best cultivators in India'.[27] The energy of Punjabis, and their readiness to engage in hard physical labour, mark them out. Punjab, moreover, has been the major recruiting ground of India's armies for close to 130 years. M. S. Randhawa estimated that the state had half a million serving or retired soldiers, each of whom had seen a little of the world and picked up skills that stay-at-home villagers would have missed. The resulting pragmatism and flexibility made Punjabis ready to try new techniques that promised profit.

The second ingredient involved the way in which land was divided in Punjab by the 1960s. When the old province of Punjab was divided between India and Pakistan in 1947, roughly 6 million Sikhs and Hindus were driven into India and about the same number of Muslims into Pakistan.[28] The Hindu and Sikh refugees who fled to India left 6.7 million acres of land in west Punjab; but the Muslims vacated only 4.7 million acres when they fled from India.[29] How were people to be resettled on 2 million fewer acres than they had left behind? One suggestion at the time was that every agricultural family, regardless of whether they were landless labourers or huge landlords in west Punjab, should be given exactly the same size of holding in resettled east Punjab. Equality should be the law. This solution was rejected, however, in favour of a system of proportional reductions. A family with up to 10 acres (four hectares) in west Punjab had its holding reduced by 25 per cent; a landlord who held more than 500 acres (200 hectares) was reduced by 95 per cent. Nevertheless, the relative class structure of west Punjab was recreated in the east.[30] But a kind of land reform did occur: consolidation. In most of rural India, generations of sale and subdivision mean that land in a village is divided into hundreds of small fields. Even though a family owns 10 or 15 hectares (25 to 37 acres), it may consist of a dozen or more different plots. This poses numerous disadvantages. Vast areas are lost to cultivation through the use of land for fences and dividing walls. Irrigation is difficult and unprofitable. A man loses time and wastes energy while he moves his plough and bullocks from one small plot to another. Disputes over boundaries arise. Cattle on one man's land stray and eat the crop on a neighbour's. Pesticides applied to one field simply drive insects next door where no spraying has been done.

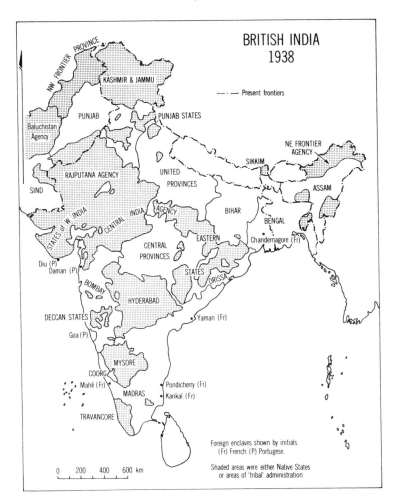

MAP 2.1   *British India, 1938*

'The blessing of the single field', Darling wrote in the 1920s, was probably the greatest advantage a cultivator could have. Darling illustrated his case with two maps of the same village: the first, a lace handkerchief of fine lines marking out 886 fields; the second, after consolidation, a striped bandana of fifty-five large blocks of land.[31]

When the upheaval of the 1947 partition made consolidation possible – 4.7 million acres of land had lost their Muslim owners – both officials and refugees grasped the opportunity to consolidate holdings.[32] By 1960, when the process was complete, cultivators in Punjab worked on sizeable chunks of land, on which it was economical to drill a tubewell, build a fence or even use a tractor. This, perhaps more than any other single ingredient, established the conditions in which the High Yielding Varieties could succeed.

REVOLUTIONS: RED?

The system of proportional cuts in the size of landholdings under which the refugees of 1947 were resettled ensured that wide class disparities remained in Punjab. By the 1970s, for example, an estimated 23 per cent of landholding families (each of whose holding was at least 4 hectares) owned nearly two-thirds of the cultivated land. This meant that 77 per cent of the landholding families divided one-third of the land among them.[33] But the class contrasts are even more stark. 20 per cent of the working population of Punjab are agricultural labourers who have no rights in land at all; they make up close to a third of the rural population.[34]

The champions of the 'green revolution' point out that the wages of agricultural labourers 'have more than doubled'.[35] They also argue that the amenities – schools, health centres, electricity, roads, buses, banks – in the areas where they live have improved. But as the author of one village survey concludes, 'the gains . . . are unequally distributed' and 'the gap between the lowest income categories [and the highest] . . . has increased'.[36] The landless third of rural Punjabis benefit only indirectly (if at all) from the 'green revolution'. They remain dependent on the landowners who give them work. Indeed, some observers argue that mechanisation makes their position more precarious than ever before and that inflation has eaten up most of the increases in wages.

Politics conducted overtly in the name of class, however, have not featured prominently in Punjab. Both the Communist Party of India and the Communist Party of India (Marxist) have pockets of strength, but they have together never managed to win more than 11 per cent of the votes cast in state elections.[37]

Though the surface of politics is dominated by personal rivalries and straightforward appeals to religion, class-based fears play a large part in influencing behaviour. The high proportion of landless labourers encourages landowners – particularly Sikhs, who predominate in the rural areas – to support parties (for example, the Akali Dal) that stress religious solidarity and thereby discourage envy of the better-off. Furthermore, Punjab's intensive agriculture of the past twenty years has created a demand for labour which migrant Hindu workers from eastern Uttar Pradesh and Bihar have filled. Some, it is claimed, settle in Punjab, thus helping to decrease the proportion of Sikhs in the state's population. In fact, it appears likely that their presence undermines class antagonisms in two ways. First, the landless Punjabis whom they replace have generally moved into somewhat more lucrative, semi-skilled jobs in the small-scale industries (mechanical repairs, for example) that have grown up around the 'green revolution'. Second, the immigrant labourers have no base in Punjab and therefore less incentive (and capacity) to take part in its politics. Being overwhelmingly Hindu, they can be used as a 'threat' to unite Sikhs of all classes.

The 23 per cent of families who own two-thirds of the land in Punjab face the problem of controlling and channelling the sense of deprivation that arises in poorer peasants and the landless. The television sets and motor cycles are there for the poor and landless to see. One way to deal with the problem is to encourage a religious fundamentalism in which all believers are invited to share equally. By financing religious buildings and organisations, the wealthy associate themselves with the faith and encourage deference from the poor. 'We are not only wealthy', such acts seem to say, 'but worthy and close to God'. The equality of such fundamentalism, however, stops short of property and wealth. Rather, the poor are invited to emulate the glorious religious postures struck by heroes of the faith in times past. In so doing, they can win admiration and acceptance from the whole community. For the large majority of poorer Sikhs, for example, there is more self-esteem to be won from acceptance as a full and admired member of a hallowed faith than in taking part in class-based organisations with purely economic goals. Class is everywhere in Punjab's politics, yet rarely in people's minds.

REVOLUTIONS: INDUSTRIAL?

Based on the figures for per capita income and gross domestic product – and indeed, on the evidence of the tractors on the roads and the television aerials in the villages – Punjab has become India's most prosperous state. But since the mid-1970s, many Punjabis have argued that the picture is misleading. Punjab's recent prosperity, they contend, is based overwhelmingly on agriculture, and the increases in agricultural production have gone about as far as they can go. Less than 25 per cent of Punjab's gross domestic product comes from industry, a share which is one of the lowest in India, even below states like Kerala (30 per cent), Madhya Pradesh (31 per cent) or Bihar (31 per cent), though the per capita GDP of these three states is far behind that of Punjab.[38]

Part of the discrepancy lies in the fact that Punjab's brilliant agricultural performance reduces the percentage share of industry in its gross domestic product, just as poor agricultural production in other states enhances the apparent importance of industry for them. Punjabis, however, see another, more sinister reason: discrimination against the state by the central government. 'We are being penalised for producing plenty', one told *India Today* in 1979.[39] According to this argument, the Government of India has diverted industrial investment away from Punjab. The great projects – steel, electronics, aircraft – are located elsewhere. In the Sixth Five-Year Plan (1980–5), the central authorities allotted Rs. 240 billion to investment in heavy industry, but only Rs. 100 million (0.04 per cent) was to be spent in Punjab.[40]

The reason often cited is that Punjab borders the old enemy, Pakistan, and that wars have been fought along that border in 1965 and 1971. It might make little sense to put a vital aircraft factory within an hour's drive of a Pakistani tank; but this is a poor explanation for the failure to locate less strategically important nationalised industries in Punjab.

Planners and politicians, however, work on their own kind of arithmetic. For the politician, Punjab sends only thirteen members to the national parliament. Uttar Pradesh sends eighty-five; Bihar, fifty-four. Parliamentary majorities cannot be based on Punjab. For the planner, Punjab is a vulnerable border state which, in any case, shows impressive economic growth, even if that growth is overwhelmingly in agriculture. Thus when central authorities have doled out the loaves and fishes, Punjab's share has been no fishes and considerably less than half a loaf.

The process of central planning and allocation affects people's lives in obvious, direct ways. If your town wins an electronics factory, the population is likely to increase, more money is likely to circulate and you as a landowner, merchant or market-gardener are likely to benefit.

But such planning also affects ideas and the way in which growing numbers of people think about themselves and others. If government becomes the referee, handing down decisions in a growing variety of matters, people are more and more likely to have cause to question some of those decisions in the following terms: 'we' have been unjustly treated, while 'they' have, as usual, managed to get what they want unfairly. People thus come to think in broader categories than they did when outside influence less often intruded on villages.[41]

Punjabis have come to feel an urgent, personal sense of injustice. Many claim that since Punjab lacks heavy industry, Punjabi youths are forced to go elsewhere in India or overseas if they are to put their skills to profit. Into Punjab, in turn, come the ill-educated agricultural labourers, mostly Hindus, whose presence threatens to alter the political balances in the state. Sikhs especially argue this case, for the orthodox among them harbour a constant fear that the Sikh majority in Punjab (about 62 per cent in 1981) will disappear and that the community will be absorbed into Hinduism.

It is, to be sure, a source of pride – and strength – that Punjab receives an estimated US $200 million a year in remittances from Punjabis overseas. Sikhs, too, proudly refer to the 2–3 million of their co-religionists who earn livings elsewhere in India and the 750 000 or more who are overseas.[42] Yet the other side of this sense of pride is a sense of indignation that 'sons of the soil' are unable to find the opportunities to prosper in Punjab. Is it not, therefore, an unjust central government that discriminates against Punjabis, knowing as it does that Punjabis will somehow look after themselves? This argument is increasingly heard in most of India's states: a prejudiced central government treats our state unfairly. For Punjab, however, it has an added potence because, for Sikhs, it can be made to blend with a sense of religious discrimination.

TWO-AND-A-HALF RIVERS

Today's Indian state of 'Punjab' is a misnomer, a shadow of its former self. The word means 'five rivers' (Persian: panj = 5; ab = water)[43] but today's Indian Punjab has no more than two and a half. Once, the word 'Punjab' described the great plain through which the five tributaries of the Indus flowed after they burst out of the Himalayas. Today, however, the Jhelum and the Chenab are in Pakistan,[44] while the Ravi forms part of the border between Pakistani and Indian Punjab. Only the Beas and the Sutlej flow for a substantial distance through the present Punjab state of the Indian Union.

The geographic area that the word 'Punjab' once described is shaped like a triangle.[45] The River Indus forms the western side; the Himalayas, the north-eastern boundary; and in the south, old Punjab disappears ill-definedly into semi-desert along a line from the town of Karnal (in the modern Indian state of Haryana) to Mithankot, 600 kilometres away in Pakistan, at the junction of the Indus and the five rivers of Punjab. (See Map 2.2, p. 40.)

This vast, flat triangle is the gateway to the Indian subcontinent, and every conqueror, except the British, began the advance into India by marching across Punjab. Alexander the Great reached the Beas in 326 BC, overran the town of Sangala, 'probably near Amritsar', and built 'twelve towering altars . . . as a thank-offering' on the banks of the river.[46] Hundreds of years before him the Aryan conquerors poured along the same route, but unlike Alexander, they pushed into the plain of the Ganges and settled. From their conquest sprang the caste system, veneration of the cow and much of what we now associate with Hinduism. Kurukshetra, where the great battle in the Hindu epic, the *Mahabharat*, is fought, lies 40 kilometres north of Karnal, the south-eastern fringe of the old Punjab. Panipat, scene of three battles (1398, 1526, 1761) which destroyed north Indian dynasties, is 30 kilometres south. Punjab has known invasion, conflict and change for at least 3000 years. 'Our society', wrote Prakash Tandon, 'adapted itself to each change until, like the exposed cross-section of an archaeological excavation, it showed layers of characteristics piled one upon the other from each external impact.'[47] Constantly faced with violence and change, Punjabis have made hardiness and pragmatism prime virtues.

In every hot country, water is precious. In India, it is usually considered sacred. It not only sustains life but purifies the body when a person is polluted by contaminating objects or people of lower castes. Ritual pollution has concerned Punjabis less than many other Indian peoples. 'There was little or no orthodoxy in us', recalled Tandon, 'nor the aloofness and complexity of the southern brahmin.'[48] But there has always been a passion about water, not so much as a ritual cleanser or an abstract purifier but as a life-giving, body-pleasing, valuable reality. Small boys rejoiced in the coming of the monsoon and 'the luxurious feeling of running out into the rain and getting soaked'.[49] Malcolm Darling had his own anecdote to sum up the practical, possessive veneration of water: 'Where the water is', a Punjabi peasant told him, 'there is God'.[50] The success of the 'green revolution' since the 1960s has depended on the ability of farmers to sink tubewells and keep their pumps running.

Close to Punjab's five rivers, cultivation was always possible, but the remainder of Punjab depended on the monsoon, and Punjab was 'on the edge of the monsoon area', its 'great agricultural possibilities . . . always limited by a lack of water'.[51] Muslim rulers built a few irrigation canals in the fourteenth and sixteenth centuries.[52] But the British in the nineteenth had at their disposal technology undreamt of by the Mughals. From the 1880s, British and Indian engineers began to construct a complicated network of canals that turned Punjab into a gigantic snakes-and-ladders board, with channels passing from one river to another, turning the country in between into highly fertile agricultural land. Prakash Tandon's father was a canal engineer. In the forty years between the early 1890s and the 1930s, he and scores of men like him built more than 15 000 miles of canals, and the cultivated area of Punjab increased by 65 per cent (from 18.8 million acres to 30.9 million).[53]

Most of these 'canal colonies', as they were called, lay in west Punjab, in what is now Pakistan. The newly irrigated land was sparsely populated by semi-nomadic pastoralists. Large sums of capital had been necessary to build the canals, and to make them pay, the British brushed aside these people and doled out the newly rich land to 'colonists' from elsewhere in Punjab. Colonists needed two qualities: proven cultivating ability and loyalty to the British government. Not surprisingly, a large proportion of them were ex-soldiers, often Sikhs, from central and east Punjab. What better way to ensure the devotion of a peasant soldier than to hold out the promise of a grant of fine land on retirement? The colonies thus allowed the British to relieve population pressure, open up a new source of taxation and reinforce the allegiance of the groups from whom they recruited a large part of the Indian Army. In perhaps the most famous of the canal colonies, the district of Lyallpur (now Faisalabad) the population increased by 38 times – from 30 000 in 1891 to 1 150 000 in 1931.[54] Darling in the 1920s wrote lyrically of Lyallpur as 'the richest tract in India, perhaps even in Asia'.[55] Picture, he asked his reader, the scene surrounding a village: 'It is early spring, and we approach it through fields of young wheat stretching away to the horizon in a sea of green splashed with the brilliant yellow of the mustard flower and broken by islets of sugar cane'.[56] Does the description sound familiar? It may well, because it includes most of the features in *India Today*'s cover photo of March 1979. Where had the family in the photo come from as refugees at partition? Lyallpur.

PARTITION

When the word 'partition' fell into a conversation in Punjab in the late 1960s, it had an effect similar to the mention of the recent death of a near-relative. There would often be a pause, or a solemn sigh, as if the speakers were reflecting on the suffering and loss which nearly everyone had known. 'For us', wrote Prakash Tandon, referring to the dispersal of his own family throughout India after 1947, 'there was no more Punjab.'[57]

By provoking an exchange of populations, the partition created 12 million refugees in Punjab alone.[58] In the course of this movement, probably 200 000 people were slaughtered.

'Communal riots', as such killings are customarily described, became for a time virtual civil war. The partition of Punjab in 1947 was based on religion. The province had a bare Muslim majority (53 per cent), concentrated in the western districts; Hindus (30 per cent) and Sikhs (15 per cent) were more heavily represented in the west. But the three religions were – almost – inextricably intermixed. A third of the population of the east Punjab districts, for example, was Muslim.[59] Once the decision to divide India was announced on 3 June 1947, there remained seventy days in which to determine the new boundaries. The stated aim of both the successor governments was that no transfer of populations should occur, but as the killing intensified throughout that particularly hot summer (the monsoon was late), Sikhs and Hindus surged towards India, Muslims towards Pakistan.[60]

The man who decided the new boundary, Cyril Radcliffe (1899–1977), a British judge, based his award on the 1941 census reports and other statistical material. He accepted submissions from Sikh, Hindu and Muslim groups, but in the end he retired to the seclusion of a bungalow in Delhi to draw the lines on the map that changed millions of lives. Radcliffe was in India less than two months. He never returned, and he refused ever to talk about his work on the boundary.

All sides expressed outrage at Radcliffe's award. Sikhs occupied large tracts of some of the most valuable land in rural west Punjab; Hindus formed the commercial class in west Punjab towns; while in east Punjab, the new boundary ignored the presence of Muslim majorities in some areas awarded to India. The boundary, concluded the geographer O. H. K. Spate (who had, it should be said, argued the case of a Muslim minority sect before the Boundary Commission), 'leans rather heavily against the Muslims and represents an attempt to appease the Sikhs'.[61] Such a statement, however, would have outraged Sikhs in 1947 – as it would today (Map 3.1, p. 68).

The partition ripped apart a political and economic entity that had existed for 150 years – since Ranjit Singh had proclaimed himself Maharaja of the Punjab in Lahore in 1801.[62] The canals and railways built during British rule criss-crossed the Radcliffe Line. It took years thereafter to reconstruct them to follow the new political boundary. The loose ends were still entangling the feet of politicians and planners in the 1980s.

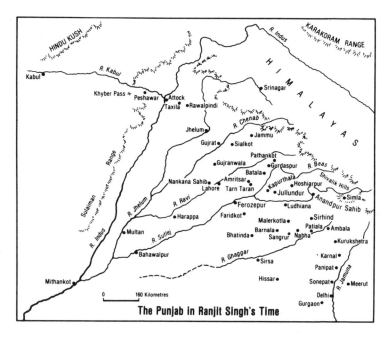

MAP 2.2 *The Punjab in Ranjit Singh's time*

When Mrs Gandhi in 1981 was promoting an irrigation project, which Sikh politicians claimed was detrimental to Punjab, she attempted to shame her opponents. With each day of inaction, she said, India's entitlement to the waters of the River Ravi – won after prolonged negotiations with Pakistan – flowed unused into Pakistan to benefit its farmers. The implication was that any group that could be so careless of Punjab's waters had no right to present itself as Punjab's defenders.[63]

IMAGES AND CATEGORIES

The violence, invasion, changing rulers and shifting political boundaries of Punjab's past have left vivid images in the present. The eighteenth century, for example, was a time of blood and anarchy. Sikhs still commemorate their martyrs of that time in the *Ardas* or daily prayer, which calls on the faithful to remember those who allowed themselves to be sawed, scalped, dismembered, turned on wheels, boiled or burnt alive by hanging from trees [*sic*], and the mothers who embraced the garlands of their children's flesh but did not waver in their faith.[64]

Prior to its destruction by the Indian Army in the assault of June 1984, the museum of the Golden Temple in Amritsar kept alive such images with a series of grisly paintings (of recent origin) depicting the deaths of Sikh heroes at the hands of Muslim oppressors.[65]

Ranjit Singh's supremacy, evidenced in the proclamation of his kingdom in 1801, ended some of the internal strife, but it did not bring tranquillity to Punjab. Indeed, that hardy warrior spent the thirty-eight years until his death in 1839 extending his empire from its base around Lahore and Amritsar. Eventually it reached into Kashmir in the north, down to the Sutlej in the south and east, and up to the Khyber Pass in the north. One of his generals became such a terror to the Muslim peoples of the frontier that another saying passed into the languages of Punjab. Even in Prakash Tandon's youth, 'whenever a Pathan woman wanted to quieten a child, she would say, "Hush, Nalwa [the general] is coming"'.[66] Such long, popular memories recall Ireland and expressions like 'the curse of Cromwell'.

Defeating Ranjit Singh's disunited successors, the British annexed Punjab in 1849, and the province assumed the political boundaries that it retained for the next ninety-eight years. The capital was Lahore, now in Pakistan. After the 'mutiny' of 1857, the British attached so much importance to the province as a recruiting ground of loyal soldiers that they made the old Mughal capital of Delhi simply a part of Punjab. Only in 1911 was Delhi separated to become the new capital of Britain's Indian empire.

The British also preserved in the Punjab plains a dozen 'princely states', territories ruled by Indian princes under British supervision. Six of these – Patiala, Nabha, Jind, Faridkot, Kapurthala and Kalsia – had Sikh rulers. Of all the Punjab states, Patiala was the largest, its prince entitled to a seventeen-gun salute under British protocol and its population in 1931 more than 1.5 million. In 1948, these states were amalgamated into the Patiala and East Punjab States' Union (PEPSU), and in 1956, PEPSU was merged with the state of

Punjab. Nevertheless, the peculiar character of the princely states affected politics in Punjab long after independence, and, indeed, in the 1980s, descendants of the princely families have become prominent politicians. Amarindar Singh of Patiala was a Congress (I) Member of Parliament and an important negotiator for Mrs Gandhi in 1982–4, while Arun Singh from Kapurthala became a close adviser to Rajiv Gandhi.[67]

In the course of 150 years, the Punjab of Ranjit Singh and the British became a reality in people's minds and vocabularies. Once that reality was shattered in 1947, however, the new Indian state of Punjab had nothing solid or sacrosanct about it. The creation of Pakistan established the fact that political entities could be based on religious majorities. The partition showed how political boundaries could be redrawn. As Table 2.1 shows, the new Indian Punjab had shrunk to 122 500 square kilometres (47 200 square miles); its population of 16.1 million in 1951 was 62 per cent Hindu, 35 per cent Sikh and less than 3 per cent Muslim, Christian and other religions.[68] Even before 1947, some Sikhs had begun to raise the cry for a Sikh majority state. After all, if there could be Pakistan, why not a Sikhistan? By the early 1950s, as we shall see, a campaign had started to redraw Punjab's boundaries again – this time to create a state in which Sikhs would be a majority.

TABLE 2.1　*The changing Punjab*

	Area sq. km.	Population (millions)	Muslim (%)	Hindu (%)	Sikh (%)	Other (%)
1941	256 600	28.4	53	31	15	1
1951*	122 500	16.1	2	62	35	1
1961	122 500	20.3	2	64	33	1
1966†	50 260	11.2	–	45	53	2
1971	50 260	13.5	–	38	60	2
1981	50 260	16.7	–	36	62	2

* After the creation of Pakistan.
† After the separation of Haryana.

SOURCES　K. C. Gulati, *The Akalis Past and Present*, (New Delhi: Ashjanak, 1974) p. 182; Pramod Kumar *et al.*, *Punjab Crisis: Context and Trends* (Chandigarh: Centre for Research in Rural and Industrial Development, 1984), pp. 39, 49; S. A. Oren, 'Religious Groups as Political Organizations: A Comparative Analysis of Three Indian States', Ph.D. thesis in Political Science, Columbia University, 1969, p. 60; FEER, 5 September 1985, p. 42.

In 1966, Punjab was divided again. This time the term used was not 'partition', which carried too many memories from 1947, but 'bifurcation'. Ostensibly, the reason was to create a state in which speakers of the Punjabi language would constitute a majority. In fact, the effect was to create a Sikh-majority state. The Hindu-majority areas, where speakers of Hindi predominated, were formed into the new state of Haryana. For the time being, the newly-built capital city of Chandigarh was to remain a territory under the central government to be used as the joint capital of the two states. The new Punjab was now whittled down to an area of 50 260 square kilometres (19 400 square miles), and a population of 11.2 million, but in 1971, more than 60 per cent of that population was Sikh.[69] In spite of fears that the influx of Hindu labourers and the emigration of ambitious Sikhs would reduce that proportion, it remained at about 62 per cent, according to statistics on religion compiled from the 1981 census.

Sikhs who campaigned for Punjabi Suba – the Punjabi-speaking state of 1966 – invoked the glories of the Sikh empire of Ranjit Singh. Although they usually couched their demand in linguistic terms – for a state in which speakers of Punjabi would be a majority – it was generally understood that Sikhs would also be a majority in such a state. Only then, the argument ran, would they be able to defend the interests of Sikhism, as Ranjit Singh defended those interests in the days of yore. The symbols of the past were called up, and adjusted to suit the politics of the present.

Between the Punjabi Suba of 1966 and Ranjit Singh's empire, however, there was at least one striking contrast, which illustrated the way in which politics had changed. Majorities and social categories meant little to Ranjit Singh. He held no elections and took no censuses. In his kingdom, although it was no doubt an advantage to be a Sikh, Sikhs probably never constituted more than 20 per cent of its population. Ranjit Singh's important subordinates included Muslims and Hindus, and the only majority he looked for was on the battlefield. Even there, the canny old soldier knew that numbers alone were seldom a substitute for organisation and morale.[70]

The British, however, left a political system in which elections and the collection of official statistics were embedded. So too were ideas about human equality, the rights of individuals and

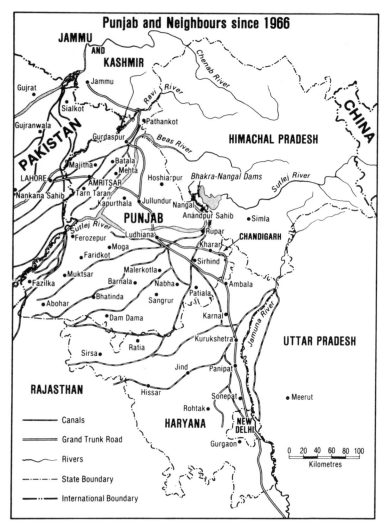

MAP 2.3　*Punjab, Haryana and Himachal Pradesh, 1966*

the correctness of working for the greatest good of the greatest number. This concern about recording, codifying and legislating led to a preoccupation with social categories – to the frequent asking of (and recording the answer to) the question: 'Who are you?'. In Ranjit Singh's time, a man might have presented himself as a Sikh at one time and a Hindu at another. But under the British, once a man appeared before an official, his religion was likely to be recorded, perhaps even on a document that also recorded his entitlement to something so vital as land or water. In former times, identities and customs were fluid; the British, on the other hand, struggled to create tangible social categories and then to freeze them. In the days of Ranjit Singh, it did not matter that Sikhs constituted only a small portion of the population of his kingdom. Legitimacy rested on conquest and continual proof of the ability to rule. By the middle of the twentieth century, however, formal majorities were crucial. When the new Punjab state was created in 1966, what mattered was the fact that within its borders a majority of the population would be Sikhs.

3 Sikhs

The only things that distinguished him from the other speakers on the platform that night were the fawn-coloured turban and the grey beard, rolled up neatly under his chin. Together, they informed anyone who saw him that he was a Sikh. But his business suit, collar and tie, and his decision to speak in English, seemed to separate him by generations from the gleaming-eyed young men – weapons in hand, turbans of electric blue, black beards cascading over loose white shirts – now featured regularly on the covers of Indian news magazines.

It was New Delhi, 31 October 1983, the last day of the worst month yet in the confrontation between terrorists, killing for Khalistan (an autonomous Sikh state), and mischievous, maladroit Congress (I) Party governments in both Punjab state and at the centre in New Delhi. On 5 October, the murdering entered a new phase when terrorists took over a bus near Amritsar, ordered seven Hindu passengers outside and gunned them down in a field. Only one survived. It was the first time terrorists had killed Hindus indiscriminately. Previous victims – often Sikhs as well as Hindus – were men who had offended terrorist groups in one way or another. But the killing of the bus passengers represented a deliberate attempt to spread insecurity among all Hindus and to provoke attacks on Sikhs. The terrorists knew that if the cycle of murder and counter-murder could be started, it would become almost impossible to stop. The example of Northern Ireland – the terrorists were well acquainted with the United Kingdom – had shown that.

The murder of the bus passengers did not lead to anti-Sikh rioting, but it had two effects. First, the central government dismissed the Congress (I) government in Punjab on 6 October and proclaimed President's Rule in the state. The state assembly was suspended, and central-government officials were inserted into key posts in the Punjab administration to rule the state under its Governor, also a central appointee.

Second, though the bus murders did not lead to riots, they hammered the wedge between Sikhs and Hindus to a new depth. 'Previously, we used to take meals together', said a young Hindu bank officer, 'and we Hindus and Sikhs would sit and talk freely and joke in the office and outside. But now we simply say "Good morning" when we come, and then go to our desks. If we talk, we talk about politics and we argue. We cannot even take tea together.' Political opinions now were assumed on the basis of whether a person wore a beard and turban.

President's Rule provided no automatic solution, and throughout October terrorists continued their attempt to intensify fear and suspicion. In Chandigarh, the drowsy, Corbusier-designed capital of Punjab and Haryana, an army hand grenade, thrown into a crowd at a Hindu festival (Ramlila, celebrating the triumphs of the god-king, Ram), killed three people. A sub-inspector of police was murdered in Amritsar district, and bombs were let off in two cinemas in Delhi and a train in New Delhi station. And on 21 October, terrorists derailed a crowded train in Patiala district of Punjab by unscrewing the rails. The technique had been widely used in the partition slaughter of 1947. Nineteen people were killed in the crash, most of them agricultural labourers from eastern Uttar Pradesh, travelling to Punjab to bring in the green-revolution harvest.[1] Terrorists were trying to show that buses, trains, public gatherings and public servants were all unsafe.

These were the circumstances that provoked the 'reconciliation' meeting in New Delhi's Vithalbhai Patel House on 31 October, organised chiefly by members of the city's urbane 'old left'. There was only one Sikh speaker – the man in the fawn-coloured turban – but what he said, and what he represented, captured a number of elements in the complex relationship between Sikhs and governments.

The speaker had a doctorate and had been chairman of an important commission of the central government. His sophisticated English – no Peter Sellers caricature, this man – testified to wide travel and an expensive education. It was difficult to see how such a man could belong to a religious community whose leaders had become fond of describing themselves as 'slaves' in 1980s India.

He revealed to the audience some details about his family.

They were not Jats, he said. Indeed, his father had converted from Hinduism to Sikhism in the 1920s, and though he had raised his children as Sikhs – witness the speaker – one daughter was married to a Hindu. Similarly, the speaker went on, one of his own daughters was married to a Hindu. At least for some groups in Punjab, the boundaries between Sikhs and Hindus were elastic, capable of stretching and contracting as people chose. Religious conviction, social advantage and administrative convenience all played a part in influencing such choices.

The speaker, however, represented a third point. Though he condemned violence, dwelt on the connections between Sikhs and Hindus and stressed the need for Indian unity, he was careful to emphasise that Sikhs had just grievances. There were problems of central-government neglect, of unjust sharing of river waters and of taking Punjab for granted. His own career and polished self-assurance seemed to belie much of what he said. Yet the importance of his remarks lay in the fact that by October 1983 virtually no Sikh could consider addressing a public meeting without giving himself some insurance against terrorists who might brand him a 'traitor' and add his name to the already infamous 'hit-lists'.

But why were such fears and suspicions possible between people who – unlike, for example, Catholics and Protestants in Ireland – had been happy even to intermarry?

JATS

In telling his audience that he was not a Jat, the speaker underlined the divisions among Sikhs themselves. Though the ten Gurus attacked the idea of caste, they did not succeed in eradicating it. For some purposes – marriage, for example – caste is important for Sikhs. There are four major categories: ex-Untouchables (sometimes called Mazhbis); artisan castes (Ramgarhias, or carpenters, for example); clerical and commercial castes (Khatris, Aroras, etc); and Jats. But Jats dominate. Today, they make up between 50 and 60 per cent of all Sikhs, with the remainder divided roughly equally among the other three categories.[2] Although all ten of the Gurus were Khatris, Jats for 200 years have provided the model for other Sikhs to emulate. Sikh Jats, moreover, seldom marry with Hindu Jats.

Intermarriage between Sikhs and Hindus has been practised chiefly by the other three categories of Sikhs.

Few observers, however, would quarrel with the proud remark of a Sikh Jat to an inquirer: 'To be a Sikh is to be a Jat-Sikh'.[3] The religion of the Sikhs and the culture of the Jats have blended closely since the eighteenth century.

The story of Jats in north India has broad similarities with that of other 'castes' throughout the country.[4] But, as with so much else with Jats, their story is lustier and more arresting. It takes observers by the shirt-front, backs them into corners and insists on being heard.

The tale of how the Jat got his mouth illustrates the boisterous vigour of which Jats are proud – and which others view with either amusement or apprehension. One day in the mythic past, the great Lord Shiva and his consort, Parvati, 'leading a bored life in the Himalayas', sculpted a magnificent figure of a man out of clay. Parvati persuaded Shiva to blow life into the man, who rose, stretched and began to move around. Only then did they realise that they had forgotten to give him a mouth. Finding only an axe near at hand, Shiva picked it up and struck the figure a great blow across the face. And that, the story goes, is how the Jat got his mouth.[5]

In the classical Hindu scheme of things, Jats had relatively low status, belonging either to the third or fourth (depending on whom one reads) of the four great *varna* or caste categories.[6] Hindu Jats sometimes experience – and resent – the condescension of higher castes. Indeed, Charan Singh, India's prime minister for a few months in 1979 and himself a Hindu Jat, ascribed some of his difficulties to the fact that higher castes did not accord him the respect he deserved.[7] But in Punjab, classical ideas of Hinduism have never been strong. Nor has the attachment of Jats to Hinduism. Status has had more to do with physical strength and skill at arms, qualities Jats prized.

The British celebrated the Jats, and unwittingly helped to shape an identity that was already recognisable to other peoples of northern India. After the British conquered Punjab in 1849, they set out to categorise and record the names, religions, castes and other attributes of their new subjects. The exercise itself was revolutionary, for it froze distinctions and labels that were previously fluid and flexible.

The ten-yearly censuses, the first of which in the Punjab was carried out in 1881, recorded not merely population numbers but as much information about society and customs as the census officers could glean, including proverbs. 'The Jat, like a wound', ran one such proverb, 'is better when bound.' A tumultuous fellow who needed tight control. 'The Jat's baby has a plough handle for a plaything', went another. A fine cultivator. 'The Jat stood on his corn heap and said to the king's elephant-drivers – "Will you sell those little 'donkeys'?" '. A man full of bravado. The recording of such proverbs not only provided a reflection of local attitudes. More important, once set down in an official publication, those attitudes acquired a life of their own and became known over a wide area. The process of recording and publishing made reputations and reinforced them.[8] It went on all over India and contributed to the growing self-consciousness of 'castes' and religions which in India has come to be called 'communalism' – social groups clashing with one another for privileges and resources.

It would be very wrong to suggest that the census officials and British ethnographers somehow 'discovered' the Jats. Jats had been in north India for a century or more before Julius Caesar 'discovered' Britain. Indeed, British officials delighted – most of them, after all, had had classical educations – in identifying the Jats as the descendants of men from Alexander the Great's armies, or as 'Indo-Scythians' who 'entered Punjab from their home on the Oxus about a century before Christ'.[9] Whatever the origins of the Jats, they were well-established and well-known in north India long before the time of Guru Nanak, much less the coming of the British. By the late nineteenth century, Jats of all religions – Sikhs, Muslims and Hindus – were thought to make up more than a quarter of the population of the Punjab.[10]

Large numbers of Jats had come to Sikhism in the seventeenth and eighteenth centuries, for it provided a faith that answered the dilemmas of the Punjab. It was a religion with which Jats could sympathise, appropriate and call their own.

SIKHISM: 'WE ARE NEITHER HINDUS NOR MUSSULMANS'

Political conditions have affected the emergence and fortunes of all religions, but perhaps in none is this more obvious than the religion of the Sikhs. The intertwining of the Sikh religion with 'the ideal of sovereignty',[11] which occurred at the beginning of the eighteenth century, bound Jats to the faith, for Jats and Sikhs had similar goals – independence from Muslim would-be overlords in Delhi. Moreover, the emphasis of the Sikh religion on equality accorded well with the proud independence which Jats prized. The Jat in the proverb, for example, asserts that even the elephants of the king are no better than 'little donkeys' and elicit no awe from a self-confident Jat.

The relationship between politics and the foundation of the Sikh religion has led foreign observers to draw parallels with Reformation Europe. They have described the Sikhs as 'the Protestants of India' and pointed out that the founder of Sikhism, Guru Nanak (1469–1539), was a contemporary of Martin Luther (1483–1546).[12] Such comparisons do no harm if they impart to Sikhism, and the period in which it arose, a concreteness for Western readers that would otherwise be lacking. But to push comparisons much further would be misleading.

Guru Nanak, 'the greatest of the sons of the Punjab', was born in a village forty miles south-west of Lahore in what is now Pakistan at a time of 'comparative peace and prosperity'.[13] Seventy years before his birth, Timur, a descendant of Genghis Khan, had torn through Punjab on his way to a great victory at Panipat in 1398 and the sack of Delhi. Nanak himself lived to see the invasion of the Mughal ruler, Babur, and the second battle of Panipat in 1526 which established Mughal rulers in India for the next 300 years.

In the villages of Nanak's youth, however, a certain stability prevailed, and he saw the uninterrupted rhythms of the agricultural seasons. The rural metaphor came readily to him throughout his life, and his teachings, like Christ's, drew on images readily familiar to his followers.[14] Even today, Nanak's hymns still relate directly to the lives of people in close touch with the land.

It is often said that Nanak strove for a religion that would draw together the best elements of Islam and Hinduism, both of which were practised in the Punjab of his time. Khushwant Singh, for example, has long argued that 'as a system of belief Sikhism is much closer to Islam than Hinduism'.[15] W. H. McLeod's view, however, seems closer to the truth. For Nanak, writes McLeod, 'conventional Hindu belief and Islam were not

regarded as fundamentally right but as fundamentally wrong
... The two were to be rejected, not harmonised ... True
religion lay beyond these two systems, accessible to all men of
spiritual perception whether Hindu or Muslim'.[16]

In the Punjab of Nanak's youth, there were a great number
of variations, or sects, within the two great religious traditions
of Hinduism and Islam. Nanak himself drew on aspects of the
religious ideas and practices he saw around him. Unlike most
Hindus, he held that there was only one God, not a multiplicity
of deities. Unlike Muslims, he believed in rebirth: if men and
women did not strive to know God, they were condemned to
be reborn into the world. Salvation lay in escaping the cycle
of births and becoming one with the Creator. To achieve
salvation, Nanak emphasised the need for meditation, yet he
held that men and women must continue to live normal lives.
'A disciplined worldliness' was the way to salvation, and he
stressed to his followers the need for 'piety and practical
activity'.[17]

Guru Nanak's followers were known as *sikhs* – learners. His
teaching took the form of verses or hymns, and these were
repeated by his *sikhs* for their enlightenment and pleasure.
These verses came to form the basis of the holy book of the
Sikhs, the Granth Sahib. The guru, or preceptor, was a common
figure in the Punjab of Nanak's day, and to know God, Nanak
held that it was necessary for people to have a guru to help
them to meditate and follow the correct path. Before he died,
Nanak appointed a follower as his successor and thereby began
the chain of the ten Gurus of the Sikhs.[18]

As a Khatri, Nanak came from what was theoretically a
warrior caste.[19] But Khatris for generations had been settled
into clerical and commercial roles in Punjab. They were
peaceable townsmen on the whole, unlike the turbulent Jats
of the villages. For its first hundred years, the religion of the
Sikhs was notable for its peaceful character. Nanak's religion
taught the way to know God, not the way to wage war.[20] These
were also relatively placid years, lived mostly in the reign of
the greatest of the Mughal emperors, Akbar (1542–1605), a
ruler fabled for his tolerant interest in comparative religions.[21]

During the next hundred years, however, Sikhism was
transformed into a faith geared for conflict and preoccupied
with the fight for political independence. The story of those

years is embedded in the consciousness of Sikhs. A calendar depicting the ten Gurus, which has been sold widely in Punjab over recent years, makes this point well and provides a telling way to visualise the change in the nature of Sikhism. Guru Nanak surmounts the calendar, the largest figure, seated cross-legged like a yogi or holy man, a halo round his head and a rosary in his hand. Beneath him and to his right are the next four Gurus standing shoulder to shoulder. But between them and the sixth Guru, Hargobind (1595–1644), successor to the martyred Arjan (1563–1606), there is a noticeable gap – and Hargobind is depicted, not with a rosary, but with a quiver of arrows over his shoulder. The next three Gurus, including the boy, Har Krishnan, are grouped with Hargobind. Then, standing alone below is the tenth and last Guru, Gobind Singh (1666–1708), a quiver of arrows on one shoulder, a bow on the other. Finally, beneath him is the eternal Guru – the Guru Granth Sahib, the holy book. It is not a bad way to picture the development of Sikhism as a social and political force.

The calendar captures all three of early Sikhism's major accomplishments. The first was the establishment of the succession of Gurus, respected teachers who could propagate the faith and bind the faithful. The second was the creation of the Granth Sahib, a distinctively Sikh scripture, though drawn from existing religious tradition in Punjab. The fifth Guru, Arjan, ordered the compilation of the Granth so that the hymns of Nanak and his successors might be available in one authoritative version. Said to have been admired in draft form by the Emperor Akbar himself, this collection was finished in 1604 and placed in the temple at Amritsar. The temple complex remains to this day as the spiritual and political centre of Sikhism.[22] By the time of Arjan's martyrdom at the hands of Akbar's successor, 'the Sikhs had become', according to Khushwant Singh, 'conscious of the fact that they were now neither Hindus nor Muslims but formed a third community of their own'. Arjan himself wrote:

I do not keep the Hindu fast, nor the Muslim Ramadan.
. . .
I will not pray to idols nor say the Muslim prayer.
I shall put my heart at the feet of the One Supreme Being.
For we are neither Hindus nor Mussulmans.[23]

The transition from Arjan to Hargobind, the sixth Guru, thus marks a turning point in Sikhism which the calendar version of the ten Gurus neatly portrays. Between Arjan and Hargobind, there is a gap, and with his quiver of arrows, Hargobind appears ready to avenge martyrdom – or at least avoid it.

The turmoil that slowly engulfed Punjab after Akbar's death, as the Mughal empire slid into intolerance, internal strife and decline, brought about the third accomplishment of early Sikhism: the creation of the Khalsa and the enthronement of the holy book as the eternal Guru – the Guru Granth Sahib. Again, the modern calendar does a fair job of depicting the transformation. Guru Gobind Singh, the tenth and last Guru, is front and centre, with his bow, arrows and a jewel-bedecked turban, almost a crown, on his head. Beneath him is the Guru Granth Sahib itself.

Even in the 1590s Guru Arjan began to attract large numbers of Jats. The Mughal empire's attempts in the seventeenth century to garner revenue and converts from the Punjab drove thousands more Jats towards Sikhism, in which they found traditions they could recognise and a set of beliefs to differentiate them from the nominal Muslim rulers. The Sikh religion in turn began to take on characteristics of the Jats.[24]

The early Gurus' attack on caste fitted well with the sense of equality that prevailed among Jats. For generations, too, Jats had accepted Khatris as teachers. There was nothing unusual, therefore, in Jats listening to the preaching of Khatri Gurus.[25] And the Gurus were Punjabis, not strangers. They illuminated their teaching with vivid rural images, and they taught that hard work was as necessary for salvation as meditation, public prayer or other forms of devotion. Here was a religion of, and for, rural Punjab. 'Sikhs who farm', a foreign scholar later wrote, 'see and feel that their religion is directly relevant to their farming.' By the late 1600s, most Sikhs were Jats.[26]

The creation of the Khalsa by Guru Gobind Singh, a Sikh historian suggests, 'was as much the result as the cause of the preponderance of the Jats among his followers'.[27] In short, Gobind Singh may well have introduced institutions that he knew appealed to Jats. He became the tenth Guru in 1675 after the Mughals' execution of his father, Guru Tegh Bahadur, whom they saw as a growing menace to the empire. For the next thirty-three years – at the same time, it is worth recalling, that English monarchs were attempting to subdue Ireland – Gobind Singh and his followers engaged in intermittent war with the lieutenants of the Emperor Aurangzeb.

In April 1699, Gobind Singh summoned Sikhs to assemble at Anandpur Sahib on the River Sutlej near the foothills of the Himalayas, nor far from today's great hydroelectric project of Bhakra-Nangal. According to hallowed tradition, he called for five volunteers, and after each had disappeared into the Guru's tent, Gobind Singh emerged with his sword dripping blood. Only after he had apparently sacrificed five men did he finally reappear with all five (he had, according to one version, killed five goats) and announce that he had been testing their faith.[28] He proclaimed the founding of a new order – the Khalsa, or 'pure' – of which these 'five beloved ones' (*panj piyare*) would be the first members. Mixing sugar and water with a two-edged sword, he initiated the five by having them drink the mixture from the same vessel, thereby emphasising that the Khalsa would not tolerate distinctions of caste. He bestowed on the five the name Singh, or lion, and laid down five symbols to be carried by members of the Khalsa – the so-called Five Ks. They were to wear their hair and beards uncut (*kesh*); they were to carry a comb (*kangha*) with which to look after their hair; they were to wear shorts (*kach*), characteristic of soldiers of the time and permitting more vigorous movement than a civilian's lower cloth; they were to keep a steel bangle (*kara*) on their wrist; and they were to carry a sword (*kirpan*). Members of the Khalsa were also forbidden to use tobacco (beloved of Muslims), eat meat killed in the Muslim way (*halal*) or have sexual intercourse with Muslim women.[29] Finally, just before his death after being stabbed by assassins in 1708, Gobind Singh is said to have proclaimed the end of the succession of Gurus and the bestowal of the Guruship on the community itself (the *panth*) and on the holy book – thus the Guru Granth Sahib.

Gobind Singh's inauguration of the Khalsa gave to the Sikh religion those outward forms that we associate with it today, particularly the beard and long hair. But the Khalsa reflected the political conditions of the time and the influx of Jats into Sikhism. The military aspects of the Khalsa are unmistakable: the testing of the first five volunteers, the use of the sword in the initiation, the fact that three of the Five Ks (the *kirpan*, *kach* and *kara*) were part of a soldier's equipment. Uncut hair was a Jat characteristic.[30]

By making the sacred book the eternal teacher of the faithful, Gobind Singh ensured that enemies could not subvert the Sikhs by setting up a puppet or capturing a recognised Guru. 'The spirit of the Guru' would now be found 'wherever members of the Khalsa . . . made decisions in the presence of the Guru Granth Sahib.'[31] It was a formula well-suited to independent guerrilla bands engaged in bitter and anarchic war. Throughout the eighteenth century, the turbulent Jat tradition asserted itself, and though the Sikh religion did not give up 'its loyalty to the teachings of Nanak', it took on 'features which derived from its Jat antecedents'.[32]

The essentials of this story are well-known to all Sikhs today, as the popularity of the calendar, described earlier, attests. Tales of yore create standards for modern conduct, standards of aggressiveness, bravery and sacrifice. To understand more fully Sikh ideals of conduct today, we need to notice three aspects of Sikh history in the years between Gobind Singh's establishment of the Khalsa (1699) and the British conquest of Punjab (1849). These are the continued sacrifices of Sikhs in a time of terror and anarchy in the eighteenth century; the tough, flexible military organisation (the *misl*) that grew out of those times; and the creation of the Sikh empire in Punjab by Maharaja Ranjit Singh in 1801. Each has a vibrant, symbolic reality for Sikhs today.

SACRIFICE

Remember the *Ardas* (pp. 40–1), the daily prayer which recalls in bloody detail the torturing and martyrdom of the faithful?[33] It refers particularly to the period after Gobind Singh's death when desperate Mughal governors sought to secure their rule by suppressing the Sikhs. Banda Bahadur, chosen by Gobind Singh to lead the Sikhs (though not as a Guru), was executed at Mehrauli on the outskirts of Delhi in 1716, along with his young son and hundreds of other Sikhs. In the 1740s, another Mughal governor of Punjab 'made head-hunting a profitable business by offering a graded scale of rewards: a blanket for cutting off a Sikh's beard, ten rupees for information of the whereabouts of a Sikh, fifty rupees for a Sikh scalp'.[34] Khushwant Sing's statement reflects the pride and indignation that even the most sophisticated of modern Sikh's feels about this time of fear and disorder. 'Abdali [the Afghan invader] spilled more Sikh blood than any others', Khushwant Singh writes, 'but he also taught them that no people can become a strong and great nation without learning to shed blood.'[35] To a Western ear, these seem curiously nineteenth-century, Bismarckian words, full of blood and iron. Yet they were published in 1963.

Sikhs seem to have stridden through these anarchic times with sure steps. Perhaps this was partly because, being well organised to stave off brigands, they were able also to indulge in a little brigandage themselves. Khushwant Singh points out that though one Mughal governor showed no mercy to Sikhs, 'they did little to deserve it'.[36] He goes on to evoke the sense of exhilaration that Sikhs still derive from contemplation of this period. Even today, the blue-clad Nihang Sikhs who wander the north Indian countryside, pepper their Punjabi with grand idioms dating from their eighteenth-century origins. To urinate is to 'see a cheetah off'; to defecate, to 'conquer the fort of Chittor'; a Sikh is a *sava lakh* – the equal of 125 000 men.[37] The language is full of pride and bravado. Even if such language is used ironically, as it is today, it suggests the placing of bets – about courage and confrontation – that may one day have to be redeemed.

The names and legacies of the period reverberate in modern Punjab. The Nihangs arose as squads of fanatical fighters after Gobind Singh's death. They wore blue, were heavily armed and became a vital component of the armies with which Ranjit Singh built his empire.[38] Today, Nihangs are occasionally laughed at as shiftless good-for-nothings who would rather stage mock battles and scrounge off villagers than do a hard day's work. But they still carry their weapons from village to village and behave as a law unto themselves.

When in April 1978 Nihangs promised to carry off and punish a religious leader who had offended them, the threat was taken seriously, the story was front-page news,[39] and the government had to declare that it would not permit such illegal acts. A few days later in Amritsar, Jarnail Singh Bhindranwale and other militant Sikhs despatched a procession to confront a schismatic sect. In the ensuing gun battle, sixteen people were killed on the spot, thirteen of whom were 'in Nihang robes or with Sikh symbols'.[40] The Nihangs represent a constant reminder of eighteenth-century glories, and because they still wander Punjab today, they imply that the standards of those glorious days are not dead.

Similarly, the Dal Khalsa – army of the pure – was founded in the 1730s to fight the Mughals.[41] In 1978, when disaffected Sikhs formed an organisation to embarrass governments and (perhaps) struggle for a Sikh state, what name did they choose? The Dal Khalsa.[42] The name had a resonance that was intended to cover up its lack – in 1978 – of much substance.

The eighteenth century also emphasised the importance of the symbols of the Khalsa – the Five Ks – in the making of a Sikh, especially the uncut hair and beard. Until this time it was enough to believe in the teachings of Nanak and the word of the Granth Sahib. From Guru Nanak to Guru Tegh Bahadur, to be a Sikh did not necessarily mean to wear a beard and long hair. However, in creating the Khalsa – the initiated among Sikhs who vowed to observe the Five Ks – Guru Gobind Singh was not only institutionalising an aspect of Jat culture (unshorn hair) but also requiring Khalsa Sikhs to become walking testimonies to their faith. As the Mughal governor's scale of rewards – a blanket for cutting off a Sikh's beard – shows, to be faithful to the symbols could mean death. Thousands no doubt were faithful; thousands of others also no doubt shaved their beards and saved their heads. What was important – and remains so today – is the distinction between *kesh-dhari* Sikhs (those who keep their hair and beards long) and *sahaj-dhari* Sikhs (the 'slow acceptors') who subscribe to Sikh teachings but cut their hair.[43] Indeed, at some periods of history, it becomes difficult for *sahaj-dharis* to gain recognition as Sikhs. Not to wear the outward symbols can be portrayed as a betrayal of all the sufferings of those who preserved the faith during its darkest days. And though *sahaj-dharis* may say that beards and long hair do not guarantee pure souls and devotion to Guru Nanak's teaching, the fact remains that people find it difficult to judge purity and devotion; beards and turbans, they can see. 'There is no such thing', writes Khushwant Singh, 'as a clean-shaven Sikh – he is simply a Hindu believing in Sikhism.'[44]

In such ways, the trials of the eighteenth century live among Sikhs today. They provide a host of symbols for elected politicians to play upon in an age when a revolution in communications invests such messages with a power unknown in the days of their origin. It is worth recalling that Guru Gobind Singh was a contemporary of James II who ruled England from 1685 to 1688 and lost his throne thirteen years before his death because he was a Catholic. There has not been a Catholic on the English throne since. And it was ten years after the breaking of the siege of Derry, which is still aggressively celebrated in Northern Ireland today, that Gobind Singh proclaimed the Khalsa. If Muslim children in Punjab were quietened even in fairly recent times with warnings about the coming of Ranjit Singh's general, Nalwa, there are people in Ireland who can remember being told to beware of 'warty Ol' – Oliver Cromwell.[45] Punjab's politics are as 'modern' as those of Belfast or the Basque provinces of France and Spain.

THE *MISL*

In 1739 Nadir Shah, the Persian, marched through the Punjab to sack Delhi, and between 1745 and 1767, according to one estimate, there were nine Afghan invasions.[46] In 1761, the southward-driving Afghans destroyed a northward-marching Maratha army at Panipat, the third of the epic battles fought at that otherwise unremarkable town. The victory, however, was so costly that it blunted the Afghan taste for deeper penetration into north India. And in weakening the Marathas, who were Hindu chiefs of central India, it allowed the British East India Company to emerge as the strongest single military power on the subcontinent.

The dates and details are not especially important in themselves (though people who knew the rugged terrain that was the Panipat bus station in the 1960s perhaps understand better than others the misfortunes of the Maratha cavalry). What is important, however, is to re-emphasise that invasion and violence were regular features of Punjab life. Out of these conditions grew a distinctive Sikh response – the *misl* – which, some argue, still influences Sikh political and social expectations today.

The *misl* resembled a territorial militia. In times of strife, local leaders gathered bands of able-bodied Sikhs and followed the leader of their *misl* to attack Afghan baggage trains, Mughal governors or – ultimately – each other. In times of peace, the bands dispersed to their villages. In theory, there were twelve *misls*, each covering a different region of the Punjab and subordinate (barring one) to the central authority of the Dal Khalsa.[47] In practice, organisation was more fluid than this description suggests. Yet the idea of the *misl* became firmly embedded in the mind of Sikhs, an accepted, recognisable way of organising for conflict: find a leader; follow him when necessary; if your enemy follows one leader, you must follow another. In her remarkable book, *Robber Noblemen*, Joyce Pettigrew contends that modern factional leaders in Punjab – and factions are fundamental to Punjab (and Indian) politics, as I shall try to show in Chapter 5 – are 'the modern equivalents of the misl chiefs . . . and . . . a continuation of an historical type'.[48] There is no doubt that every Sikh knows about the eighteenth-century *misls*, and this knowledge sets a pattern for – and legitimises – modern factional politics. 'We are behaving', people may say to themselves, 'as our forebears did when one *misl* struggled against another in former, glorious times.'

MAHARAJA RANJIT SINGH (1780–1839)

When Partap Singh Kairon (1901–65), the commanding Chief Minister of Punjab between 1956 and 1964, toured villages to promote the Congress Party and denounce his Akali Dal opponents, he would tell his audiences: 'I am the first Jat to have brought power to Jats in Punjab since Maharaja Ranjit Singh'.[49] Kairon consciously chose to associate himself with 'the most popular hero of Sikh history' – 'what . . . Bonaparte [is] to the French'.[50]

Ending the struggles between the *misls*, Ranjit Singh built a Sikh-ruled empire in Punjab with its capital in Lahore from 1801. (Consider the anguish among Sikhs when Lahore fell on the Pakistan side of the Radcliffe Line at partition in 1947.) At fifteen, he came into the leadership of the Shukerchakia *misl* and before his eighteenth birthday had captured Lahore.[51]

When he died in 1839, his empire extended from the Khyber Pass to the Sutlej and from Kashmir almost to Sind. He embodied a number of characteristics that Sikh Jats held dear: he could hunt, ride and drink with the best. The Sikh empire did two things. First, it made a reality of Guru Gobind Singh's cry: *raj karega Khalsa* – the Khalsa shall rule. Though Ranjit Singh was careful not to offend his Muslim and Hindu subjects, and though Sikhs did not constitute a majority of the population, the idea of a state ruled by Sikhs branded itself into the minds of Punjabis. What had happened once could happen again.

Second, because Sikhs ruled, it made sense to be a Sikh and to wear the symbols of the Khalsa.[52] To belong to the religion of the rulers brings advantages. People converted to Islam under the Muslims, and were to convert to Christianity under the British, for the same reasons. With the religion of the Sikhs, however, there was a difference, because Hindus regarded it simply as a sect. Though large numbers of Hindus adopted the Five Ks, they felt able to retain practices – like cow-worship and concern about caste distinctions – that the Gurus had deprecated.

This raised a problem that remains with Sikhism today. The policies of governments to a certain extent determine the number of bearded Sikhs. If governments encourage the Five Ks, larger numbers choose to adopt them. If governments are neutral, however, the numbers of Sikhs who choose to wear the long hair and beard decline. The religion of the Sikhs is thus subtly and intricately entwined with the question of political rule. Of all the legacies of the period 1699–1849, that is perhaps the most important.

'A QUEER POSITION': THE SIKHS AND THE BRITISH

In relation to the Sikhs, wrote a European intelligence officer around the time of the First World War, the British were 'in a queer position'. The Sikhs, he continued, 'have been fostered and petted and taught to regard themselves as a great nation'. This had two results: 'while it has kept the banner of Sikhism flying to the great advantage of the government, it now appears to be likely to be used as an instrument to scourge us'. His fear was 'neo-Sikhism', Sikh revivalism aimed against British rule, which raised the possibility of 'active rebellion'.[53]

After Ranjit Singh's death in 1839, it took the East India Company ten years, two bloody wars and the work of some of its ablest officers to annex the Punjab kingdom. Dissensions and treachery at the Punjab court nullified the hard fighting of Punjab's soldiers on the battlefields. An understandable respect grew up among the British for the sturdy soldiers able to give and take hard knocks. Thus began what a Sikh today refers to as 'the long imperial romance between the Sikh and the Raj'.[54] Between the end of the Second Sikh War in 1849 and the outbreak of the 'mutiny' in 1857, the British skilfully brought order to the Punjab countryside and won the approval of a large section of their new subjects. When the revolt came in 1857, Sikhs sided with the British and were invaluable in defeating the 'mutineers' and their supporters who came largely from the central plain of the Ganga River (the so-called United Provinces or UP). In the aftermath, Punjabis generally, and Sikhs particularly, replaced men from the UP in the remodelled Indian Army. Even today, Punjabis retain this importance in the armies of both India and Pakistan.

Indeed, British patronage after 1857 helped to maintain the outward symbols of Sikhism. Immediately after the British annexation of the Punjab in 1849, many Sikhs began to abandon the beard and uncut hair and become to all intents and purposes, Hindus. Dalhousie, the Governor-General, noted that one of his officials 'used to say that in 50 years the sect of the Sikhs would have disappeared'.[55] Since Sikhs lived among Hindus and were drawn from Hindu castes, there were constant temptations to foresake both Guru Nanak's teachings about a single God and the evils of caste and Guru Gobind Singh's injunctions to keep the hair uncut. Many men required more practical encouragement, which the British Indian Army soon began to provide. It became a rule that Sikhs who joined the army 'should not be permitted ... to drop [the practice of keeping long hair and beard]'.[56] The British thus provided incentives to Sikhs to hold fast to the symbols of the Khalsa.

Indeed, this emphasis continues in Sikh regiments of the Indian Army to this day. After the mutiny of some Sikh troops following the storming of the Golden Temple in June 1984, Lt-Gen Harbaksh Singh, the longest-serving colonel-in-chief of the Sikh Regiment, wrote a public letter listing the ways in which the Indian Army still uses the religion of the Sikhs to bind Sikh soldiers. They take their oath of loyalty on the Guru Granth Sahib; the symbols of Guru Gobind Singh are everywhere in the Sikh Regiment; a *gurdwara* (place of worship) is part of every barracks; and the Granth Sahib itself is carried into forward areas.[57]

Ranjit Singh, the British and the government of independent India all found it judicious to encourage the outward forms of Sikhism, which fostered a martial spirit and kept turbulent men loyal to – and at the disposal of – the state. To many British army officers, Sikhs became 'one of our most loyal Indian sects', providers of soldiers who were 'loyal, brave and trust-worthy'.[58] At some stages of British rule, Sikhs may have made up as much as a fifth of the Indian Army.[59]

The army made men mobile. Old soldiers, as we have seen, were often rewarded with grants of land in the newly-opening canal colonies of west Punjab. The army also sent men overseas – to 'no less than six theatres of war', as a proud British officer of a Sikh regiment put it.[60] Partly through the old-soldier connection, Sikhs learned of opportunities throughout the British empire and the world. By the beginning of the twentieth century, they were migrating to British Columbia, California, east Africa, south-east Asia and Australia.[61]

This mobility often brought Sikhs into conflict with the most blatant forms of racial prejudice and imperialism, victims of white governments trying to exclude non-white migrants. In one of the most celebrated examples, the *Komagata Maru*, a chartered Japanese ship carrying more than 300 Sikhs, was forced to sit for two months in 1914 in the waters between Vancouver and Victoria, British Columbia, while Canadian governments refused permission for the Sikhs to land. Eventually, the ship was forced back to sea, first to Hong Kong, then Singapore and finally Calcutta. There, some of its passengers linked up with the ill-fated Ghadr movement that attempted a revolt against the British government in India in the early months of the First World War.[62]

Singapore, Hong Kong, Vancouver. The names suggest a Jules Verne saga and hint at the breadth of experience that some Sikhs were acquiring. This promoted a growing self-consciousness and resentment of British rule.[63] From the time of the First World War until today, the migrant experience has played a key role in encouraging Sikhs to define who they are, to formulate sweeping political goals and to confront established governments in India. That overseas influence briefly drew the attention of a huge audience after Mrs Gandhi's assassination when a few unwise Sikhs in London and New York popped champagne corks for television cameras.

During the First World War, more than 100 000 Sikhs fought for the British. Initially, this seemed to testify to astonishing loyalty, for the total Sikh population was only about 3 million.[64] In the longer term, however, the seeing-of-the-world that went with military service had the same effect on many returned soldiers as it had on other Sikh migrants: they became more self-conscious, assertive and sometimes, angry. The 'ambiguity' of British feelings about the Sikhs grew increasingly clear. Though the British 'admired Sikh virility and bravery', they 'never quite trusted the Sikhs', and doubts nagged them that the 'Sikhs were about to reclaim their lost kingdom'.[65]

At the end of the war, these doubts intensified as India throbbed with tales of revolution in Europe, expectations of political reform, and the effects of inflation and influenza. Punjab's special qualities, its violent nature – 'A Jat, like a wound, is better bound' – were at the heart of the massacre at Jallianwalla Bagh, a few minutes' walk from the Golden Temple in Amritsar, on 13 April 1919. The British general, Reginald Dyer (1864–1927), who ordered the firing which killed at least 400 people, later explained his actions by the need to set an example that would cow the whole of the turbulent Punjab.[66] The Governor of Punjab, Sir Michael O'Dwyer (1864–1940), who whole-heartedly backed Dyer, was murdered in London twenty-one years later by a Sikh.[67]

By the middle of 1920, the Gandhian nationalist movement confronted the British with the most serious challenge to their rule since 1857. Imbibing the spirit of challenge, Sikhs put forward demands of their own, which produced the two institutions which dominate their politics today – the Akali Dal and the Shiromani Gurdwara Parbandhak Committee (SGPC).

THE AKALI DAL AND THE SGPC

After Gobind Singh proclaimed the Granth Sahib as the eternal Guru, the building in which the sacred book was housed assumed an even greater importance. Known as the *gurdwara* ('the door of the guru'), it became the centre of Sikh social life. Wherever Sikhs settled, they established *gurdwaras* which were frequently endowed with valuable properties. Regular collections from the congregation helped to maintain the *granthi*, or reader.

But again the question of Sikh identity arose. Many *gurdwara* supervisors (*mahants*) abandoned the outward symbols – the Five Ks – and became indistinguishable from Hindus. The properties of the *gurdwaras* came to be recorded in their names and were passed on from father to son.[68] By the beginning of the First World War, the sharpened sense of identity among Sikhs who kept the beard and turban led to growing demands that the *gurdwaras* should be controlled by genuine Sikhs, not shaven Hindus.

In November 1920 an estimated 10 000 Sikhs met in Amritsar to establish a committee to draft new rules for the management of the Golden Temple. This became the Shiromani Gurdwara Parbandhak Committee. Within a month, the Akali Dal – 'army of the faithful' – was formed as a central organisation to co-ordinate local *jathas*, or bands, that were already attempting to wrest control of *gurdwaras* from the *mahants*.[69] During the next four years, the Akali Dal sent volunteers to occupy *gurdwaras* and turn out the apostate proprietors. The *mahants*, initially supported by the British government, resisted. In one famous encounter in February 1921, the toughs employed by the *mahant* at the *gurdwara* of Nankana Sahib near Lahore slaughtered more than a hundred Akali demonstrators.[70] The *gurdwara*, however, quickly passed into the hands of the SGPC, and the 'Nankana holocaust', brightly reflecting the spirit of sacrifice of the Akali Dal, became part of Sikh tradition, worthy to be mentioned in the same breath as the deeds of Guru Gobind Singh.

The role of travelled Sikhs was noteworthy. According to one estimate, 10 per cent of 15 500 Akali volunteers of this period were either ex-soldiers or returned emigrants.[71] For many Sikhs, experience of a wider world, far from weakening their attachment to the symbols of the Khalsa, heightened it and suggested the need for change in the way the Sikh religion conducted its affairs in Punjab.

All this was happening at a time when the British were desperately trying to suppress the Gandhian non-co-operation movement throughout India. Although the Gandhian challenge collapsed in February 1922, British officials were appalled at the prospect of a permanent rift with the 'loyal' Sikhs. Given the large number of Sikhs in the army and the possibility that the army might have to be used against future nationalist upsurges, the British moved for a settlement with the Sikhs. In doing so, they institutionalised the SGPC and made it in effect 'the Religious Parliament of the Sikhs', which it remains today.[72]

The Sikh Gurdwaras and Shrines Act of 1925 placed more than 200 places of worship under the control of an SGPC that was to be elected every three years by all adult Sikhs living in Punjab. At that time, the annual income of religious properties was estimated at Rs. 2 million; by the early 1980s, it was said to be more than Rs. 70 million (US $6 million).[73] The funds available to the SGPC, as well as its influence over religious life, made it a magnet for ambitious Sikh politicians. In the Sikh-majority Punjab formed in 1966, the SGPC became an organisation which could create and destroy governments.

LEADERSHIP AND PARTITION

After the passage of the Gurdwara Act, four strands of affiliation ran through Sikh politics. Most obvious were the semi-aristocratic families who held large estates and supported the Unionist Party. The Unionists, representing Muslim, Hindu and Sikh landlords, governed Punjab in comfortable harmony with the British from 1923 until the elections of 1946.[74] The Akali Dal represented the second strand. Its influence lay among the Jat peasantry, and after 1925 it was often preoccupied with internal feuds and battles to control the SGPC. Sikhs who supported the Indian National Congress formed the third strand. They were never large in number, yet some Sikhs were always found in Gandhi's movement.[75] Finally, a still smaller group of Sikhs attached themselves, in the tradition of the

Ghadr revolutionaries of 1914, to revolutionary movements and ultimately to the Communist Party.

Most Sikhs, however, tilled their land, went abroad, entered government service or joined the army. Historians have since written of a 'Sikh indifference to politics' in these years.[76]

In this sense, the partition of India in 1947 caught Sikhs unaware. The demand for the creation of a Muslim state – Pakistan – grew in other areas of India, not in Punjab. Indeed, in Punjab, Muslims constituted a small majority, and the lesson of Punjab legislative politics seemed to be the one which Maharaja Ranjit Singh had recognised long before: to govern the Punjab, one needed the co-operation of all religions. The Unionist Party represented just such a coalition based on the class interests of landlords.

Yet the partition ripped through the Punjab as it did through no other area except Bengal. The reason was bound up with the bureaucratised, legalistic, head-counting government established by the British. In India as a whole, the census reports showed that Muslims were a minority (about 21 per cent). In some provinces, they did not hold as many places in the government service as Hindus, nor was their rate of literacy (for example) as high. How were such inequalities and injustices to be remedied? By the creation of a state – a 'Pak'-istan, a land of the pure – in which Muslims would be a majority. The idea virtually began as an acronym – **P**unjab, **A**fghania, **K**ashmir, **I**ndus, Baluchi**STAN** – among Muslim students in London in the 1930s.[77] By March 1940, the Muslim League had met in Lahore and passed a resolution making the creation of Pakistan its ultimate goal. When the British left India, the League declared, a Muslim state must be established in those areas where Muslims were a majority.

The fact that the resolution was passed in Lahore was significant. The Muslim League was still not a power in the Punjab, but to adopt the resolution in Lahore was to give the idea of Pakistan far wider publicity among Punjabi Muslims. And if Pakistan was to be achieved, Punjab would have to be its core. Between 1937, when the League won only one seat in the 175-seat Punjab legislature, and 1946, when it won seventy-five seats, the idea of Pakistan passed from pipe-dream to impending reality.[78]

Sikhs had no answer to this drive for a Muslim state, even

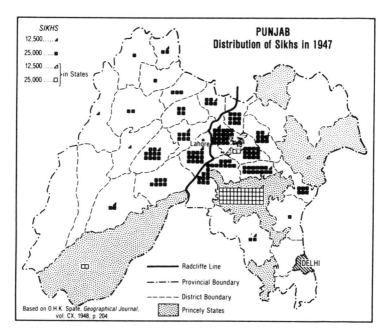

MAP 3.1   *Punjab: Sikhs and the Radcliffe Line, 1947*

though two undesirable outcomes were early apparent.[79] Either
Sikhs would find themselves in an undivided Punjab that was
part of a Muslim-dominated country, or Punjab would be
partitioned and a section of Sikhs would be left in Pakistan.

After the outbreak of the Second World War in 1939, the
two major strands of Sikh politics – the Unionists and the
Akali Dal – eventually supported the British government and
successfully urged Sikhs to join the army. Thousands were
taken prisoner by the Japanese after the British débâcle in Malaya
and the surrender of Singapore in February 1942. Large
numbers of Sikh prisoners-of-war later joined the Indian
National Army (INA) to fight with the Japanese against the
British. But although participation in the INA has since
provided another symbol of Sikhs' militant commitment to
their (and India's) freedom, it did nothing to improve the
political prospects of Sikhs in Punjab.[80]

From 1942, most Sikhs who supported the Congress were in
jail; those who backed the Unionist Party watched complacently
as its influence withered under pressure from a burgeoning

Muslim League; Sikhs who were Communists now backed the British government and the 'people's war' to save the Soviet Union from Nazi Germany; and the Akali Dal itself urged Sikhs to join the army. Yet to most observers, it was clear that India would be independent soon after the war and that a Muslim state was increasingly likely.

Sikh politicians appear to have thought very little about the consequences of independence and partition. In August 1944, various Sikh representatives met under the Akali Dal leader Master Tara Singh (1885–1967) in Amritsar and established a committee to 'evolve a scheme for the establishment of an independent Sikh State in case India was to be divided'.[81] The demand for an independent Sikh state was raised frequently over the next three years, but little effort was made to work out what it might entail. Neither was it used effectively as a bargaining counter with the British, the Congress or the Muslim League. As one advocate of a Sikh state explained in April 1946, 'I am not giving a Blue Print of the demand. That . . . is left to natural political leaders aided by practical experts'.[82]

The demand for a 'Khalistan' or 'Sikhistan', moreover, differed from the Muslim cry for Pakistan in one vitally important respect; in no district of the Punjab were Sikhs in a majority. Claims that their stake as major landholders and taxpayers ought to justify the inclusion of areas of west Punjab inside the boundaries of a Sikh state were easily brushed aside. The best that advocates of the Sikh state could do was to suggest that 'the demand rests on an . . . exchange of population'.[83] However, no political organisation was prepared to consider population transfers until the killing of August 1947 forced millions to move.

Mountbatten arrived in India in February 1947 – the last Viceroy, charged with extricating the British from the subcontinent. He had, it appears, already decided that partition was the only way. Sikhs were simply one small part of the huge puzzle, and they received only scant attention. By 3 May 1947 even Master Tara Singh of the Akali Dal, rejecting suggestions from the Muslim League that Sikhs would be better off in a united Punjab inside a big Pakistan, was resigned to partition: 'division of the Punjab is the only way to a peaceful settlement'.[84]

The killing had in fact begun in March 1947 when Sikhs in

Rawalpindi were murdered in large numbers by Muslim mobs. Caught by surprise in the west Punjab areas where their numbers were fewest, Sikhs began to arm themselves in the east and central Punjab. There was talk, though not very well thought out, of using the Sikh princely states as the basis for carving out a Sikh state by force of arms in the chaos that might follow partition. In the event, however, the slaughter of August, September and October 1947 owed more to fury than to grand strategy.[85] The killing brought about the transfer of

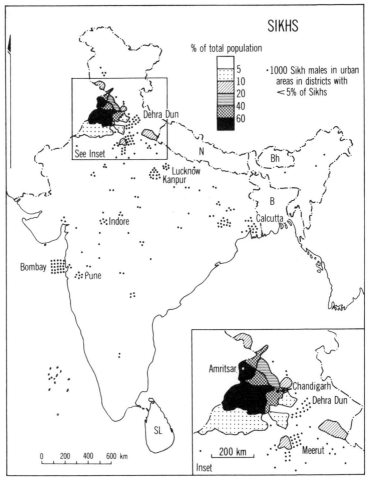

MAP 3.2   *India: distribution of Sikhs, 1971*

populations that, earlier, no one had been prepared to talk about.[86]

Thus by the end of 1947, Sikhs were numerically more concentrated than they had ever been before. But close to 2 million of them were in refugee camps and had lost everything in their escape from Pakistan. Their resettlement, and the dynamic remaking of Punjab over the next twenty years, constitute one of modern India's notable achievements.

The successes of the refugees contrast strikingly with the failures of Sikh political leaders and recall a remark of Malcolm Darling. Sikh Jats, Darling claimed in an Indian Civil Servant's sweeping style, do 'splendidly, whether with sword or plough, as long as conditions are adverse'.[87] The phrase highlights a point about Sikh leadership which was often made in the aftermath of partition. There were, according to this argument, too many attractive opportunities for able Sikhs. The best men joined the army or the civil service or took up land in the canal colonies or went abroad. The pool of clever lawyers – men like Gandhi, Nehru, Jinnah, Vallabhbhai Patel, Rajendra Prasad, to name only a few – who were the essence of national political life, did not exist among Sikhs.[88] Thus Sikhs were out of their depth when 'pitted against more capable leadership of . . . sister communities'.[89]

There was no doubt something to this analysis. Master Tara Singh, the leading Akali Dal spokesman, had been a comparatively humble school teacher (thus the 'Master'), and British officials were distinctly unimpressed with the grasp of wider issues which he and other Akali leaders displayed.[90]

But there was more to it than this. Trevaskis hinted at it in the 1920s when he wrote that 'good leaders had always been few amongst the democratic Jat Sikhs'.[91] M. S. Randhawa noted the same quality: 'Everyone regards himself as a leader, and is unwilling to follow others'.[92] There is, wrote Joyce Pettigrew, 'a particular cultural tradition among the Jats: they did not regard themselves as subordinate to any other person.'[93] This fierce egalitarianism has meant that the struggle for political power among Sikhs has been especially bitter. Charges of religious betrayal, or cries that the Khalsa is in danger, have proved to be two ways to outbid rivals in the contest to attract followers.

A man who attempted to assume a position of superiority

over other Sikh Jats did so either at his peril or after having made very certain of his support. As we shall see in Chapter 6, factions, which characterise rural politics throughout India, acquire a peculiar intensity in Punjab.

This spirit of undisciplined equality, coupled with the fact that spokesmen for Sikh interests in the 1940s were not the most sophisticated men the community had produced, contributed to the plight in which Sikhs found themselves at the end of 1947. Darling's conditions could not have been more adverse.

4 Innovations

On 4 November 1979 an odd procession moved off from one of the outer buildings of the Golden Temple complex in Amritsar towards the temple itself. A black-bearded Sikh in his thirties, having had garlands of flowers placed round his neck by his two daughters, carried a large radio on his head. Behind him came an older, grey-bearded Sikh, a small black box clutched to his stomach like a hot-water bottle. Together they represented 'Radio Golden Temple', an illegal transmitter which began its first broadcast a week later with greetings to 'our listeners all over the world'.[1] Its 25-watt signal could be picked up as far away as 250 metres.

This venture into radio blended hallowed symbols, 'modern' communications and immediate political schemes. The timing, and the choice of the Golden Temple as the venue, disclosed a good deal about what was happening to Punjab.

Although the Golden Temple got its famed copper-gilt roof only in 1802 under Ranjit Singh's empire, a place of worship dear to the Sikhs, inaugurated by the fifth Guru, Arjan, had stood on the site since 1589. It was here that he installed the newly-compiled scripture, the Granth Sahib, in 1604. Thirty years later Sikhs were forced to abandon Amritsar, and Guru Gobind Singh is thought never to have visited the town.[2] However, from the early eighteenth century, it once again became a Sikh centre, made legendary by their enemies who a number of times in the epic years between the 1740s and 1760s destroyed temples built on the present site. In the time of Ranjit Singh, the temple became and remained golden – 'the Mecca of the Sikhs ... the St Peter's at Rome ... the Jerusalem of Sikhism'.[3] In 1979 it was a revealing place for a radio station.

Governments have monopolised broadcasting in India since 1930. The British passed the Indian Wireless Act, which today still controls radio, towards the end of M. K. Gandhi's civil

73

disobedience movement in 1933. Gandhi's Salt March of 1930 had galvanised India and shown how politically potent a simple walk, and a few dozen talks, in the countryside could be. As far as the British were concerned, the new medium of radio, and its capacity to talk to millions, needed to be tightly controlled. All-India Radio (AIR), the national service, began in 1936, and since 1947 the central government of independent India has jealously controlled it. Neither independent companies, nor state governments, have the right to run their own stations.[4] By the early 1980s, AIR operated about 130 medium-wave transmitters and sixty-five stations throughout the country, but critics complained of a ponderous, unresponsive, government-manipulated service. During the 'emergency' of 1975–7, AIR came to be known as 'All-Indira Radio': its news, critics said, was all about Indira Gandhi.[5]

The General Overseas Service of AIR, the short-wave division, which, like the BBC World Service and the Voice of America, broadcasts to the world, also has a reputation for hidebound boredom. Yet hundreds of thousands of Indians overseas, particularly in Britain, yearn for programmes to keep them in touch with what they value most at home. For many, that represents, in part at least, religion.

Every Indian government since 1947, however, has been committed to 'secularism'. This means that only AIR may produce religious broadcasts, and these are carefully checked and balanced to prevent offence and forestall charges that particular groups are favoured. Though the policy is reasonable in a country of such diversity, it cannot satisfy everyone, and it has usually been applied with little imagination or flexibility. Moreover, since close to half – the figure is amazing, but apparently accurate – of Indian migrants in Britain come from Sikh backgrounds,[6] the desire for Punjabi culture and Sikh religious ceremonies on short-wave radio has been far stronger than AIR has been able to satisfy.

When Surjit Singh Barnala, a member of the Akali Dal and Minister for Agriculture in the central government, visited London in May 1978, Sikhs appealed to him to set up a short-wave transmitter to broadcast devotional songs from the Golden Temple. Punjabis in London offered to collect the money to pay for the project, and the Akali Dal in Punjab later passed a resolution supporting it.[7] But although Barnala represented the Akali Dal in Prime Minister Morarji Desai's ministry, the central government rejected the request in December 1978.[8]

By November 1979, however – the timing now becomes important – Morarji Desai's government had collapsed, and a weak caretaker ministry held office during the September–December election campaign that was to bring Mrs Gandhi back to power. In Punjab, although the coalition between the Akali Dal and Janata Party had also broken up in August, the Akali Dal continued to hold office; but it was split into two warring factions, unable even to co-ordinate its campaign for the coming election to the national parliament of Punjab's thirteen members.[9] In such slippery times, there was no telling what a 25-watt radio transmitter, installed in the sacred precincts of the Golden Temple, might achieve.

The grey-bearded man who carried the small black box in the procession of 4 November 1979 was Dr Jagjit Singh Chauhan (born about 1927). He was later to acquire notoriety outside India when in a radio interview with the BBC after the Indian Army's storming of the Golden Temple in June 1984, he called for Mrs Gandhi's assassination.[10]

A qualified medical doctor, Chauhan was a political gadfly. He began his career as an Akali but deserted to become Finance Minister in a renegade minority government in Punjab in 1967–8, which the Congress supported as a way of undermining the Akalis. Chauhan left India in 1970 or 1971 and spent time in Britain and the USA. In October 1971, as the tension mounted between India and Pakistan over the guerrilla war in East Pakistan (now Bangladesh), Chauhan engineered a half-page, 1500-word advertisement in the *New York Times* under the heading: 'The Sikhs demand an independent state in India ... [sic] the only guarantee for peace on the sub-continent'. The Sikhs, it proclaimed, live 'in constant fear of genocide', persecuted by 'a brute, unfeeling, racist Hindu majority'. The advertisement, which called for a demonstration (which does not seem to have occurred) in front of the United Nations the following day, commanded little attention at the time. What it now highlights, however, is the quality of romantic bombast and exaggeration which characterised Chauhan. ('Nearly 80 per cent of the Indian army consists of Sikhs', the advertisement informed readers.)[11] He remained in Britain during the 1975–7 'emergency' and later liked to talk about this period as his 'exile'.[12] He returned to India after the election of the Janata Party in March 1977.

The 'installation' of the radio transmitter was a clever gimmick, intended to draw attention to Chauhan who was angling for a way to re-enter Punjab's politics. Styling himself as president of a breakaway party, the Akali Dal (Revolutionary), he told his Golden Temple audience of his disappointment that no members of the ruling Akali Dal greeted him on his return from 'exile' in Britain. He added ominously that he was no threat to any of them since he was not seeking a seat in either the state legislature or parliament. However, as a rueful Akali Dal worker said, Chauhan appeared to want to become a 'third force when there were already two factions in the Akali Dal'.[13]

Radio Golden Temple, which had not yet gone on the air, made the front page of the *Tribune*, Punjab's oldest and largest English daily, the next morning, even though the story carried the headline 'Transmitter Threat Flops' and veteran correspondent Prem Mohindra dubbed the episode 'a damp squib'.[14] But Chauhan and his handful of followers had already toured a number of towns in Punjab, and they carefully timed their appearance at the Golden Temple to coincide with the large crowds celebrating the birthday of Guru Nanak. They thus ensured that thousands of curious onlookers saw their procession.

When Radio Golden Temple began to broadcast on 12 November, it 'created a sensation' and 'young Sikhs rushed to the temple to see the actual working of the radio station'. There was not much to see. A journalist found it 'housed in a small room' – 'jumbled wires and three small gadgets'. Hooked up to the Golden Temple's loudspeaker system, the transmitter broadcast morning and evening prayers which eventually could be heard up to 1500 metres away. People brought their transmitters to the area to 'enjoy the fun . . . and satisfy their curiosity'.[15]

Meanwhile, the central government agonised over the illegality of the transmitter and the virtual immunity bestowed on it by virtue of its being inside the Golden Temple precinct. A feeble electioneering government hoped, one suspects, that the problem would go away. In fact, it did.

On 1 December, Chauhan announced that he and his followers were handing over the transmitter to the SGPC, the committee that manages all Sikh *gurdwaras* (places of worship) in Punjab, which would henceforth carry on the campaign for a full-scale radio station.[16] The SGPC stopped the broadcasts. By the end of the month, moreover, Mrs Gandhi's Congress (I) Party had won the general elections and twelve of the thirteen seats in Punjab.[17]

In January 1980, Chauhan was hobnobbing with Zail Singh, a Sikh, who was Home Minister in the new Congress (I) government in Delhi. He also wrote letters to Mrs Gandhi herself and arranged to meet her son Sanjay, ostensibly to pursue the demand for a radio transmitter for the Golden Temple.[18] By March, leaders of the Akali Dal were denouncing Chauhan as 'an agent of the Congress (I) . . . instigated by [its] . . . leaders . . . including Mr Zail Singh'.[19] His task, they said, was to divide the Sikh vote in the impending elections to the state legislature by preaching wild ideas about an independent Sikh state. Indeed, in another symbolic act in March, Chauhan had raised a replica of Ranjit Singh's yellow banner (made in London, his followers told reporters) outside the great *gurd wara* at Anandpur Sahib and vowed to open an office of the 'Khalistan government' inside the Golden Temple. In May, Chauhan returned to Britain, and in June, the Congress (I) narrowly won the state elections in Punjab over a divided, feuding Akali Dal.[20]

In an attempt to understand events in Punjab, the 'toy' radio station fulfils two functions.[21] First, it introduces the question of 'factions' which are the essence of Punjab's (and India's) politics and which Chapter 6 explores in detail. Chauhan's manoeuvres were thrusts and parries in well-understood, long-standing duels for power. Second, the station symbolises the innovations that have spread throughout Punjab since the mid-1960s, altering the consequences of familiar actions. The old contests go on, but now in radically different circumstances and with outcomes that veteran participants may not foresee.

It is important to note how Chauhan, the man behind the radio stratagem, flirted first with the SGPC and the Akali Dal – even trying to exploit the latter's name by calling his own group the Akali Dal (Revolutionary). Later, however, he courted Mrs Gandhi's party so avidly that fearful Akali Dal politicians

branded him a Congress (I) agent. Joyce Pettigrew captures
the spirit of such politics: 'Whenever a man had enough
economic resources, and the political conditions were suitable,
he could aspire to collect a following around himself'.[22]
Ideology – including the doctrine of Khalistan – was considerably less important than personal rivalry. Chapter 6 tries to
show how intense rivalries, long a part of Punjab's way of life,
exploded out of control in the late 1970s and led first to the
battle of the Golden Temple in June 1984 and ultimately to
Mrs Gandhi's assassination in October.

   The key reason for their explosion also relates to the tale of
'Radio Golden Temple'. By the mid-1970s India generally,
and Punjab especially, were experiencing a revolution in
communications that was changing the rhythms of daily life
and politics. Ideas spread faster and to more people. More
people moved faster and to more places. And more places
experienced the effects of a market economy that surged into
more and more areas of daily life. Once, for example, a person
picked a twig from a particular tree (the *neem* in Punjab) each
morning and chewed it to clean the teeth. By the 1970s,
however, even small towns had hoardings advertising the glory
of toothpaste.

UNDERPINNINGS AND INFRASTRUCTURES

'There has indeed been a revolution in the Punjab', concluded
a foreign scholar who returned in 1978 to the village in which
he had lived in the mid-1960s. The revolution was a 'change
in the relation between villagers and the state'.[23] In short,
government had begun to do something for villagers – it had
effectively propagated the measures necessary for the 'green
revolution' – and villagers now began to feel 'their interests
identified with the interests of the state'. They also experienced
'increasing wealth and widely-shared rising living standards'.
All these together, the writer suggested, were likely to play 'a
very important part' in fostering 'political stability'.[24]

   At one level, he was right. In spite of the buffeting that
Punjab has experienced in the mid-1980s, its farmers continue
to produce record harvests. Unrest has not got in the way of

agriculture.[25] On the other hand, 'political stability' is not the first – or second – phrase that springs to mind to describe the politics of Punjab since 1980.

The 'green revolution' brought widespread government activity, and considerable wealth, to Punjab. In the wake of the drought and hunger of 1965 in north India, governments desperately needed to increase food production, and when Punjab farmers reponded so eagerly to early attempts to promote the 'green revolution', they received (until about 1973) further encouragement. Once, 'government' had consisted of little more than a distant revenue office, police station, post office or school. By the 1970s, however, 'government' meant banks, co-operative societies, agricultural extension offices, bus routes and colleges.

It is worth emphasising, too, that what was happening in Punjab was also happening in lesser degrees throughout India. 'Many people hope', wrote a scholar in the 1970s, that where Punjab has led, 'India will follow.'[26] What other areas lacked, however, was the momentum and acceleration that so marked the 'development' of Punjab from the mid-1960s.

Roads were perhaps the most obvious aspect of such change. When the 'green revolution' became technically possible in the mid-1960s, close to half of Punjab's villages were still not served by sealed roads. To fulfil the new possibilities of agriculture, roads were essential. In the entire span of the Third Five-Year Plan (1961–6), the state had built only 2280 kilometres of road, but in the single year of 1969–70, it added 1920 kilometres. 'No other development programme', wrote M. S. Randhawa, 'received such unanimous support from the rural people.'[27] By 1970, Punjab had 10 000 kilometres of sealed road; by 1975, 25 000; and by the end of the decade, 95 per cent of its villages were linked by sealed roads.[28]

Randhawa extolled the extensive effects of the road-building programme:

> The farmers market their produce with facility and . . . purchase fertilisers . . . from the market town with ease . . . Villagers who have had no experience of growing commercial crops . . . adopt them easily . . . Roads also promote industry . . . Villagers who have never used bicycles purchase them . . . Tractors can command larger areas for cultivation . . .

The sons and daughters of the farmers ... take advantage of educational facilities in the towns.[29]

Coupled, as it was, with the 'green revolution', the expansion of the road network produced a demand not merely for bicycles but for motor vehicles of all kinds. At least a sixth of India's tractors are in Punjab. Punjab cultivators, one story had it, bought tractors not because they needed them for agriculture but because they wanted to transport their marriage-parties in style during the wedding season.[30] Roads broadened horizons and enhanced expectations.

The need for financial credit also went with the 'green revolution'. Punjab in the late 1970s had the highest ratio of banks to population of any of the Indian states: a bank branch for every 11 000 people. The national ratio was only half this: one branch for every 22 000 people.[31] The extensive banking system was also needed for remittances from Punjabis living overseas. A study conducted by Punjabi University, Patiala, estimated that 200 000 families in Punjab's three border districts alone received US $400 million annually from abroad.[32]

On the surface, these expanding connections with the wider world seem beneficial. But they have another side. The 'green revolution' made cultivators heavily dependent on conditions elsewhere over which they had no control. (Recall, for example, the increased prices for fertilisers and diesel fuel resulting from the oil crisis of 1973). Similarly, once people acquired the knack of dealing with banks, they could feel aggrieved when banks did not give them the credit they needed at the terms they wanted, particularly when it was 'commonly believed that about two-thirds of Punjab's bank deposits get invested outside Punjab'.[33] Even money from abroad had drawbacks: the Punjabi University survey concluded that much of it was spent on alcohol and soft drugs.[34]

EDUCATION: 'THE COW IS A USEFUL ANIMAL'

Most people still agree, I think, that education is a Good Thing. 'A more highly qualified work force should be more productive', hypothesised a team of social scientists who analysed the correlation between literacy and agricultural productivity in India.[35] In fact, however, they found that the proposition did not hold: high literacy was associated with *low* productivity. What their investigations did show was that in areas where agricultural productivity increased, then literacy later rose. People who were more prosperous could afford to release their children from household tasks and even pay school costs. Sending children to school was a sign of status – perhaps a little like secluding women (putting them into purdah) in former times. It was a way of saying to the neighbours: 'We can afford to do this; we don't have to have them work'. Punjab's education system, a scholarly critic wrote, 'has contributed little to the recent economic development of the state'.[36]

The effects of a system may be considerably different from its aims. Schools everywhere transmit a lot of information behind the bicycle-shed at recess, and though little of it relates to the formal syllabus, it often makes a greater impact on the recipients. People who have been to school for a few years are likely to approach life differently from those who have not. Their new perspectives may not be the ones which the education system seeks to impart, nor are they necessarily 'modern' or 'enlightened'. But simply having experienced 'the system' – and learned to read – makes people different from their contemporaries who have done neither. In Punjab today more children go to school than ever before, because their parents can now afford to send them.

Electricity (available in every village by 1976), mechanisation and surplus income have accompanied the 'green revolution' for many of Punjab's rural families.[37] Sewing machines and electric grinders free girls from long hours over needle and thread or mortar and pestle. Methane units, fuelled by vegetable waste and animal excrement, provide cooking gas for wealthier households and mean that fewer children from dependent families are needed to make cow-dung pats by hand for fuel.

By 1974, 78 per cent of primary-age children in Punjab were attending school, the second highest figure in the country, exceeded only by southern Kerala (96 per cent) – India's most literate state.[38] Reflecting this demand, the number of primary school teachers rose from 23 000 in 1966–7, as the 'green revolution' began, to 34 000 in 1970–1.[39] In the same period, the number of middle-school teachers nearly doubled. By 1974, virtually the entire rural population had a primary school within 2 kilometres, and more than 80 per cent had secondary schools within 8 kilometres.[40]

Indeed, greater wealth and leisure made secondary and college education popular. To have one's children at such institutions brought prestige and might also bring profit. An 'educated' girl could expect to require a smaller dowry; an 'educated' boy might secure a salaried job. The number of college students increased from 35 000 in 1964–5 to 100 000 in 1968–9 and 110 000 in the mid-1970s.[41]

Take as an example a village of 1400 people in Gurdaspur district. By 1976, the village had '20 graduates and more than 50 matriculates'. Although 'the spread of education is the largest among the landowning families', four graduates and six matriculates came from completely landless families. 'The recent trend is that many girls are receiving education', and 'a large number of girls' attended secondary school in the town of Gurdaspur, 4 kilometres away, a clear illustration of the way in which schooling encouraged movement and with it, the spread of ideas.[42]

There was nothing progressive about the education system. It was rough, overcrowded and rigid. Corporal punishment was a daily event in classes which often contained fifty or more pupils sitting outside on mats under the shade of a mango tree in summer or in the sun in winter. Memorising chunks from textbooks and privately published 'guides' or cribs, they reproduced these at the examinations, where similar questions had appeared for years. Indeed, there was great outrage if the hoary favourites prepared by the pupils did not turn up. In the first year of English, for example, a favourite essay topic was 'The Cow', and a company called Swan's Guides of Jullundur had produced a crib which began: 'The cow is a useful animal. It has four legs and one tail. It gives us milk'. Thousands of cow essays were carefully memorised each year.

Whatever the defects, the education system bestows qualifications that open up the possibility of desirable jobs. Even parents who are illiterate themselves want to see their children go to school, and 'the importance of the school in local religious and political affairs' has steadily increased.[43] Schools have thus become another thread in the growing web of connections between thousands of rural families and the government. In one key area, Punjab's education system has been moderately successful: it has increased literacy. In 1961, 27 per cent of its total population – and 24 per cent of India's – could read and write. (See Table 4.1.) By 1981, literacy in Punjab had risen to 41 per cent – 47 per cent for males and 34 per cent for females. These figures, moreover, are for the total population, but roughly 40 per cent of Indians in the 1980s are under the age of 15. If we eliminate boys under 10 from the calculation, we may estimate that three out of five men in Punjab can read and write in the 1980s.

TABLE 4.1 *Comparative literacy, shown as percentage of total population, 1961–81*

	1961	1971	1981
India	24.0	29.5	36.2
Punjab	26.7	33.7	40.7
Kerala*	46.9	60.4	69.2
Rajasthan†	15.2	19.1	24.1

NOTE Excludes Jammu and Kashmir.
* Highest state in 1981.
† Lowest state in 1981.

SOURCES *EPW*, 11 April 1981, p. 644; *Times of India Yearbook*, 1979, p. 266.

Literacy does not make people wise, but it exposes them to more information than most illiterates can ever know. It constantly invites them to think about a wide range of matters of which they have no personal, direct experience and thereby encourages flirtations with new ideas – the previously 'unthinkable'. At the same time, mass schooling indicates that a society now affords more opportunity for leisure. Schooling brings young people together and gives them time to talk, read and discuss. Out of these twin processes, new attitudes emerge about one's identity, future and the fairness of the political system in which one lives. All this helps to explain the role of young, literate Sikhs in recent events in Punjab.

READING THE NEWS AND MAKING IT

Punjab by 1981 had about 6.8 million literates who sustained an expanding newspaper and publishing industry. As Table 4.2 shows, the circulation of daily newspapers in the Gurmukhi script increased from 34000 in 1967, when the new Punjabi-language state was formed, to 79000 during Mrs Gandhi's 'emergency' when the press was closely censored. And in the hunger for information after the 'emergency', circulations rocketed up to 218000 by 1979, an increase of 541 per cent in the period after the formation of the new Punjab and the beginning of the 'green revolution'.

TABLE 4.2 *Circulation of daily newspapers published in Punjab*

	1967	1976	1979	% Increase 1967–79
All languages	108 000	260 000	445 000	312
Gurmukhi script	34 000	79 000	218 000	541

SOURCES *Press in India*, 1968, 1979, 1980.

In August 1978, the Tribune Trust, which publishes the *Tribune*, Punjab's dowager English daily, started sister Hindu and Gurmukhi dailies from Chandigarh. Within weeks, the Punjabi edition built up a circulation of 30000, surpassing all the management's hopes. Prem Bhatia, the *Tribune* editor, marvelled at the fact that 'a gold mine has remained unexploited ... an untapped reservoir of Punjabi readership ... has been waiting to be wooed'.[44] By the 1980s, Punjabis were buying half a million newspapers in various languages each day, a ratio of about one daily for every twenty people over the age of 15. The increases in the circulation of other periodicals were also noteworthy. (See Table 4.3.)

The statistics illustrate the fact that today more Punjabis are exposed to a wider array of external influences than ever before. The growth of Gurmukhi newspaper circulations, moreover, has been most dramatic. This relates directly to the Sikhs, for Gurmukhi is the script of their sacred literature.

TABLE 4.3 *Circulation of all periodicals published in Punjab*

	1967	1976	1979	% increase 1967–79
All languages	389 000	600 000	873 000	124
Gurmukhi only	276 000	599 000*	754 000	173

* 1977 figure; 1976 would have been considerably lower.

NOTE   Figures for Gurmukhi include periodicals published elsewhere in India. These are numerous in Chandigarh and Delhi.

SOURCE   *Press in India*, 1968, 1978, 1980.

Access to newspapers and periodicals, like universal education, may well be beneficial. In theory, it produces well-informed citizens able to make rational judgements about the problems confronting their societies. But few people who have looked at the *Sun* in Britain or the *Post* in New York would want to push that argument very far. The ability to read does not make people rational or humane. The printed word may simply spread rumours more widely, engrain prejudices more deeply and lend dignity to outlandish tales.

In April 1978, there was a gun-battle in Amritsar in which eight people died.[45] Some observers contend that it set up a chain reaction of violence that reached its climax in Mrs Gandhi's assassination in October 1984. In any case, the slaughter in April 1978 produced 'deadly venom and unabashed hatred' in the Gurmukhi and Hindi press of Punjab.[46] Newspapers exchanged 'half-truths and blatant lies', revived 'ancient myths and phobias' and reopened 'old scars and wounds'.

The killings involved two groups: on the one hand, orthodox militant Sikhs, including Nihangs, whose supporters comprised most of the dead, and on the other, a schismatic sect called the Sant Nirankari Mission, which, its adversaries claimed, represented an affront to true Sikhism. In the newspapers, however, the dispute reduced itself to provocative stereotypes. Hindu newspapers played down the killings, tended to defend the Sant Nirankari Mission and called for a judicial inquiry into all the events of 13 April. Sikh newspapers demanded the immediate arrest of leaders of the Nirankari Mission and steps to defend Sikhism.

The Punjab government, a coalition of the Akali Dal, ostensibly the party of the Sikhs, and the Janata Party, primarily representing the interests of urban Hindus, picked its way through the crisis gingerly but with some skill. When it went out of office nearly two years later, no further killing had occurred in Punjab. At one point, however, after a battle between orthodox Sikhs and members of the Sant Nirankari Mission in Kanpur in Uttar Pradesh in which eleven people were killed, the state government was forced to impose 'a brief spell of censorship' on 'all but one of the twelve Jullundur dailies'.[47]

It is worth emphasising again that roughly three out of five men in Punjab now were able to read, close to a million students were in high schools and more than 100 000 in colleges. The resulting hunger for information and entertainment sent newspaper circulations shooting upwards. But this also meant that more people than ever before were capable of being angered by reports of events many miles away or attacks on their beliefs written by distant strangers weeks or months before.

The newspaper wars of April 1978 had two long-term outcomes. First, both Sikhs and Hindus were embittered. This bitterness was rubbed in deeper because invective that would simply have been whispered (or, at worst, shouted) even fifteen years earlier now was recorded in print, where more Punjabis than ever before were able to read it and agonise over it at their leisure.

Second, the 'challenge of the Sant Nirankari Mission' spurred on a re-examination of Sikh history. Stated so baldly, this may conjure up a picture of grisled villagers sitting in the winter sun avidly reading the Princeton University Press edition of Khushwant Singh's *History of the Sikhs*. The process is less obvious and more subtle than that, yet it goes on – not merely in Punjab and among Sikhs, but throughout India's regions and among scores of 'caste' and religious groups. Essentially, it represents the attempt of increasingly literate societies to explain their relationships to the governments with whom they increasingly have to deal and to the wider world that increasingly affects their lives. The compulsion to record who you are – and who you are not – is irresistible.

HISTORY-MAKING

History-writing – explaining momentous past events, or the evolution of large social groups – can be dangerous. All cultures, whether literate or not, have stories to explain their origins. These may not be written down, and they may not stand up well to the tests of Western-style history-writing as it has developed over the past 200 years. Nevertheless, people know such stories, believe them and hold them dear. Anyone who questions or 'misinterprets' them is likely to provoke angry replies.

The printing press changes story-telling. Throughout the world over the past hundred years or more, peoples ruled by foreign imperial powers first experienced the printing press as an arm of the government. The press issued notices, recorded laws, produced textbooks and spread a version of the past that reflected well on the colonial government. The printed word literally carried the stamp of authority. Almost simultaneously, sections of the subject peoples began to use the press to propagate their own stories. What was History to one side was often myth to the other. Because the printed word lasts, it nips and gnaws at people's souls as no word-of-mouth story can. Moreover, printed matter provokes spoken comment which itself may be published and thereby provoke further comment – and so on. History-writing thus generates history-writing, because one version of events so often clamours for correction or refutation. In the process, conflicts sharpen, ideas spread and identities are defined as never before. We need only consider the concern with which newly-independent governments approach the subject of their own and their people's pasts to sense the explosiveness of printed story-telling.[48]

Let me try to illustrate how these general statements apply to Punjab. As well as the attacks and counter-attacks in 'the vituperative Jullundur vernacular press',[49] the killings of 13 April 1978 produced a host of other publications. One of these, an English pamphlet entitled *The Nirankari Mandal's Challenge to Sikhism*, published by the official *gurdwara* management committee (SGPC), aptly demonstrated how words on paper hardened identities and challenged governments.[50]

The pamphlet attempted to show the Sant Nirankari Mission's responsibility for the 'pre-designed massacre' of 13 April

and to expose the Mandal's 'conspiratorial challenge to ...
Sikhs'. In brief, it claimed that the Mission was perverting
elements of the Sikh religion 'to mislead and beguile' Sikhs,
with the aim of enabling Hinduism 'to absorb Sikhism'.
The pamphlet listed seven areas of blasphemy ranging from
disregard for the long hair and beard to 'relegation of Guru
Granth'. The essence, however, was that Gurbachan Singh,
the head of the Nirankari Mission, had put himself above Guru
Nanak and the Guru Granth Sahib. The Mission retained
the outward form of some Sikh ceremonies, but introduced
elements that were offensive to devout, orthodox Sikhs. At
the time of initiation into the Khalsa, for example, Guru
Gobind Singh laid down that devotees should drink a mixture
of sugar and water stirred with a two-edged sword. The
Nirankari Mission retained the ceremony, but demanded that
its adherents drink 'the water in which the feet of the Nirankari
Head are washed'. The pamphlet hinted that this plot to sap
the essence of the Sikh religion was backed by the Congress
central government.

More important than the pamphlet's charges, however, was
its use of language. The Sikhs were not simply 'a religious
community'; Guru Gobind Singh had transformed them 'into
a nation'. The pamphlet dwelt on Guru Gobind Singh's political
achievement, and the last line affirmed the 'identity of the
Sikhs as a nation'.[51] But if Sikhs were 'a nation', then what
was India? And what was the place of Sikhs in India?

This brings us back to the innovations of the 1970s and
1980s – the spread of schools, increase in literacy and the
growth of the Punjabi and Hindi press. Since Maharaja Ranjit
Singh's time, Sikhs undoubtedly carried 'the idea of Sikh rule
in the Punjab not as a plot but as a romantic yearning'.[52] Now,
however, the idea was acquiring a concrete quality through its
constant discussion in the press and the fact that evidence was
now available – through newspapers, radio and the television,
which Punjabis could also pick up from Pakistan – that such
goals had been attained elsewhere.

By October 1981, Sikh extremists were referring to themselves as 'a PLO-type organisation' and the leading figure,
Jarnail Singh Bhindranwale, was described as 'a religious
fundamentalist in the mould of Iran's Ayatollah Ruhollah
Khomeini'. Later, journalists asserted that 'Bhindranwale owed

his meteoric rise in no small measure to the rise of Khomeini'. The reasoning was that the Ayatollah's triumph in Iran made religious fundamentalism respectable in the eyes of many better-educated Sikhs who would formerly have dismissed Bhindranwale as a bumpkin.[53] News of international events, now accessible to more Punjabis than ever before, began to colour attitudes and mould opinions.

Struggles to define Sikh identity in print began in Punjab in the 1870s when Dayananda Saraswati, the leader of a Hindu sect, the Arya Samaj, published a book with derogatory references to Sikhism. 'Nihangs . . . threatened to assassinate [him].'[54] In 1899, an expensive legal case hinged on the question of whether a deceased Sikh was also a Hindu, at least for purposes of inheritance. The courts ruled that he was and set off a cascade of pamphleteering: *Sikhs Are Hindus*, declared one; *We Are Not Hindus*, a Sikh writer replied. *The Tribune* loftily remarked that 'calling others by names does not make a nation, a people or religion'. As a recent historian notes, 'the printing press which now permanently recorded religious controversies magnified them'.[55]

Governments cannot simply eliminate modern communications, however much they might wish to do so. But they can seek to control them (witness All-India Radio). In Punjab, as elsewhere in India, government sponsorship of history-writing – and contests between politicians for the 'custody' of newly-potent historical symbols – have been a regular aspect of public life, especially during the past twenty years.

The Punjab government celebrated the 300th birthday of Guru Gobind Singh in 1967, the 500th birthday of Guru Nanak in 1969 and thereafter a 'succession of anniversary celebrations'.[56] These were often commemorated by conferences of 'professional historians' and by substantial publications. For example, the 300th anniversary in 1975 of the martyrdom of Guru Tegh Bahadur, the ninth Guru, resulted in a lavish, art-paper edition of his orders or directives to his followers (*Hukumnamas*), produced in Punjabi, Hindi and English.[57]

History, however, is not the property of a single group. There is a contest to appropriate major figures for particular modern causes. The celebrations of the 200th birthday of Maharaja Ranjit Singh in 1979–80 provides a telling example.

In May 1980, a Congress government was elected in Punjab, and its Chief Minister, Darbara Singh, a Sikh Jat, set out to show that the Congress revered Sikh heroes every bit as deeply as did the Akali Dal. Part of the rhetoric of the celebrations involved constant reiteration of the claim that Maharaja Ranjit Singh was 'the founding-father of secularism', because he had used Hindus and Muslims, as well as Sikhs, to run his state. The aim was to build up in the minds of Sikh voters the idea that the Congress, not the Akali Dal, was the rightful heir to the glories of Ranjit Singh's kingdom and the best custodian of Sikh interests.

Some people, however, were sceptical. A Sikh speaking at one celebration, confessed that 'frankly, I find it very hard to accept' the claim that Ranjit Singh had been a founder of 'secularism'. The speaker went on to say that he had recently attended a meeting, which included the Chief Minister and other members of 'the present ruling party'. The speeches about Maharaja Ranjit Singh were so sugary that they suggested 'almost ... that he was a god on earth. This may be all right for the politicians, and for the general public, but I think we [historians] have to give Maharaja Ranjit Singh what is his due, no more and no less'.[58] Politicians, on the other hand, were striving to associate themselves and their causes with the 'general public's' memory of Punjab's greatest heroes.

The SGPC, the *gurdwara* management committee, controlled by opponents of the Congress, followed the same strategy. In 1977 it began publishing colourful, illustrated children's books on Sikh history in Punjabi, Hindi and English. 'I am confident', wrote the president of the SGPC, Gurcharan Singh Tohra, in his preface to a book about the martyrdom of Guru Gobind Singh's two elder sons in 1704, 'that on reading such heart-sending [*sic*] episodes of Sikh history, a real spirit of a just and righteous struggle for justice will be infused in the community.'[59] The first in the series was published in April 1977, immediately after the end of Mrs Gandhi's 'emergency' in which hundreds of members of the Akali Dal, the political party linked to the SGPC, had been imprisoned.[60]

The books had an indirect but discernible link with the economic changes accompanying the 'green revolution'. At an obvious level, more children now had the ability and the leisure to read, and, as Prem Mohindra noted in the *Tribune*, it was important for political groups to 'catch the youth young.'[61] In addition, these children were part of an expanding class of cultivating families, tied to the world of banks, markets and other external influences.

It was significant that the booklets on Sikh history acknowledged the inspiration and 'expert advice' received from the chairman of the Punjab and Sind Bank, the major Sikh-controlled bank. An urbane man, directing a modern institution that dealt daily with thousands of agriculturalists, he felt compelled to interest himself in the propagation of history. Indeed, according to a Sikh historian, his 'effulgent passion to promote the cause of Sikh History and Culture' was remarkable.[62]

In the children's books, no Sikh (in the English versions, at least) ever dies or is killed. Sikhs 'slaughter' their enemies, but they themselves 'attain martyrdom' or 'sacrifice their lives'. Guru Gobind Singh, for example, encourages his followers with remarks like: 'Each drop of blood shed by us will lay firm foundations for our community' or 'When this mortal life reaches its limits, may I die fighting with limitless courage'.[63]

The stories of Gobind Singh's exploits had always been known, but now the dignity and durability of print reinforced them, and coloured illustrations enlivened them. Moreover, the stories now were told, not by family elders who might give each tale their own twists and emphases, but in standardised, semi-official form, suggested by the chairman of a leading bank and introduced by a powerful politician.

This contest to appropriate popular symbols was entwined even with the road-building programme that was so important for promoting the 'green revolution'. An Akali Dal government in 1969 began a 640-kilometre road to join Anandpur Sahib in the north-east of the state, Damdama Sahib in the south-west and eighty-nine places along the way, all of them associated with the exploits of Guru Gobind Singh. The Governor of Punjab later wrote, almost as an afterthought, that the road also served 'the communications requirements of those who live on either side'.[64] The Congress government of Zail Singh, which was in power in April 1973 when the route was completed, exploited it cleverly. The Chief Minister led a three-day procession which involved four army and police bands, 1000 trucks and buses, 5000 cars, a fly-past by three

planes and 'flower-bedecked' buses and trucks bearing the
Guru Granth Sahib and sacred relics of Guru Gobind Singh,
including 'arrows . . . and a dagger'. Faced with the dilemma
of whether to boycott the procession, the Akali Dal eventually
decided to take part. The party president was seated in the bus
carrying the Granth Sahib, and Parkash Singh Badal, the
former Chief Minister, 'made it known that the project was
started during the Akali regime'. Most observers agreed,
however, that the event increased the popularity of the Congress 'even in villages which were Akali strongholds'.[65] The
procession dramatised what was an increasingly regular occur-
rence: the world was coming to rural Punjab.

The use of modern technology to mould old stories to new
purposes – the reshaping of history – goes on throughout India.
It goes on because it appears to work. People everywhere want
to think well of themselves – to believe that their ancestors
were noble and that they themselves command status and
respect. Few politicians would risk the gamble, for example,
of giving 'Maharaja Ranjit Singh what is his due, no more and
no less'. They find it makes more electoral sense 'to say that
he was a god on earth'.[66]

Every region has its own distinctive stories and characteristics. Punjab is unique, for example, because it is the home
of Sikhism and has a particularly violent tradition, the product
of frequent invasion and frontier conflict. These aspects have
blended with the rapid innovations of the past twenty years to
produce a particularly explosive cocktail.

Jarnail Singh Bhindranwale expanded his following by putting his message – including the names of people who, he said,
had betrayed Sikhism – on cassette tapes. When he and his
followers called demonstrations, they made sure of large
attendances by sending auto-rickshaws (three-wheeled, two-
passenger taxis) 'fitted with loudspeakers', into the countryside.
They printed pamphlets and put up posters.[67] When officials
claimed that Bhindranwale's followers were getting training in
modern firearms, he replied that 'the Sikhs had not committed
any sin since arms training was part of the Sikh tradition'.[68] To
young Sikhs, eager to serve their religion, his advice was to
buy a revolver and motorbike.[69] The visions belonged to Guru
Gobind Singh and the eighteenth century; the implements, to
the twentieth.

WEAPONS: 'A COTTAGE INDUSTRY'

Many areas of rural India have never been so heavily armed as they are today. The illegal manufacture of grenades and firearms has in some places 'assumed proportions of a cottage industry'.[70] A single district in western Uttar Pradesh in 1980 was estimated to have more than 22 000 *licensed* guns. The extent of illegal gun-manufacturing can be judged by the fact that a police drive against rural gun factories in UP in June 1980 closed down more than 100, the 'mere tip of [the] iceberg'.[71] One factory, specialising in high-quality ammunition, conducted its business in a busy commercial area of Lucknow, the state capital.[72] In some districts of Bihar, 'the fire power of mafias ... is superior to that of police'.[73] Bandits (called dacoits) plague large areas of rural north India, often working in collaboration with landowners and local politicians, who value their help at election time. In a district of Bihar, 'possessing illegal arms and maintaining a private army consisting of at least five persons is considered a mark of social status'.[74] People who rhapsodise about non-violence and the peaceful essence of Hinduism misread the realities of the Indian countryside.

In addition to cottage-industry manufacturers, there is another way of acquiring arms: on the black market. Such weapons may have been smuggled into India across the borders with either Pakistan or the north-eastern neighbours, or they may simply have 'leaked' from the paramilitary police forces, or (less likely) from the army itself. Armed police have increased greatly in the past twenty years. Their training and discipline are much more lax than that of the army, and there appears to be a regular weapons trade involving elements of the armed police and civilian buyers.[75]

The problem has an international dimension which again emphasises the revolution in communications. There are more arms in the world today than at any time in history. One international arms salesman, as Anthony Sampson discovered in 1977, was 'still making profits out of the residue of the Second World War'. Moreover, the proliferation of long-range aircraft means that arms bought, for example, in Manchester, with money from Libya, can reappear within days in the Philippines.[76] In the Punjab, wars in 1965 and 1971 left guns behind in the countryside, and the porous border with Pakistan makes smuggling a common occupation. Today, firearms are more readily available, from more diverse sources, than ever before.

In Punjab, in the past, 'the cultivator followed the plough with a sword in his hand'. Now, in some districts, Joyce Pettigrew writes, 'a farmer drives his tractor with a rifle slung across his shoulder or a revolver beside him, and rarely leaves home without a weapon of defence in his possession'.[77] The home of Parkash Singh Badal, twice Chief Minister of Akali Dal-led governments, is located in one such area, and in the 1980 assembly elections, he and his opponents had 'the backing of numerous armed groups'.[78] The police estimated that there were 500 000 legal and illegal arms in Punjab.[79] The favoured weapon is no longer a good revolver or an army .303 but a sten-gun.

Murders and vendettas have been part of Punjab life for a very long time, as we shall see in Chapter 6. But by the 1980s something had changed: the pace had quickened. Compare the murders, sixteen years apart, of two prominent men.

On 6 February 1965, Partap Singh Kairon, Chief Minister of Punjab from 1956 until eight months earlier, was shot dead on the Grand Trunk Road about twenty miles north of New Delhi. His three companions were also murdered. The motive appears to have been a personal feud. Their car was 'attacked by four armed men . . . at a spot where it was travelling at slow speed because of road repairs'.[80] The assailants were on foot; Kairon's car had to be made to slow down; the killers escaped on foot across the fields.

Contrast this with the murder of the 82-year-old Hindu newspaper proprietor, Lala Jagat Narain, on 9 September 1981. Narain, a long-time Congress politician and once an ally of Kairon, had been especially derogatory towards Sikh political demands in his Jullundur-based newspapers. Returning to Jullundur from Patiala, his car was fired on and pursued by three Sikhs riding a motor cycle. Though the car driver tried to escape, the motor-cyclists bore down on the car and killed Jagat Narain with sten-gun bursts from close range.[81]

On 22 September a similar technique was used in the market area in Jullundur in retaliation for the arrest of Jarnail Singh Bhindranwale in connection with Jagat Narain's murder. Supporters of Bhindranwale sped through the market on a motor cycle, spraying the market with sten-gun fire, killing four people and wounding eleven. The government's response was not to announce a crash programme for motorising the police, but rather to proclaim a dusk-to-dawn ban on male pillion passengers on motor cycles.[82]

INNOVATIONS AND VALUES

Punjab has long been a violent place, but in the past fifteen years or so, the accelerated movement of ideas, people and objects has begun to change the way in which violence is directed. 'More' ultimately becomes 'different'. Let me first attempt to explain the basis of this violence, then to account for the changes, the effects of which we shall see in Chapters 6 and 7.

First, Punjab is a frontier area, over which there have been constant battles. Indian and Pakistani tanks in 1971 battled on the same ground across which Alexander the Great's troops marched more than 2000 years ago. People have long carried arms, seen them used and themselves known how to use them.

Second, Punjab is still largely a peasant society and most peasant societies, I suspect, are violent. People who live close to nature must kill animals and pests to survive. Because their sole resource is often the land and what it produces, they cannot afford to be cheated of their share of a crop or their corner of a field. They have a life-or-death interest which may lead them to take a spade to a thief or a traducer, an impertinent inferior or a cruel master.

Third, society in Punjab is based on links of dependence which tie most people to a patron and may thus involve them in the patron's struggles and the patron in theirs. These concrete ties intertwine with the code of honour of the fiercely egalitarian Sikh Jats. It is not that all Sikh Jats *are* equal; rather, that they believe they ought to be. *Robber Noblemen*, Pettigrew calls her book about them. Offence is quickly taken; scores must be settled. Turning the other cheek is not part of the code, which, Pettigrew writes, demands 'murder in revenge for murder'.[83] In many parts of the countryside, 'scores are settled on the spot without reference to the arm of the law and without fear of consequences'.[84] These characteristics bear similarities to those of feudal Europe, where dependents, wrote the great French historian Marc Bloch, saw 'precious advantages' in 'the patronage of a powerful man in a highly anarchic society', and where 'the primary duty of the kinsman was vengeance'.[85] In Punjab, too, the connections between men, and the values they hold to be important, enjoin violence.

In the past, two other things kept violence in Punjab within bounds. One was technical, the other (I believe) ideological. First, people's movements were limited and their arms were basic. An American scholar, for example, pointed out that Punjab's murder rate was higher than that of the USA, although in Punjab 'there is less access to efficient weaponry with which multiple murders might be committed'.[86] Second, most people were tied to their villages and immediate neighbourhood. If one killed, the possibility of flight was less thinkable and feasible than in more mobile societies. Similarly, one's victims were likely to be one's neighbours, not unknown people in a distant place.

This leads to the second point. Joyce Pettigrew contended that face-to-face rural life meant that 'a man was never so detached from others that either his concern about them or his hatred for them became an abstraction, i.e., a product of his ideas and values rather than of his interactions'.[87] On the other hand, she suggested, industrialised, bureaucratised societies (mass societies) had become so specialised – people so identified with their formal 'jobs' – that they were capable of immense crimes. The death camps of Nazi Germany were perpetrated by 'ordinary' people whose excuse was 'that they only obeyed orders and did their duty because they couldn't devolve their *bureaucratic* responsibility further and thus were coerced by their system into cruelty'.[88] Implicitly, Pettigrew argued that at least the man who killed a personal enemy knew the value of an individual life, because in taking life, he knew he was risking his own (as the Nazi bureaucrat never could). The murderer in Punjab also had a direct, self-interested reason for killing his victim, and this limited the extent of killing. Individual hatred is at least confined to individuals; mass hatred is almost limitless.

The innovations that have spread so widely through Punjab since the mid-1960s, however, have begun to corrode the old wire fence that kept violence within bounds. The sten-gun and motor cycle, used for the indiscriminate killing in the Jullundur market on 22 September 1981, symbolise the change. Expanded communications networks now bombard Punjabis with information that enables them to treat other people as abstractions and, in the worst event, to hate (and kill) whole groups whose members, as individuals, are unknown. This new potential, characteristic of mass societies, meets and mixes with Punjab's violent traditions and the powerful Sikh heritage of resistance to would-be rulers. The personalised, face-to-face qualities that previously kept violence within manageable bounds are gradually being stripped away.

5 Politics, 1947–77

The two men brought together for a reconciliation in 1956 seemed to have only two things in common: they were both Sikhs and they were both short. For a Jat, Partap Singh Kairon was remarkably small, but his size did not prevent him from reminding listeners that he was the first Sikh Jat to wield power in Punjab since Maharaja Ranjit Singh. Nor did he discourage comparisons between the Maharaja and himself.[1] Kairon, however, was the Congress Chief Minister of Punjab, allied with Jawaharlal Nehru in New Delhi and dedicated to the integrity of the Indian state. If anyone was a 'nationalist', then Kairon appeared to be.

Master Tara Singh, on the other hand, seemed the embodiment of the 'separatist tendencies' seen by both foreign scholars and national leaders as a threat to the unity of independent India.[2] Since 1948 he had been a bitter critic of India's national government, which, he said, was scheming to enforce the will of the Hindu majority and absorb Sikhs into Hinduism. In February 1949, he became the first high-ranking non-Communist politician to be arrested by the government of independent India (to prevent him from taking part in protests against the alleged denigration of Sikhs and the Punjabi language). By 1952, he had made a speech that 'virtually called for the assassination of Nehru' and was demanding a 'Punjabi Suba', a new state in which the interests of the Punjabi language and of Sikhs would be properly safeguarded.[3] His statements were ambiguous – or simply vague? – about whether such a state was intended to have a Sikh majority or whether its main consideration was Punjabi, a language spoken by virtually everyone who lived in the Punjab regardless of religion.

In contrast to Kairon, Tara Singh was a Khatri, not a Jat. He had been born in the frontier district of Rawalpindi, now part of Pakistan, into a Khatri tradition which accepted that members of the same family could adopt either the Hindu or

Sikh identity. He himself did not assume the latter until he was a high school pupil aged about 15. Too small, as he later claimed, to be admitted into medical college, he studied for an Arts degree and became a schoolteacher about 1908 – hence the title 'Master' which he carried for the rest of his life.[4] He demonstrated the zeal of a convert. From the 1920s, he was one of the most fiery advocates of what he saw as Sikh interests, a leading figure of the Akali Dal and often president of the SGPC.

At the time of their meeting in 1956, Tara Singh and Kairon had been 'antagonistic for the last 16 years', yet in the 1930s they had fought the British together as colleagues. Both were imprisoned for their parts in M. K. Gandhi's civil disobedience movement of 1930–4, and in the mid-1930s Kairon was an official of the Akali Dal under Tara Singh.[5] The Akalis and the Congress co-operated to contest elections in 1937, and Kairon remained with the Congress even after Tara Singh and others broke with it in 1940. While Tara Singh gave qualified support to the British war effort, Kairon opposed it and went back to prison for supporting the 'Quit India' movement in 1942. The years of nationalist challenge to the British helped to mould both men.[6]

Their meeting in 1956 was occasioned by the approach of the 1957 general elections and the Akali Dal's decision to merge for a second time – it had done so from 1948–50 – with the Congress. Congress leaders in return promised a new deal in Punjab – a 'regional formula' that would guarantee Punjabi rights and establish committees of the assembly to oversee legislation relating to the Punjab-majority and Hindi-majority areas of the state. But Master Tara Singh was sceptical – about the agreement and about Kairon whom he regarded as 'a great opportunist' and 'most unscrupulous'.[7] Kairon, who had a degree in political science from the University of Michigan and had lived for nine years in the USA in the 1920s, might have been slightly flattered. He was once quoted as saying: 'I've not only read Machiavelli, I've mastered him'. One suspects, however, that he found Tara Singh infuriating, for even the Master's admirers have conceded that he could be 'indecisive' and 'very confused'.[8]

Their meeting, intended to iron out their differences and enable the new union of Akalis with the Congress to work smoothly, lasted two hours. At the end, both admitted it had been 'a failure', and they 'parted greater enemies' than before.[9] By 1960, Master Tara Singh had succeeded in dragging most Akali sympathisers out of the Congress Party and had begun a campaign of civil disobedience for the creation of a Punjabi Suba, a state in which the Punjabi language (and Sikhs) would be supreme.

Kairon and Master Tara Singh are splendid, flamboyant characters; tales about them abound. For our purposes, moreover, they dramatise three aspects of Punjab's politics which are vital for an understanding of what happened in the 1980s – indeed, of what's happening to India.

First, the two men were inescapably involved with India's national government and the rules it laid down. Kairon chose to proclaim his loyalty. Tara Singh, on the other hand, railed against the national government as the would-be destroyer of the Sikhs. Yet neither man could ignore the national rules; each had to tailor his aims to take them into account.

Second, Kairon and Tara Singh were both products of the Gandhian nationalist movement. Tara Singh by the 1950s attacked the Indian state, but he could not deny his own readiness to heed Gandhi's call in 1930. But there was something more subtle and pervasive than that, something which was common to all of India, not just Punjab. This was the Gandhian model of protest, which emphasised non-violence, civil disobedience, boycott and fasting. The power of this nationalist model, consecrated by thirty years of struggle against the British, was too great for most movements to reject in the years immediately after independence. Tara Singh used all the techniques. Yet the attraction of this Gandhian model, too, had eroded, like the federalism of the constitution, by the 1970s.

Third, the story of Kairon and Master Tara Singh has a twist to it, revealed later in this chapter, which illustrates an essential element of Punjab (and Indian) politics – the importance of faction.

By the early 1970s, national rules and veneration of nationalist models were both fast dissolving. In Punjab, because of the effects of the 'green revolution' and the fact that the ideas of M. K. Gandhi had never exercised much sway over Punjabi peasants, the process was faster than elsewhere. Untrammelled factionalism, now exploiting external ingredients unknown previously, led to the explosions of the 1980s.

NATIONAL RULES: RELIGION AND LANGUAGE

For men like Jawaharlal Nehru, India in 1948 was passing through a nightmare. The partition of 1947 destroyed the possibility of a united secular state whose goal would be economic well-being. The partition also brought the deaths of hundreds of thousands and created more than 12 million refugees. The partition, too, was responsible for the murder of M. K. Gandhi by a Brahmin assassin in 1948. The assassin fervently believed that Gandhi had betrayed Hindu India by giving in to Muslim demands. Religious antagonism, which Gandhi desperately tried to overcome and which Nehru angrily deplored, raged in the first months of independence. Thereafter, the India state under Nehru's direction used its propaganda organs (All-India Radio and the education system, for example) to propagate ideas of 'secularism' and to deprecate 'communalism' – popularly, the mixing of religion and politics. The state had been torn apart once by the 'monster of communalism', advocates of this argument would say; Pakistan must not be repeated. The Indian state would tolerate no overt connections between religion and politics.

These rules of the national game were particularly chafing for Sikhs, who in prayer each day repeated the words '*raj karega Khalsa*' – 'the Khalsa shall rule' – and nurtured the stories of Guru Gobind Singh's exploits and Maharaja Ranjit Singh's empire. Moreover, in 1948 close to half of all Sikhs were refugees, who had just seen a religiously-based state – Pakistan – take shape before their eyes and then drive them from their homes. Now they were being told that religion and politics were an illegitimate mixture.

They had further reasons for dismay. It soon seemed to some of them that the national propaganda about even-handed treatment for all religions was hypocritical eyewash. Hindus, who were more than 60 per cent of the new Punjab, quickly set off a 'wave of communalism' against Sikhs 'in official and public life'.[10] Militant Hindu groups, confident of their own numerical edge in the new Punjab, referred to the Sikh religion as an offshoot of Hinduism and declared that 'the Sikhs should come back to the Hindu society and be absorbed by it'.[11] The national sermonising about keeping religion out of politics did not seem to apply to Punjabi Hindus.

The basis of the problem lay in the close connection between language and religion. People may speak one language in their daily affairs, use another for writing and official purposes and have their religious scriptures in a third. Modern English speakers find it difficult to comprehend the linguistic complexities which many Indian children take for granted. 'By the age of ten', wrote Prakash Tandon, who was born in 1911, 'I was learning English and Persian, my curriculum was in Urdu and I spoke Punjabi at home and outside.'[12]

Before the nineteenth century, Muslims, Hindus and Sikhs all spoke Punjabi in daily life, but only Sikhs wrote it. Persian, in the Arabic script, was the language of official business and most written communication. Sikhs, however, wrote in Punjabi, using the Gurmukhi script of their sacred book, the Granth Sahib.

When the British arrived in the Punjab, they introduced English and Urdu, the basic language of the Gangetic Plain, which was written in the Arabic script. From the late nineteenth century, people of various religions began to write Punjabi in this Arabic script which had become familiar through schools and offices.

Until 1947, Urdu was the language learned by most people who went to school in Punjab. At the same time, Punjabi Brahmins knew Sanskrit, the language of the Hindu sacred texts; they and revivalist Hindus began to promote the modern north Indian language, Hindi, written in the Devanagari script of Sanskrit. Literate Hindu women in Punjab in the twentieth century often learned Hindi in order to read religious books. 'In my mother's generation', Tandon recalled, 'there were many women who could not communicate with their husbands when they were away from each other, as they could only write in Hindi and their husbands only in Urdu or English.'[13]

Through all this, devout Sikhs read the Guru Granth Sahib, recorded entirely in the Gurmukhi script and identified in the popular understanding with the Punjabi language. In this sense, Sikhs were the only people with an emotional attachment to the written Punjabi language. Indeed, Punjabi was often dismissed as some sort of semi-barbaric dialect – 'nothing but rustic Hindi, only crude, a little unpolished and rustic in its character'.[14] Just the sort of language, cultivated Hindus seemed to imply, that you would expect to be spoken by rough (Sikh?) peasants. Yet a British linguist had made the practical judgement in the 1880s, that the Gurmukhi script and the Punjabi language were no more '"barbarous" [than English] . . . when it superseded Latin and French'.[15]

Though virtually everyone in Punjab in 1947 *spoke* Punjabi, few non-Sikhs chose to write it, and if they did so, they used the Arabic script, made familiar by having learned Urdu at school. Only Sikhs wrote Punjabi in the Gurmukhi script. Thus to disparage and devalue Punjabi was to ridicule Sikhs and undermine their religion. Examples of such denigration were easy to find. The Punjab University senate in June 1949, for example, rejected a proposal to introduce Punjabi as a language of instruction.[16] The Constituent Assembly, which was drafting India's new constitution in 1948 and 1949, produced passionate speeches advocating Hindi as the national language but tending to dismiss other languages. Hindi in the Devanagari script was eventually adopted, though with the provision that English would continue for fifteen years.

The national rules – one of which was that 'thou shalt not mix religion and politics' – and the complexity of Punjab's languages forced Sikhs to identify more and more closely with the Punjabi language in the 1940s and 1950s. By October 1949, Master Tara Singh was claiming the 'right of self-determination' for Sikhs, who had 'a culture different from the Hindus' – 'Gurmukhi culture'. Moreover, he went on, 'the language of the Sikhs was different'.[17]

Militant Hindu organisations responded to such demands by organising a campaign to induce all Hindus in Punjab to record Hindi, not Punjabi, as their mother-tongue in the census of 1951. They reasoned that if Hindi were shown to be the language of the majority in most of Punjab, no attempt to alter the borders and create a Punjabi-language state could succeed. They feared such a state because it threatened to increase the importance of Sikhs – even though Sikhs would have been a minority in a state constituted on a genuine Punjabi-language basis. Throughout the 1950s, however, Punjabi Hindus increasingly educated their children in Hindi and affirmed that Hindi was their mother-tongue. Thus the demand for a Punjabi Suba – a Punjabi-language state – came to be the demand for a Sikh-majority state. 'The shift of Punjabi-speaking Hindus', Paul Brass writes, was 'more dramatic' than any linguistic choice previously made in Punjab 'because it was an overt and deliberate political act.'[18]

The national ethos after partition, and the 1950 constitution which declared India a secular state, made religion an illegitimate basis for political demands. Even Master Tara Singh felt the need to acknowledge this, and though he sometimes spoke of a Sikh state and lingered on the glorious right of the Khalsa to rule, he more often spoke ambiguously about a state in which Punjabi would be able to develop and flower.

As early as 1920 Gandhi himself had been responsible for reorganising the Congress into provinces based on language, and in theory the party was committed to language-based states. How else were ordinary people to be able to deal with their government except in their mother tongue? Multi-language states would only encourage the retention of English. Yet in 1947, in the aftermath of the partition, Nehru was reluctant to engage in more boundary-drawing exercises, and the Constituent Assembly agreed to delay the consideration of language-based states until some unspecified future time.[19] The demands, however, were irresistible, and a reorganisation on the basis of language began with the creation of Andhra Pradesh (a Telugu area) in south India in 1953. Wide-reaching changes, particularly in south India, followed in 1956, the result of the report of the States Reorganisation Commission which had held hearings, and generated excitement, throughout the country in the previous two years. But, though the commission's conclusions resulted in new states based on the Malayalam (Kerala), Kannada (an enlarged Mysore), Telugu (an enlarged Andhra) and Tamil (Madras) languages, it did not recommend the creation of a Punjabi-language state. For many Sikhs, the conclusion seemed obvious: 'No status is given to the Punjabi language, because Sikhs speak it. If non-Sikhs had owned Punjabi as mother-tongue then the rulers of India would have seen no objection in establishing a Punjabi state'.[20]

Linguistic states, sanctified by the Congress from 1920, were a legitimate demand. Religious-based states and calls for secession were not. These were the rules that Nehru's national government laid down, and it showed by its actions that it would tolerate no defiance. When Sheikh Mohammad Abdullah (1905–82), the Prime Minister of Kashmir, began angling for greater autonomy in 1953, he was arrested, detained until 1964, and permitted to re-enter the state's politics only in 1975.[21] No wonder that Master Tara Singh couched his demands in terms of the Punjabi language and permitted himself only occasional ambiguities about Sikh rule.

The Punjabi-language state was finally achieved in 1966 only after the death of Nehru, the fall from power of Master Tara Singh, and a war with Pakistan, fought on the Punjab border, in which Sikh soldiers were among the outstanding heroes. It was only achieved, too, after Tara Singh's successor – in contrast to the Master – 'adopted a consistent position' that it was 'a language demand'. Under the national rules (perhaps bent a little by circumstances like Nehru's death and war with Pakistan), such a demand was legitimate.[22]

NATIONALIST SPIRIT: THE DECLINE OF THE FAST

As well as the national rules, underwritten by force and the threat of punishment, a certain nationalist spirit pervaded India in the years after 1947. When Gandhi was assassinated in January 1948, he left a style of political protest that emphasised non-violence, boycott, fasting, civil disobedience and jail-going, all justified by referring to one's readiness to suffer for a righteous cause. (A political scientist has referred to this as the 'saintly idiom' in Indian politics.)[23] Indeed, there was a widespread sense that the techniques and slogans imparted righteousness to any cause that used them.

Throughout independent India, these methods glowed with sanctity. Whether the demand was for better food in a college hostel or new state boundaries that might affect millions of people, the protesters used the techniques of fasting, boycott, disruption and 'courting arrest' and constantly emphasised their dedication to 'non-violence'. The nationalist movement had left a recipe which virtually every group cooking up a protest in the years after 1947 found expedient to adopt.

So powerful an influence did this 'saintly idiom', or nationalist model, exert that even in Punjab Master Tara Singh and his followers often felt compelled to adopt it. In the 1960s, they ranked among India's most frequent fasters.

Yet the emphasis on non-violence, which was the essence of Gandhi's programme, does not accord well with the picture of Punjab as a turbulent frontier region. To be sure, urban Punjabi Hindus recognised aspects of Gandhian non-violence and admired the fame and respectability it had won. But non-violence had little relevance for the majority of rural Punjabis, particularly Sikh Jats, for whom 'killing and violence were facts of existence'. Indeed, as a Sikh historian wrote, 'immolation by fasting was a novelty in Sikh tradition'.[24] But for more than twenty years of independence, Gandhian language and techniques influenced the way in which even the Akali Dal conducted its activities. Only in the 1970s was the nationalist ethos so eroded – the Gandhian recipe so discredited by adulterated ingredients – that groups with grievances increasingly abandoned it.

Consider the example of Master Tara Singh and the demand for Punjabi Suba – a Punjabi-language state. As the States Reorganisation Commission completed its report in 1955, the Akali Dal pressed its demand for such a state in the time-honoured Gandhian way – by slogan-shouting and noisy protest meetings. In April 1955, the Congress government of Punjab unwisely chose to ban the shouting of slogans advocating the Punjabi state. The Akali Dal responded gratefully: Master Tara Singh was the first to break the law and be arrested on 10 May, and by July thousands of protesters, using the Golden Temple as their headquarters, had followed him to jail. On 4 July the police entered the Golden Temple itself to make arrests, and the resulting furore led eventually to the withdrawal of the ban on Punjabi Suba slogans, an apology by the Hindu chief minister and his eventual fall from office. His successor was Partap Singh Kairon, who, some hinted, had manoeuvred his Hindu chief into the blunder of sending police into the Golden Temple.[25]

The Akali Dal felt it necessary to adopt the Gandhian methods because those methods still exercised a certain mystique throughout India. Yet the 'fit' with Jat Sikh custom was sometimes uncomfortable. When the Akalis organised a huge demonstration in support of the Punjabi state in Amritsar in February 1956, the procession attracted cultivators from miles around, stretched for 5 kilometres and took five hours to pass. Estimates put the number of marchers at between 100 000 and 200 000.[26] Such processions were a standard technique of Gandhian protest. But the Amritsar march added an un-Gandhian feature: the marchers came 'armed with shining swords and axes'.[27] Guru Gobind Singh was unlikely ever to give way to Gandhi.

The example of fasting illustrates even more vividly both the magnetism of the Gandhian example and its decline. Fasts and the threat of fasts dominated Sikh agitational techniques in the 1960s. The 'fast-unto-death' became overworked and discredited, part of the withering throughout India of the flowers of Gandhian idealism.

Fasting, indeed, proved the undoing of Master Tara Singh. In 1956, the Akali Dal accepted the 'regional formula' proposals and merged with the Congress to fight the general elections in 1957.[28] This had occasioned the 'reconciliation' between Kairon and Master Tara Singh. Some Akalis soon claimed, however, that the 'regional formula' was not genuinely implemented and was in fact all part of the plot to absorb Sikhs into Hinduism. In March 1960, Tara Singh called on those Akalis elected to the legislature as Congress candidates to resign. Only five out of twenty-four did so, thus underlining his contention that in a Hindu-dominated state, Sikhs would be lulled into betrayal of their faith. In April, he launched the Akalis on a civil-disobedience campaign for a Punjabi Suba, again stressing the linguistic nature of the demand, yet at the same time leaving little doubt that such a state would have a Sikh majority. 'We shall either win or die', he declared. 'We shall not be defeated.'[29] He was soon arrested, but throughout the remainder of the summer and the monsoon season – when cultivators have more time available – thousands of Sikh demonstrators were arrested and jailed for their ritual law-breaking.[30] The model of behaviour for both the police and demonstrators had changed little since Gandhi's non-co-operation movement of 1920–2.

By November 1960, the protest seemed to be petering out as peasants returned to their land to plant next season's crop. Master Tara Singh was still in prison. At this point, his recently recruited lieutenant, Sant Fateh Singh (1911–72), wrote to Nehru – as Gandhi had written to British Viceroys in the past – to announce that he would go on a 'fast-unto-death' from

18 December unless Punjabi Suba were granted. The central government made no promises, but it released Master Tara Singh who claimed he had won concessions and advised his follower to give up his fast in January 1961.[31] The agitation, however, had shown few results, and the third general elections were only a year away.

In August 1961, Master Tara Singh himself went on a 'fast-unto-death' which failed. Neither extracting concessions from the central government, nor dying, he 'was persuaded to end his fast' on 1 October.[32] His admirers later claimed that he broke the fast only after having received 'certain assurances' from the central government and the promise of an inquiry into Akali demands. His detractors, however, ridiculed him for having pulled out of the fast to save his life, and the custodians of the Golden Temple, to whom his case was referred, instructed him to clean cooking utensils as penance for having broken his vow.[33] Although he was re-elected president of the SGPC, more than half the delegates boycotted the elections. The decline of his authority – and that of urban, non-Jat Sikhs – in Akali politics had begun.

At this point, we need to follow two threads: the erosion of respect for the techniques and symbols of the nationalist movement (the story of fasting is an excellent example); and the decline of non-Jat influence within the Akali Dal. The latter coincided with the eventual attainment of the Punjabi Suba in 1966. The two stories are closely linked, because the hefty body of Sant Fateh Singh strides through both.

SANT FATEH SINGH AND THE RISE OF THE JATS

The Sant and the Master were about as different as two Sikhs could be. As an urban, non-Jat Sikh, Master Tara Singh had always required a lieutenant who could appeal to Jats. It was for this role in about 1959 that he 'dragged into Sikh politics' Sant Fateh Singh who was to become his nemesis.[34] Although the Sant's clientele were Sikh Jat peasants, his own caste is uncertain. Sometimes it is said he was a Gujjar (a lower caste), not a Jat. At about the age of 10, he was sent off for religious training with a sant. They established themselves among Sikhs in Rajasthan, and Fateh Singh acquired popularity by his ability to sing hymns and play the harmonium. Eventually, he too earned the title of 'sant', but he had no 'normal schooling'.

Unlike Master Tara Singh – and confirming many of the stereotypes about the differences between 'strong' rural Sikhs and 'effete' urban ones – the Sant was physically powerful, able in his youth to lift a 100kg weight with ease, 'crush a brick with his fist' and 'walk 30 miles at a stretch to attend religious gatherings'. Like all good Punjabis, he kept up his strength by drinking milk – 'daily ten kilos'. If that were true, it was twenty times even today's Punjab average and forty times more than was good for him. His death in 1972 resulted from a series of heart attacks. Had early excesses with the milk pail built up a disastrous cholesterol level?

Sant Fateh Singh turned fasting into farce. Yet the fact that he used the ploy at all indicated the hold that nationalist models of behaviour still exercised in the 1960s. In August 1965, he announced a death fast for Punjabi Suba, but called it off when war with Pakistan began in September. In December 1966, after the concession of the new Punjabi-language state, he fasted to demand that the city of Chandigarh be awarded to Punjab. He added a new technique, apparently in imitation of Buddhist monks in Vietnam (and already used by Tamil protesters in south India): at the end of a set period, he said he would burn himself to death. Again, he withdrew the fast after the carefully timed eleventh-hour arrival in Amritsar of the speaker of the Lok Sabha (a Sikh) with Mrs Gandhi's offer to arbitrate. His final fasting threat in January 1970, again over the ownership of Chandigarh, also ended with promises of arbitration by the Prime Minister.[35]

Only one 'fast-unto-death' in Punjab actually ended in death: that of Darshan Singh Pheruman (1884–1969) who died on 27 October 1969 after a fast of seventy-four days aimed to force the central government to award the city of Chandigarh to Punjab.[36] His fast was not simply the sublime gesture of a stubborn old man. Rather, it was closely connected to the factional manoeuvring of Punjab politics and with efforts to embarrass Sant Fateh Singh. By January 1970, after all, the Sant had been ready four times in the previous ten years to 'fast-unto-death', but he was still vigorously alive. Rivals could – and did – cast doubts on his courage.

Fasting has not figured prominently in Punjab politics since

Sant Fateh Singh's last attempt in January 1970. The abandonment of the technique was evidence of a widespread disillusionment (not just in Punjab, but throughout India) with the national model. There had been both an erosion of respect and an immense increase in outside influences. For example, the addition of burning to the fast-unto-death ritual indicated the way in which an increasingly literate and newspaper-reading population was imbibing ideas from throughout the world. With the nationalist ideals and techniques so discredited, many people were ready to adopt methods suggested by international events.

Sant Fateh Singh also represents the rise of Jat Sikhs within the Akali Dal, and this too is similar to processes going on elsewhere in India. Landowning peasant castes, often in the past regarded as fairly low in status, have been translating their numbers and growing wealth into political power over the past thirty years. In doing so, they have been elbowing aside 'higher' urban, commercial and clerical castes who in 1947 were more important politically than they are today.

In the 1950s, the Akali Dal relied heavily on urban, refugee, non-Jat Sikhs like Master Tara Singh, and it was such people, not Jats, who persistently raised the cry of 'Punjabi Suba' and talked of an independent Sikh state. In having lost their shops and businesses in west Punjab in 1947, urban refugees were at a greater disadvantage than peasant refugees. The latter (mostly Jat Sikhs) were allotted land and started again. Agriculture demanded land, labour, and skill; they had all three. Commerce, however, needed capital, and urban Sikh refugees had to compete with Hindu commercial people already living in east Punjab. It is not surprising, therefore, that urban Sikhs dreamed of a state in which they would be able to offer themselves some of the advantages that Punjabi Hindus seemed to have. The campaign for a Punjabi state, argues Joyce Pettigrew, was characterised by 'Jat apathy and urbanite commitment'.[37]

Urban Sikhs, however, were fostering a process that led to the diminution of their influence. In the past, the links between urban Sikhs and Jat Sikhs in the countryside had never been close. Indeed, Jat Sikhs sometimes referred to their urban co-religionists as 'Bhapa' Sikhs, a term carrying 'a perceptible degree of opprobrium'.[38] Similarly, the other two major social categories of Sikhs – artisan castes and ex-Untouchables (Mazhbis) – were generally treated as inferiors both by Jat Sikhs and urbanites. However, the Punjabi Suba agitations of the 1950s and 1960s began to build 'a sense of identity'[39] through the greater Sikh community. Though the ideas, grievances and leaders may at first have come from urbanites, they eventually spread to others. Any agitation involving Sikhs touched the pride of rural Jats, and, as one told Joyce Pettigew, 'the spark is ignited to that deep faith'.[40] By drawing Jats into the political process of independent India, the campaigns of the 1950s and 1960s readied them to take over a role befitting their numbers and wealth. Jat models of conduct have become increasingly potent and pervasive. 'The *Jats* will not even touch you (the Hindu)', an urban Sikh remarked to a Punjabi Hindu in the 1950s about the future in a reorganised, Punjabi-speaking state, 'but they will certainly *Jaatise* [*sic*] us (the urban Sikhs)!'[41]

In 1957, a survey estimated that nearly half of the Akalis elected as Members of the Legislative Assembly (MLAs) (recall that they had merged with the Congress for the elections) were non-Jats. In 1962, however, after Master Tara Singh's embarrassing withdrawal from his 'fast-unto-death', Sant Fateh Singh's followers ousted the Master from both the Akali Dal and the SGPC. After the elections of 1967, the large majority of the twenty-four Akali MLAs were Jats.[42] The fall of Partap Singh Kairon in 1964 also encouraged the movement of Jat Sikhs from Congress towards the Akali Dal. Kairon was ostentatiously a Jat, and 70 per cent of Sikhs elected as Congressmen in Punjab in 1957 were Jats. But by the mid-1960s, it was increasingly clear that 'the main base of Akali support . . . is among the Jat Sikh peasantry'.[43]

The Jat Sikh peasantry was becoming more and more likely to send its children to schools, read newspapers, travel overseas and watch television. The message of endangered Sikh interests, which urban non-Jat Sikhs shouted with such vigour in the 1950s, found ears that were increasingly inclined to hear. For their part, Sikh Jats brought to the new style of politics their own traditions of faction, violence and readiness for sacrifice.

112

TABLE 5.1 *Punjab election results, 1952–80*

| | Seats won | | | | | | | |
	1952	1957	1962	1967	1969	1972	1977	1980
Congress	60	71	49	48	38	66	17	63
Akali Dal	31	–	19	24	43	24	58	37
AD (Master)				2				
Jana Sangh	0	5	4	9	8	0		
BJP								1
Janata	–	–	–	–	–	–	25	0
CPI	6	3	9	5	4	10	7	9
CPI (M)	–	–	–	3	2	1	8	5
Others	13	7	5	13	9	3	2	2
TOTAL	110	86	86	104	104	104	117	117

SOURCES P. R. Brass, 'Ethnic Cleavages in the Punjab Party System, 1952–72' in M. Weiner and J. O. Field (ed) *Electoral Politics in the Indian States. Party Systems and Cleavages* (New Delhi: Manohar, 1975) pp. 13–15; Dalip Singh, *Dynamics*, pp. 248–51.

TABLE 5.2 *Punjab elections, 1952–80: percentage of valid votes*

	1952	1957	1962	1967	1969	1972	1977	1980
Congress	35	48	44	37	39	43	34	45
Akali Dal	15	–	12	21	30	28	31	27
AD (Master)				5				
Jana Sangh	5	9	10	9	9	5		
BJP							–	6
Janata							15	3*
CPI	5	14	7	5	5	7	7	7
CPI(M)	–	–	–	3	3	3	4	4
Other parties	15	5	10	4	5	1	–	1
Independents	25	24	17	16	9	13	9	7
TOTAL	100	100	100	100	100	100	100	100

* Combined vote for three groups.

SOURCES Dalip Singh, *Dynamics*, pp. 240, 242–3, 246, 248, 251.

PARTY AND FACTION

At the beginning of this chapter, I wrote that the relationship between Kairon and Master Tara Singh illustrated the way in which faction pervaded Punjab's politics. Factions, indeed, form a major theme of the next chapter, in which I try to explore them in more detail. Here, however, it is possible to set the stage by unfolding the surprising last act in the story of Kairon and Tara Singh. Until this point, they will have appeared as inveterate foes, deeply divided on firm ideological grounds. Did not Kairon, in defence of the Indian state, crush Tara Singh's Punjabi Suba agitation of 1960?

In 1965, however, the fortunes of both were waning. Sant Fateh Singh had driven the Master from the Akali Dal. Kairon had lost the chief ministership. Elections to the SGPC were held in January 1965, and Tara Singh and his followers contested them in a desperate bid to regain lost power. Their 'strongly communal policy' emphasised the need for a Sikh state. But whose support did they have in their campaign? They had, in fact, 'the backing of . . . Mr Kairon and certain other Congress leaders'.[44] The old enemies, groping in the political wilderness, had fallen briefly into each other's arms. It did no good, however. Master Tara Singh's group lost the elections, and within a month, Kairon was murdered.

The vignette illustrates the fundamental importance of factions. Party labels and allegiances take second place to them. Indeed, the success of parties is often based on the factions that (temporarily) line up within them and against them.

Since independence, the Congress and the Akali Dal have had a symbiotic relationship – the existence of one requires the existence of the other. The factions that penetrate down to most villages in Punjab make it so. If your enemy already has links with a political party, you can thwart him only by lining up with his rivals within that party or with another party altogether.

It is not surprising therefore that the creation of the Punjabi-language state of Punjab and the Hindi-majority Haryana on 1 November 1966, did not bring with it an era of tranquillity and stable government. Chandigarh was made a Union Territory and joint capital of both states, a decision that pleased no one. Though the Prime Minister, Mrs Gandhi, awarded the city to Punjab in January 1970 (as part of a proposal that Sant Fateh Singh used to explain the ending of his fast), this has never been implemented. Nor, indeed, was another part of that award: the transfer of territory around Fazilka, on the border with Pakistan, from Punjab to Haryana.

Within fifteen months of the creation of the new state, Congress control of Punjab's politics was broken. At the general elections of February 1967, it was reduced to forty-eight seats in a legislature of 104, and a United Front of all non-Congress parties, led by the Akali Dal, took office. The story of the next five years highlights again the role of faction in the state's politics. Consider the list of ministries and their duration, which is compiled in Table 5.3.

In some ways, the list speaks for itself. The horse-trading and deal-doing are frankly chronicled in the memoirs of the Governor of the day, D. C. Pavate, who had the task of deciding the validity of rival claims to form governments.[45]

One of these ministries, however, deserves further comment, because the circumstances of its creation so well illustrate the way in which factions work and because some of its legacies continue into the 1980s. Its Finance Minister, for example, was Dr Jagjit Singh Chauhan, today's champion of 'Khalistan'.

TABLE 5.3   *Punjab governments 1967–72*

Dates	Government	Chief Minister
March to November 1967	United Front, led by Akali Dal	Gurnam Singh
November 1967 to August 1968	'Janta Party', minority, supported by Congress	Lachhman Singh Gill
August 1968 to February 1969	President's Rule	
February 1969 to March 1970	Akali Dal–Jana Sangh coalition	Gurnam Singh
March 1970 to June 1970	Akali Dal (Sant Group) – Jana Sangh coalition	Parkash Singh Badal
June 1970 to June 1971	Akali Dal (Sant Group), supported by Jana Sangh	Parkash Singh Badal
June 1971 to March 1972	President's Rule	

SOURCE   Dalip Singh, *Dynamics*, pp. 93–111.

On 25 November 1967, Lachhman Singh Gill (1917–69) who 'graduated into politics via real estate',[46] became Chief Minister, having deserted from the Akali Dal with sixteen supporters. In the 1950s, he had been a close lieutenant of Master Tara Singh and vice-president of the SGPC. But after Tara Singh's failed fast of 1961, Gill led the group that destroyed the Master's hold on the Akali Dal.[47] In 1967, Gill wanted to be Chief Minister, while the Congress Party in Punjab wanted to dislodge the United Front government. The Congress, under Gian Singh Rarewala (1901–79), an old rival of Kairon, agreed to back Gill's little band of defectors. Though supported by the Congress, Gill also allied himself outside the legislature with the remnants of Master Tara Singh's supporters (who were still advocating a Sikh state) to try to win control of the SGPC. Meanwhile, within the Congress, Rarewala faced a strong challenge from Giani Zail Singh, who became Chief Minister from 1972 to 1977.[48]

Charges are still made – and to judge from the Governor's account, they are true – that the Congress promoted the Gill government and keenly exploited divisions among the Akalis. Moreover, the fast of Darshan Singh Pheruman, which ended in his death in October 1969, was portrayed as an example of an old man being manipulated by rival political groups. Pheruman's fast embarrassed Sant Fateh Singh, who had been drawing back from death fasts for ten years. Akalis claimed that his fast was set up by Giani Zail Singh of the Congress (President of India since 1982), Jagjit Singh Chauhan (self-proclaimed 'president of Khalistan' since 1982) and others to divide the Akali Dal.[49] The allegations are worth recalling when we consider the formation of the Dal Khalsa in April 1978, in which both Chauhan and Zail Singh are said to have been involved.[50]

Political alliances are fluid, factions join and divide for advantage and the labels of 'Akali Dal' and 'Congress' are often matters of convenience. They allow those who use them to portray themselves as defenders either of Sikh interests or of national interests. The choices depend on the circumstances of the time.

EMERGENCY AND ENFORCED TRANQUILLITY

The five years of unbroken administration between 1972 and 1977 owed a good deal to national events. In 1971 Mrs Gandhi won a surprisingly heavy victory in general elections for the national parliament fought on the slogan 'banish poverty' (*garibi hatao*). Even in Punjab, where the Akali Dal government was in power, Mrs Gandhi's Congress Party won ten out of thirteen seats.[51] The failure of Akali candidates underlined the divisions in the party; the success of the Congress indicated that voters were passing out of the control of local bosses and were able to listen to politicians' messages for themselves. They were slowly dispensing with middlemen or 'interpreters'.

In December 1971, India defeated Pakistan in a twelve-day war that resulted in the emergence of Bangladesh as a sovereign state. Again, there was heavy fighting on the Punjab border, and again Sikhs were glorified as defenders of the Indian state. The officer who commanded the Indian Army in the victory over the Pakistanis in Bangladesh was Jagjit Singh Aurora, a non-Jat Sikh.

The Akali Dal government had collapsed in June 1971, and the threat of war led the central government to maintain President's Rule in the Punjab until March 1972. The Congress won a resounding victory in state elections in Punjab (as it did even in opposition strongholds like West Bengal) taking sixty-six out of 104 seats (see Table 5.1). Giani Zail Singh formed a government that ruled until 1977.

Mrs Gandhi's 'emergency', imposed on the whole country in June 1975, helped to keep the government in power by providing it with an excuse for censorship and detention without trial. Legislators who thought of changing sides had good reason to think again. At the same time, however, the 'emergency' provided another example of the ability of the Akalis to rally large numbers of people for agitations. After secret negotiations over possible support for the 'emergency' broke down in July 1975,[52] Akali demonstrators regularly defied the bans, and more than 40000 are said to have been imprisoned.[53] This would make the Akali protest, which operated from the *gurdwaras*, the most sustained opposition to the 'emergency' offered anywhere in India. It is a story about which little seems to have been written.

The loathing generated by the 'emergency' in north India swept the Congress away in the national elections of March 1977. In Punjab, the Congress could not win a seat, and in the state elections in June, the Akali Dal took fifty-eight out of 117 seats, the best result in its history. It formed a coalition government with the Janata party, with Parkash Singh Badal as Chief Minister.

The Congress now was farther from power than it had been after the elections of either 1967 (when it resorted to the Lachhman Singh Gill stratagem) or 1969 (when it appears clandestinely to have encouraged the death-fast of Darshan Singh Pheruman). In such a predicament, the tactics for Punjab politicians were obvious, for they had been developed in the course of forty years' experience of legislatures and elections. The factional building-blocks of Punjab governments were lying about waiting to be jostled into new alignments.

What was different, however, was the volatility of Punjab society. Messages now moved faster and reached more people, who could, if they wished, mix the exhortations of Guru Gobind Singh with the methods of the Palestine Liberation Organisation, the Italian Red Brigades or the Irish Republican Army. The barriers that in the past kept factional rivalries confined and intelligible were now increasingly broken, with the result that once-predictable actions were now producing outcomes that few could foresee.

In 1977, Parkash Singh Badal, Akali Chief Minister of India's most prosperous state, was noted for his long commitment to 'communal harmony and . . . complete Hindu–Sikh unity'.[54] By February 1984 he was being arrested for burning the Indian constitution. What had happened?

6 Faction

The newspaper photographs of his arrest show an unlikely looking rebel with little about him of either Gandhi or Guru Gobind Singh. Under his jacket, Parkash Singh Badal wears a collar and tie and a woollen sleeveless pullover of the kind Punjabi women spend their winters ceaselessly knitting. The button of the jacket strains across an ample stomach, made more obvious by the pressure of a Sikh policeman's finger as he tries to guide his distinguished prisoner gently through the crowd.

It is 27 February 1984, and in front of the Bangla Sahib Gurdwara in New Delhi, located opposite the international telecommunications centre where foreign journalists file their reports, Badal and four others have just burned copies of the Indian constitution. Under the Insults to National Honour Act, the offence carries a penalty of up to three years in prison.[1] To elude the police, Badal had earlier slipped into New Delhi disguised as a truck driver.

Born in 1926, Badal has twice been Chief Minister of Akali-led coalition governments in Punjab (1970–1, 1977–9). He is, according to Pavate, the former Governor, 'a country gentleman … a big farmer by profession, quite rich by inheritance, well educated and modern in outlook, with a charming and gifted wife'. His family are Jat landlords of longstanding in Ferozepur, a turbulent yet fertile district on the frontier with Pakistan. His native village of Badal lies in a sandy area near the Rajasthan and Haryana borders. He was first returned to the legislature as a Congress candidate in the general elections of 1957 after the Akali–Congress merger. Later, he became the urbane lieutenant so badly needed by the rustic Sant Fateh Singh.[2]

By February 1984, however, Badal was fighting for his political life – indeed, perhaps even for his life itself. In the

118

week before he burned the constitution, fifty people were murdered in Punjab. Most of the dead were Hindus; most of the killers were Sikh youths 'riding motor cycles and carrying Sten guns'.[3] But Sikhs, too, were being killed: in reprisal, in the neighbouring state of Haryana; and for 'treachery' in Punjab itself. The men with the guns decided what constituted treason.

Badal was the victim of a political system that had come adrift. Bitter factional rivalry characterised by intimidation and violence have long been the essence of politics in rural Punjab. John Malcolm recorded in 1805 that 'there are few, if any' of Punjab's villages, 'the rule of which is not contested between brothers or near relations'. The resulting turmoil, wrote Malcolm, 'in a country where the infant is devoted to *steel* and taught to consider war as his only occupation', was there for all to see.[4] As we have seen, two things contained violence in the past. First, the animosity was personal: you assaulted or murdered – often with your own hands – personal enemies, and you knew that by doing so, you probably identified yourself to their families and thus put the lives of your family in danger. Second, weapons were old-fashioned and communications slow. The only customs you followed – your only 'models' – were those of the elders under whom you grew up.

Since 1947, appeals against 'oppression of Sikhs' and demands for a 'Sikh state' – whatever these may mean in any given context – have been a feature of Punjab politics. But until the early 1960s, the Akali Dal, which broadcast these cries, was in many ways an organisation dominated by urban, non-Jat Sikhs. Jat Sikh cultivators, in the landed security of their fairly isolated villages (as they were at that stage), could be excused for not being greatly interested. Personal rewards and enmities preoccupied them. But with the 'green revolution', as more villages acquired link roads, more children went to primary and then high school and more and more newspapers and travellers passed through the villages, the ideas of a wider world increasingly spread into the countryside. The chief of the Punjab police force in 1984 lamented one of the great achievements of the 'green revolution': 'Our problem is [that] there is a network of link roads in the Punjab countryside which makes it impossible to chase and trace the killers'.[5] Violence and faction remained; but the cables of face-to-face intercourse and inward-looking rural life, which previously kept them anchored, had now been cut.

FACTIONS: RELIABLE RELATIVES

I have written a good deal about 'factions' up to now and claimed that they are central not just to Punjab's politics but to the politics of all India's regions. But how do they work? Why? Are they unique to India?

The word 'faction' has been part of British political vocabulary for 400 years. Edmund Burke equated it with a 'mean and interested struggle for place and emoluments'.[6] Today, parliamentary parties are often said to be divided into factions – 'wet' and 'dry' in Mrs Thatcher's Conservative Party, the so-called 'Tribune group' in the British Labour Party, the various well-organised groups within the Australian Labour Party or even the 'Red Tories' of Canada's Progressive Conservative Party. All these examples, however, are divisions within parliamentary political parties and all have an ideological base. None is primarily concerned with distributing patronage to its members. These examples from urban, industrial societies differ from the Indian phenomenon which I have used the word 'faction' to describe.

Factions in India exist in virtually every village. They are based on two things: on personal affections and hatreds and on distribution of favours and rewards. Poor, low-caste men follow wealthy high-caste men who can offer them land to cultivate or protection from other mighty personages. In return, the powerful acquire dependents they can call on in a fight. 'When the landlords war against each other', a scholar writes of a Punjab village in the 1970s, 'the landlords' Scheduled Castes [formerly 'Untouchables'] are formed into small militias to defend their landlords and to do mischief against the opposing side.' Two Scheduled Caste men had been killed in such clashes in the past five years.[7] Thus the wealthy vie with each other for power and prestige. 'Quarrels', wrote Malcolm in 1805, 'have been transmitted from father to son.' In the 1970s, Joyce Pettigrew noted that in every institution, 'there had always been two opposed factions'. Concerning elections, for example, another observer declared in 1982: 'If the chief of a family is an Akali, often the Congress is able to field his brother or uncle or nephew against him'.[8]

Reasons of economic organisation explain why factions pervade India. Indeed, I suspect that factions similar to those of Punjab are found in most peasant societies. First, such societies generally have few officials or bureaucratic institutions. The landlord, who lets you till a piece of his land, probably also controls wells and water, determines building restrictions (who may build what) and involves himself in settling village disputes. Such a big man and his family fill the roles of various agencies and officials in urban, industrial societies. Thus poor men need patrons to safeguard their multiple needs, and patrons need dependents to swell their numbers and enhance their prestige against rivals.

The coming of electoral, legislative politics to India at the beginning of this century added another dimension to factions. Numbers now became even more important. The weak, the elderly – even, eventually, women – who would be no use in a fight, were just as good at the ballot box as a broad-shouldered, 20-year-old son. Legislatures, moreover, created governments, and governments dispensed patronage. To control government was to tap a great reservoir from which a man could irrigate his followers. The politics of legislatures thus blended well with the long-standing factions of villages.[9]

Indeed, legislative politics and the expansion of government activity reinforced such factions. The growing need to deal with government institutions brought village people into touch with a complicated outside world. How else to deal with it except with the help of your patron? The humble man cannot command the bureaucrat's attention; but the humble man's patron can.[10]

Looked at in this way, factions become less exotic, less specific to the 'Mysterious East'. Big men always needed followers. Now they needed them all the more, because votes – raw numbers – won elections and controlled legislatures. In recent times, the politics of India's states often appear to be nothing more than 'intrigues to capture the [government]' which 'clutter the history . . . with trivial detail and obscure the deeper issues'. A political leader's eminence has seemed to be 'measured by the number and reliability of the relatives he controlled'.[11] This observation, however, is not a political scientist's about modern India. Rather, it is the historian, J. H. Plumb, describing British politics in the eighteenth century.

It is worth pointing out as well that the legislative politics of the so-called 'white Dominions' in the nineteenth century were similarly based on factions and on continual attempts to pull down governments and set up·new ones. In its first thirty-five years of responsible government between 1856 and 1891, for example, the Australian colony of New South Wales had twenty-three ministries.[12] Punjab in the thirty-five years between 1947 and 1982, had thirteen ministries (and five spells of President's Rule).

Why, then, did factions of the kind just described disappear from the legislatures of Britain and the 'white Dominions' and why do they remain so much a part of Indian politics today? First, factions are, I think, the product of societies where communications are not highly developed and where it is difficult to organise interests – class interests or ethnic group interests, for example – over wide geographical areas. Thus local notables provide the links between people in the country-side and higher levels of government. This presupposes a largely peasant society. As a greater proportion of the popu-lation moves into towns and cities, organisation becomes physically easier, and people are less hampered in organising around interests rather than patrons. (In India today, about 25 per cent of the population is urban; in Britain, 30 per cent of the population was urban by 1801.) Marx and his followers believed that class interests would inevitably drive together urban factory workers of industrial-revolution Europe into a homogeneous class-for-themselves, able to revolt and over-throw capitalism. Yet the 'interests' that have affected the behaviour of urban Indians have often involved religious, language or racial – in short, ethnic – identities. Nevertheless, such behaviour was different from the close attachment to a faction leader or patron.

Urban and industrial life has also meant more specialised services. The person from whom you rent your rooms is not necessarily the same person for whom you work or who lends you money or to whom you go if you need to deal with officials. People have separate, specialised roles; patrons, in contrast, hold dozens of threads in their hands alone.

Industrial societies also began to develop forms of social

security – pensions, unemployment payments, health insurance. In peasant societies, a patron who is able to grant a loan or find a son a job may be the only safety net in times of crisis. In industrial societies a family may have other alternatives.

Finally, as populations become more literate and more familiar with communications, they are better able to deal with governments and officials for themselves. With less need for the 'mediatory functions' of a patron or faction leader, people gradually come to depend on him less.[13]

These reasons, I think, go some way towards explaining the prevalence of faction in Indian politics. Peasants everywhere need patrons. Legislative politics in slowly industrialising societies, where it is difficult to create majorities out of interest groups, also sustain factional rivalry. Village needs and legislative needs reinforce each other.

There are no doubt aspects of Indian culture which also support factions in politics. The ancient relationship between the *guru* (preceptor or teacher) and *chela* (disciple or follower), for example, may provide a model of behaviour, both for the factional leader and his followers. The leader's role is crucial, and the followers cluster round him with great deference. Scholars of India debate whether factions are based primarily on such personal loyalties to leaders (and hatreds between leaders) or on 'rational calculations of personal and group interests'.[14] I suspect that both standards apply – that there are some enmities no reward can overcome, and some rewards so sweet that any enmity can be (for a time, anyway) overlooked.

Factions appear in the boldest colours in Punjab. But they pervade most of village India. 'The faction', writes Paul Brass about Uttar Pradesh, 'belongs to the traditional order.'[15] He then demonstrates how such factions have linked up with struggles in legislative politics. Other scholars have studied factions in Maharashtra in western India and Orissa in the east, while Joyce Pettigrew's enthralling book establishes a special place for them in Punjab. She writes that, in struggles among Sikh Jats, 'violence was taken for granted ... power was transient, possessions were transient, and the basis of power and wealth was force'. And force was based on faction, the 'means whereby certain powerful families attempted to consolidate their power and . . . weaker families were provided with links necessary for the preservation of their property and other interests'.[16]

What happened in Punjab – and increasingly elsewhere – since the early 1970s is that a host of innovations have overtaken the old ways in which factional struggles have been carried on. The old barriers that restricted communications and violence are disappearing. Yet factions still exist; they still attempt to destroy rivals and bring down governments. Now, however, all the devices – ranging from murder to raising the ideological bets (for example, 'I am a "better" Sikh than you') – have far wider ramifications.

The processes that will increasingly erode the basis of factions in India are well under way. Bureaucracy, a communications revolution, urbanisation and industrialisation cannot be turned back. They are accompanied by evidence that ordinary citizens and voters are gradually becoming prepared and able to dispense with 'intermediaries' or 'patrons'. Election results since 1971 suggest that national leaders can project messages which large sections of the population can receive, and approve or reject, without the influence of local go-betweens.

Politicians and landlords raised in the tradition of factions find it difficult to conduct their politics in any other way, even when it becomes apparent that their stratagems do not bring the desired results and may produce consequences, as in Punjab, that few people wish or foresee. Let me try to explain how factions in Punjab, operating in new and poorly understood conditions, produced the crises of the 1980s.

PUNJAB: QUESTIONS OF PRESTIGE

The links between villages and factions in the Punjab legislature in Chandigarh run like a conveyor belt. Messages and support pass up and down. In skilfully tracing this process, Joyce Pettigrew showed how the Chief Minister, Partap Singh Kairon, himself played a part in village struggles in the 1950s and 1960s. Moreover, in the same villages lived families allied with Kairon's deadly rival, Gian Singh Rarewala.[17] The careers of both men illustrate the fact that party and ideology were far less significant than power and honour. Both men changed parties and took their factional allies with them.

Parkash Singh Badal came up through this system, and all the factional compulsions were still operating when the Akali Dal and its partners swept the Congress out of office in June 1977. The Akalis won fifty-eight out of 117 seats and 31 per cent of the vote (see Tables 5.1 and 5.2). Their allies, the Janata Party, which was essentially the old urban-Hindu Jana Sangh, took twenty-five seats and 15 per cent of the vote. Congress, which had governed the state under Giani Zail Singh from 1972 until Mrs Gandhi's fall in March 1977, managed 34 per cent of the vote but only seventeen seats. Badal became Chief Minister of a coalition government for the second time, faced with the difficult task of satisfying his own close supporters, fending off rival groups among the Akalis, dealing with his urban Hindu partners and preventing Sikh factions in the Congress from raiding the Akali fold as they had wolfishly done in the past.

The Congress Party was deeply divided and dangerously out of control, its candidates unable to win a single seat in the parliamentary elections in March. In those elections, it was 'an open secret' that the supporters of Zail Singh, the Chief Minister, 'did everything' they could to ensure the defeat of 'at least six Congress candidates'. Aggrieved Congress officials accused Zail Singh of having 'provided men and money to defeat the Congress candidates' and having made it 'a question of prestige to get the Akali candidate elected'.[18]

Why should a Congress Chief Minister have worked against his own party's parliamentary candidates? Zail Singh's behaviour nicely illustrates the considerations on which faction leaders base their calculations. By early February 1977, it was increasingly evident that Mrs Gandhi's party was going to lose the national elections called for mid-March. In this light, Zail Singh's behaviour represented an attempt to shore up his own faction in state politics. Having helped to get Akali candidates elected, he could then explore the possibility of a coalition with the Akalis in Punjab. This would have had the double advantage of confounding rivals in the Congress and at the same time ensuring that his own group stayed close to power in the difficult days that would follow Mrs Gandhi's defeat.

The Akali Dal–Janata Party victory in Punjab's state elections, however, was so overwhelming that they did not need to consider possible allies among Congress factions. The latter faced a long period out of power. And to be out of power meant that your enemies were likely to be *in* power and able to direct all the mechanisms of government against you.

Desperate straits had called for desperate measures in the past. In the 1960s, for example, there was plenty of evidence of 'Congress sponsorship of factions inside the Akali Dal'. The 1967 Akali-led government was brought down by similar devices.[19]

The technique developed in the late 1970s was to encourage dissatisfied Akali factions to start a campaign 'for complete autonomy of Punjab' and to accuse their own government of failure to look after Sikh interests. This would anger Hindus in the Janata Party, put Akali ministers in the position of having to qualify their devotion to their religion and thus divide Parkash Singh Badal's government. In the ensuing disarray, it might be possible to 'bring in a Congress (I) [Indira] government'.[20]

RESOLUTIONS FROM ANANDPUR SAHIB

Towards the end of 1973, the outlook was not brilliant for politicians attached to the Akali Dal. The Congress government of Giani Zail Singh was stealing Sikh religious thunder with projects like Guru Gobind Singh Marg, the road linking places associated with the tenth Guru. Cultivators still enjoyed good prices for their crops and relatively cheap inputs. The oil crisis, and the resulting rise in the price of diesel fuel and fertilisers, began only with the Israeli–Egyptian war of October 1973. The fortunes of Akalis seemed at such a low ebb that an attempt to hold a conference in the town of Malerkotla in November was 'described by political observers as a flop'. The *Tribune* gave it only three paragraphs.

Even more remarkable, the meeting of the working committee of the Akali Dal, which is said to have endorsed the 'Anandpur Sahib Resolution' on 17 October 1973, apparently went unreported. Although the Resolution has since become the focus of so much debate, it was not mentioned in the *Tribune* of October or November 1973.[21]

It is not surprising, therefore, that when the Resolution was revived (or rediscovered?) disagreement arose over what the original document said. The journalist Kuldip Nayar, for example, was told that the 1973 version was drafted in English by Kapur Singh, an ex-official, and 'explained' in Punjabi to Sant Fateh Singh. The irony of this story lies in the fact that Sant Fateh Singh had been dead for a year when the Akali working committee is supposed to have met at Anandpur Sahib in October 1973.[22]

The story emphasises the uncertainty about the origins and the 'correct' version of the Resolution. What seems possible is that the Akali working committee met at Anandpur in October 1973 and discussed various possibilities for reviving the party's fortunes. In the course of these deliberations, someone drafted proposals about greater autonomy for Punjab and about Sikh 'nationhood'. People who attended the meeting doubtless recalled discussion of a 'resolution', but during the next five years, there was little incentive or opportunity to be specific about it or to publicise it. In 1974–5, Akali leaders like Parkash Singh Badal were working for a new alliance with the Jana Sangh, whose backing among urban Hindus enabled the formation of Akali-led coalitions in 1967 and 1969.[23] In such negotiations, a 'resolution' emphasising Sikh pre-eminence needed to be played down or completely forgotten. In 1975, Mrs Gandhi's 'emergency' brought strict press censorship and the imprisonment of many leading Akalis. Whatever the 'resolution' of 1973 said, it was intended as a bargaining tool and therefore had no role to play if bargaining was banned.

The 'resolution' was revived in August 1977, after the Akali-led coalition came to power in Punjab.[24] But it became prominent only in October 1978 when a rare 'all-India' conference of the Akali Dal, which attracted 500 000 people according to journalists' estimates, met in Ludhiana.[25] The meeting endorsed twelve resolutions which came to be known collectively as the 'Anandpur Sahib Resolution'.[26] At the time, however, the *Tribune* referred to them as individual resolutions, unrelated to whatever may have happened at Anandpur Sahib in 1973. For our purpose, however, it is enough to emphasise that by the early 1980s, at least three versions of the 'Anandpur Sahib Resolution' were circulating.[27] A politician could choose the one that best suited his particular purposes.

The conference in 1978 was significant for two other reasons. First, Akali leaders effectively silenced Sant Jarnail Singh Bhindranwale and his supporters when they tried to disrupt a session. Bhindranwale and his friends, however, were not angry about the questions of Sikh nationhood. Rather, they were protesting against the Punjab government's allegedly soft line towards the 'anti-Sikh' Sant Nirankari Mission. The Bhindranwale group may have been fanatics, but even if this were so, their interest at this stage was religion, not politics.[28]

Second, in reviving the 'Anandpur Sahib Resolution' and calling for greater autonomy, Akali Dal leaders were at pains 'to dispel fears and misconceptions' about the party's connection 'with separatist elements'.[29] To this end, the president of the national Janata Party, Chandra Shekhar, was invited to address the conference, and the president of the Punjab branch of the Janata Party garlanded prominent Akalis at a public function.[30] Having recently been roughly handled by Prime Minister Morarji Desai, and themselves embroiled in a factional feud, Akalis were using the demand for greater state independence as a lever against the central government and as a device in Punjab politics. It also served to divert attention from Bhindranwale's attempt to have a virtual war declared against the Sant Nirankari Mission. The demands, asserted Akali leaders, were no different from those made by the Communist Party of India (Marxist) [CPI(M)] government of West Bengal.

At the time of the 1978 meeting, the only talk of a separate Sikh state came from an unknown organisation called the Khalsa Mukti Fauj, whose spokesman attacked the Janata–Akali Dal coalition, praised Indira Gandhi and Jawaharlal Nehru and called for 'the formation of a Sikh State'.[31] Such evidence is far from conclusive, but it suggests that the Congress (I) Party was already trawling in Punjab waters, hoping for trouble. Indeed, within a week, a crisis in the central government led its two Akali ministers to resign briefly. In Punjab, stories circulated about the possibility of an alliance between the Congress (I) and a section of Akalis.[32] At this stage, therefore, the 'Anandpur Sahib Resolution' was simply one of a number of bargaining counters.

By the early 1980s, however, once the Congress (I) had returned to power in Punjab, the Resolution began to acquire the stature of holy writ. First, however, it was necessary to decide which Resolution one was discussing and what in fact it said. The version deemed authentic by the president of the

Akali Dal, Sant Harchand Singh Longowal, in 1982, spoke of guarding and propagating the Sikh faith. It called for the addition to Punjab of various pieces of neighbouring states and for greatly increased autonomy from the central government, not just for Punjab but for all the Indian states. 'Central intervention', the approved version of the resolution declares, 'should be restricted to Defence, Foreign Affairs, Post & Telegraphs, Currency and Railways.' The resolution criticised Indian foreign policy under the Congress as 'useless and harmful ... Our foreign policy should not be tagged along with any other country [a reference to the Soviet Union]'. It also vowed to achieve justice for Sikh employees of the central government, to strive to have the *kirpan* (sword) made part of the uniform of Sikh soldiers, to ensure that every Indian who was not a criminal 'be allowed to keep a fire-arm without license', and to work for 'prohibition and ban on smoking at public places'.[33] It was a confused and confusing document, hinting at semi-autonomy in places and stressing in others the need to look after Sikhs in the army and other central-government services.

Perhaps its most important feature was the fact that it carried the name of Anandpur Sahib, one of the most sacred sites of the Sikhs, associated with Guru Gobind Singh's days of lonely adversity and spiritual triumph. Thus to be against the Anandpur Sahib Resolution was almost to be opposed to the Sikh religion itself.

BHINDRANWALE: 'A UNIVERSITY ON THE MOVE'

In addition to the well-understood factional contests for power, widespread unease and anxiety touched rural Punjab in the late 1970s. The innovations of the past ten years unsettled lives, and altered, subtly yet fundamentally, the consequences of long-familiar actions. Buses, widely-circulated Gurmukhi newspapers, scores of literate village youths – together these allowed the tale of (for example) a murder committed in a remote village to be spread throughout the state by the following morning. A member of the Sant Nirankari Mission complained that orthodox Sikhs, coming from far and wide to harass the Nirankari headquarters in Amritsar, arrived in 'a jeep, a car and two mini-buses loaded with arms'.[34]

In the late 1960s, elderly Akalis at the Golden Temple used to reprimand young Sikh visitors who trimmed their beards about the sin of cutting hair. One suspects, however, that the dilemma had long confronted Sikhs: to trim or not to trim. Indeed, about 1803 John Malcolm nearly provoked murder by joking with a *kesh-dhari* Sikh about shaving.[35] By the late 1970s, however, anxiety about such deviations – and the thrill that young rustics perhaps derived from trying them, as young people everywhere like to alarm their elders – reached deep into the countryside. 'Trimming of beards is becoming a general tendency', wrote one observer, who pointed out the dismay this caused among older people and the pillars of the Akali Dal. The latter's influence, after all, rests on their claim to be the only true representative of an unsullied Sikh tradition.[36] If the tradition fades, so too might Akali authority.

One result has been a growing revivalism, an attempt to bring Sikh youth back to purity. There appear to be at least two major influences at work. First, knowledge of international affairs, resulting from the innovations of the 'green revolution', has spread throughout Punjab and made Sikhs aware of the so-called Islamic revival in Muslim countries. Punjab has a higher ratio of television sets than any other state, and Pakistani television signals can be received in Punjab. Since General Zia ul-Haq came to power in 1977, Pakistan has promoted itself as an Islamic state and emphasised the resurgence of Islam. Sikhs have seen some of this on television, read about the Ayatollah Khomeini and the Iranian revolution in their newspapers, and a few have said in effect: 'Anything they can do, we can do'.

Second, people throughout India are being drawn into a more complex world. Though the process goes on everywhere, the pace has been faster in Punjab. This world holds out the possibility of prosperity, but it often makes it difficult to observe time-honoured religious practices. This has led people to look for new, convenient ways to show themselves and their neighbours 'that their traditional values are as relevant today as ever before'.[37] In Hindu areas, one scholar suggests, this has resulted in the increasing importance of 'god-men' or *swamis* like Sathaya Sai Baba, the frizzy-haired, red-robed holy man popular with millions of Indians and many foreigners. In a changing world, 'in which order has disappeared, controls have been lifted and self-indulgence is rife', such a *swami* acts as 'a cultural broker between traditional answers and contemporary problems'.[38] Such *swamis* illustrate the need of many people to feel they are retaining their religious traditions even in times of unsettling change. A similar process has also been at work in Punjab.

The collision of two different elements of that process combined with old-style factional manoeuvres to produce the gun-battle in Amritsar on 13 April 1978 in which eighteen people died. You may recall (Chapter 4) that on that harvest festival day (Baisakhi), two large gatherings were being held in Amritsar. One was the customary Sikh celebration of one of Punjab's favourite festivals. The other was a conference of a god-man sect, the Sant Nirankari Mandal or Mission, which though outwardly Sikh, appeared to many Sikhs as heretical and subversive. Yet the Nirankari Mission was attracting a following, particularly among urban, non-Jat Sikhs and ex-Untouchables.[39] Focusing as it did on a living teacher (its leader, Baba Gurbachan Singh) it satisfied the same needs as other Indian god-man cults. But its deference towards an individual, and its lack of deference towards the Guru Granth Sahib, put it at bitter odds with conventional Sikh values. It was militant orthodox Sikhs, themselves fired by a sense of revival, who marched to the Nirankari Mission's conference to warn it against denigration of the true Sikh religion. Supporters of the Nirankari Mission were prepared, and most of those killed were Sikh demonstrators.

Although the sincere religious beliefs of many Sikhs were a contributing factor in the clash, it was apparent at the time that some politicians were attempting to serve immediate political ends as well. Within the Akali Dal, a 'faction ... trying to project itself as the better defender of Sikh interests'[40] welcomed (perhaps encouraged) the conflict as a way of undermining Badal's government. Factions associated with the Congress played a double game. They encouraged aggressive orthodox Sikhs as a way of tearing apart the government, but at the same time, they 'condemned the violence on peaceful Nirankaris'.[41] It was only a year since Mrs Gandhi's defeat and the fall of her disciples throughout India. For those of them in Punjab, a return to power looked a long way off unless they could destroy the Badal-led ministry, as previous coalitions had been destroyed in 1967 and 1969, and as Kairon had absorbed the Akali opposition in 1956 and abetted its feuds in 1960–2.

As a focus for the forces of orthodoxy, the gun-battle of 13 April 1978 brought to prominence for the first time Jarnail Singh Bhindranwale, whose name became a household word throughout India during the next six years. On the day itself, the Nirankari Mission held a morning procession through the streets of Amritsar to the grounds where between 50 000 and 100 000 devotees had gathered for a meeting.

Meanwhile, at the Golden Temple, the normal Baisakhi celebrations were going on under the patronage of the state government and with an Akali Dal minister in attendance. Once the Nirankari Mission's procession passed off peacefully, the large numbers of police alerted for the day appear to have relaxed. In the early afternoon, Bhindranwale 'and some of his followers' asked the minister to stop the Nirankari Mission meeting. The minister, who himself had a reputation at one time as a Sikh-state advocate, apparently replied that the procession was over 'and there was no need to do anything now'. At that point, about 200 members of various groups, including some of Bhindranwale's supporters, marched to the Nirankari Mission gathering with the aim, they said later, of asking them 'not to say anything against the Sikh religion'. The police did not keep the two sides apart, firing broke out and fourteen of the demonstrators were killed along with four from the Nirankari Mission. Dozens were wounded and more than thirty kept in hospital. Badal, the Chief Minister, hastened back to the Punjab from official business in Bombay and later cancelled a planned visit to the USA.[42]

Bhindranwale himself does not appear to have been present at the gun-battle, and of the dead, only a few belonged to his group; but at the cremation of the fourteen dead two days later, he gave a public warning 'that he would not allow these deaths to go in vain'. The dead were quickly dubbed 'martyrs', and a former president of the Akali Dal, now a Member of Parliament, declared that he was 'prepared to lead an agitation to save the honour of his religion'. The incident provided a convenient opportunity 'to strike hard at [Badal's] political supremacy within the [Akali Dal]'.[43]

But who was Jarnail Singh Bhindranwale? Most of Punjab wanted to know. Though only 31, he was already referred to as a 'sant' or holy man. He had followers ready to carry out his suggestions and influence enough to be able to speak to government ministers. Dalbir Singh of the *Tribune* recorded what was probably Bhindranwale's first major interview towards the end of April 1978. (Dalbir Singh himself became a follower of Bhindranwale and went underground after the Indian Army's capture of the Golden Temple in June 1984.) Later, Bhindranwale was pursued by representatives of national and international news agencies, but on this occasion he was still a little-known sant from a remote corner of Punjab, and he was talking to someone he trusted.

Even at this stage, however, he had a sense of what his followers and potential followers expected – a sense of flair and the theatrical. The photograph accompanying the interview showed him in full black beard, blue turban, long loose white shirt – and carrying the iron arrow that came to be his trademark. It harked back to Guru Gobind Singh and heightened the sense of romance and revival that Bhindranwale so successfully conveyed.

His background was similar to that of generations of sants. Like Sant Fateh Singh, Bhindranwale as a boy was placed under the instruction and care of a Sikh holy man in a *gurdwara*. His father admired Sant Kartar Singh, the head of a group once linked to a village called Bhindran in Ferozepur district. Thus the chief of the group was known as 'Bhindranwale'. As the youngest of seven sons in a Jat Sikh family, 'I had little work to do', Jarnail Singh said. The family could spare him, so when Sant Kartar asked for recruits to study the sacred texts, Jarnail Singh was sent with him.[44] His formal studies ended in the fifth class at about the age of 10, and he never learned English. But he had 'a rare command over the Punjabi language', wrote the *Tribune* correspondent, 'and can wield it to express complex ideas'. He had been married at 19 and had two sons, born in the early 1970s, but religious duties had superseded those of husband and householder. In August 1977, Sant Kartar Singh was killed – 'mysteriously', according to one of the quickly produced books of 1984[45]—in a car accident, and Jarnail Singh became leader of the group and acquired the title Bhindranwale.

He and his followers worked from 'a spacious and majestic gurdwara' near the large village of Chowk Mehta, 40 kilometres east of Amritsar. There they maintained a hostel for forty teenage students who studied Sikh scriptures, history and music. From this base, Bhindranwale and his escort (two of whom were armed with '.12 bore licensed guns') travelled throughout Punjab to give readings of the sacred Sikh texts. 'We are a university on the move', he told the *Tribune* correspondent. 'All the time we are busy teaching the correct reading and meaning of the Guru Granth Sahib, preaching the Sikh religion and bringing within the Sikh discipline all those who are interested in it.'[46]

Sants are part of Punjab rural life. In the past, they relieved the monotony of the village by carrying news and reading the sacred texts in a polished, entertaining way. A British army officer in the 1920s noted that virtually every Sikh village welcomed sants and encouraged them to stay. The British, however, also recognised their political potential, and the police 'nervously tracked wandering Sikh preachers'.[47]

In 1978, Bhindranwale was very much a part of this tradition; but there were striking innovations. The *Tribune* correspondent noted, for example, a much-used tape-recorder near at hand. Moreover, Bhindranwale seemed to have a steely edge that distinguished him from the sant of former days who spent 'most of his time in seclusion meditating on holy things'.[48] Bhindranwale named a member of the Nirankari Mission as responsible for the killings of 13 April and demanded that the man 'be handed over to us as Jehanghir [the Mughal emperor] had handed over Chandu who was responsible for the martyr-dom of Guru Arjan Dev [in 1606]'. Later, Bhindranwale vowed that 'we will enforce our socially acceptable justice on the culprits and we will pay any price for that'. In all his statements, the *Tribune* reporter wrote, Bhindranwale was 'the image of self-assurance'.[49]

At this stage, Bhindranwale appears to have been his own man, doing the things Sikh sants had long done, but doing them with notable aplomb. His tall, striking good looks, command of Punjabi and theatrical self-assurance (witness his iron arrow) gave him a greater appeal than other sants. His readiness to use a tape-recorder to spread his message and enliven his readings indicated an understanding of the changes in rural Punjab. People still wanted to hear the old messages, but television, films and cassette tapes made them look for drama and novelty. A sant had always had to be an entertainer; Bhindranwale understood that now the competition was different.

As a Jat Sikh from southern Punjab, Bhindranwale was also familiar with violence. Even in 1978, he travelled with an armed guard, and his group had been involved in fights with followers of the Sant Nirankari Mission as early as 1973. Bhindranwale reacted to the killings of 13 April 1978 not with a sense of revulsion or dismay – it would, I think, have been a mistake to have expected such a reaction – but with vows of revenge.

In 1978, Bhindranwale did not appear to be allied with any of the factions involved in legislative politics in Punjab. Although some members of the Akali Dal itself were attacking Badal and the government for being too soft on the Nirankari Mission, Bhindranwale refused to criticise the ministry in the immediate aftermath of the gun-battle in Amritsar.[50] We shall probably never know for sure whose idea it was to send the small procession to the Nirankari Mission's meeting place on 13 April. Certainly it went with Bhindranwale's blessing, but whether someone had whispered the suggestion in his ear is impossible to determine. In any case, after the killing, it was clear that a new and potentially powerful piece had appeared on the Punjab political board.

According to one version, Zail Singh, the ex-Chief Minister, first attempted to use Bhindranwale as a pawn capable of dividing the Akali Dal government. Though out of power, Zail Singh still had influence in his home area of Faridkot, and he prevailed upon its police superintendent, who was an ally, to issue as many gun licences as Bhindranwale's supporters asked for.[51] Indian journalists vouch for the truth of this assertion, and there is no doubt that policemen have long been part of factional politics in Punjab and have issued arms licences to benefit their allies.[52]

At this point, Bhindranwale is reported to have come to the notice of Sanjay Gandhi, Mrs Gandhi's younger son, the evil genius of the 'emergency', whose wife, Maneka, was a Khatri Sikh. In 1978 Mrs Gandhi and her family were facing their darkest days. Inquiry commissions were probing the crimes of the 'emergency', and the Janata Party government still looked fairly firmly in power. An indefinite period out of office – and

even prison sentences – were real possibilities. In neighbouring
Pakistan, after all, the former prime minister, Z. A. Bhutto,
was in jail and eventually executed in April 1979. In Sri Lanka,
the former Prime Minister, Mrs Sirimavo Bandaranaike, was
also facing inquiries and was to lose her civil rights in 1981. In
these desperate times, Sanjay Gandhi is said to have asked a
Sikh friend 'to get a dynamic young Sant who could challenge
the Akali leaders' in Punjab. Pressure needed to be applied to
the Janata government at as many points as possible.[53] It was
here that Bhindranwale came in, and the path that led to both
his and Mrs Gandhi's deaths began.

SGPC: 'THE ONLY SURE STEPPING STONE'

The urgency of deal-making in Punjab increased throughout
1978 because elections to the Shiromani Gurdwara Parbandhak
Committee (SGPC), repeatedly postponed since 1965, were
imminent. 'The only sure stepping stone for ascendancy among
the Akalis', the SGPC controls 700 *gurdwaras* and shrines in
Punjab, Haryana, Himachal Pradesh and Chandigarh, and a
budget of close to US $6 million a year.[54] Though in theory
the SGPC is simply a committee of management, in fact it also
deals with both doctrine and politics. The president of the
SGPC, concluded a journalist, is 'virtually a parallel Chief
Minister'.[55]

The aim in 1978 was to hold the long-overdue elections while
an Akali Dal-led government was in power in Punjab, and
then have the central government pass an act to bring every
gurdwara in India under the SGPC's control. In theory, this
would foster unity and rational management; in practice, it
would give the SGPC access to wealthy *gurdwaras* in other
parts of the country. 'The coming elections' were therefore
'rightly imagined', according to the usually well-informed
'Analyst' in the *Tribune*, to be 'crucial in determining the
course of Sikh politics for the next decade'. To gain an
advantage, one Akali faction was 'trying to project itself as the
better defender of Sikh interests than the present leadership'.
It was 'playing for very high stakes'.[56]

Thus against the background of fundamental changes in rural
society in Punjab, a dozen or more pieces manoeuvred on the

political board in 1978. There were at least two factions of Akalis in the legislature, each with links stretching into the countryside as such factions always had. Within the Congress Party, some factions were aligned with Zail Singh, the ex-Chief Minister, and some with his rivals. There were groups of urban Hindu politicians owing allegiance either to the Congress or the Janata Party. There were tiny groups of overseas Sikhs with stars in their eyes and glib talk of Sikh independence on their tongues. And in New Delhi there was the desperate family of Indira Gandhi, keenly interested in Punjab because of its proximity and Sanjay Gandhi's contacts there. Mrs Gandhi's strategy was said to be to break up the Akali Dal–Janata Party coalition, and to do this, her supporters were happy to encourage aggressive Sikh claims that would destroy the Akali alliance with urban Hindus.[57]

In August 1978, a twentieth-century 'Dal Khalsa' was founded in Chandigarh and pledged to achieve an independent Sikh state. The first meeting was widely believed to have been financed by Zail Singh and the Congress (I). In its report, however, the *Tribune* mentioned neither Zail Singh nor Jagjit Singh Chauhan's National Council for Khalistan. The newspaper summed up the announcement of the Dal Khalsa in five paragraphs, noting that its young founders said they were 'completely disillusioned with the leaders of various parties including . . . the Akali Dal who failed to get pride of place for Sikhs'.[58]

Elections force differences to the surface. The SGPC elections of March 1979 laid bare some of the factions struggling in Punjab and revealed the strange bedfellows such struggles made.

The SGPC and its elections are probably unique among the world's religions. They are conducted under central-government legislation (the act of 1925), and every adult Sikh in the Indian areas of the old Punjab is entitled to vote in one of 140 territorial constituencies. For a Sikh aiming at political power, membership of the SGPC is both a foundation-stone and a stepping-stone.

The elections of 1979 were the first ever held with the Akali Dal in government. In the past, Akali candidates usually won and controlled the SGPC, but they had the advantage of being able to point to the threat posed by a sinister Congress ministry and the need to protect Sikh interests. Now, however, it was factions associated with the Congress (I) who could use the SGPC elections to try to undermine the Akali-led government.

Badal set out to register a resounding success for the Akali Dal – and especially for his own faction in the party. He was at once confronted by his major rivals: Gurcharan Singh Tohra (b. 1924), president of the SGPC since 1973, and Jagdev Singh Talwandi (b. 1929), party president of the Akali Dal. Eventually, the three compromised, and each nominated most of the candidates for his own home areas. Two or three other leading Akalis won for themselves the same privilege.[59] More than a hundred disappointed erstwhile Akalis, who did not get their party's endorsement, were expelled for indiscipline. Some either contested as independents or supported opposition groups.

The latter attempted to put up a united front, but they were a diverse array. As well as Akali dissidents, they included Jagjit Singh Chauhan and his National Council for Khalistan who campaigned for a Sikh state, Bhindranwale who pledged to purify the faith, Baba Santa Singh, a roly-poly Nihang who had long feuded with the Akalis, Santokh Singh from Delhi, who had supported Mrs Gandhi during the 'emergency' (as, too, had Santa Singh) and various members of the Congress (I), including Zail Singh as an adviser.[60]

The subsequent careers of the allies are revealing. Chauhan went to Britain where he has since propagated 'Khalistan' and savaged the Congress (I) and Mrs Gandhi. Bhindranwale died when the army stormed the Golden Temple in June 1984. Santa Singh made the cover of *India Today* two months later when Mrs Gandhi's agents found him to be the only Sikh available who would help the government to repair the damage in the Golden Temple complex.[61] Santokh Singh was murdered in New Delhi in December 1981. And Zail Singh became Home Minister of the Government of India in 1980, and President of the republic in 1982.

The Akali Dal's candidates swept the SGPC elections, winning 133 of the 140 seats, with about 65 per cent of votes cast. Only 3.7 million Sikhs, of the 6 million estimated to have been eligible, registered to vote, and of those registered, only about two-thirds voted.[62] Bhindranwale, however, managed to get four of his candidates elected in Amritsar district, even though his close associate Amrik Singh, president of the All-India Sikh Students' Federation and the son of Bhindranwale's mentor, was defeated by an Akali minister. As evidence of the flexibility with which factions approached elections, Amrik Singh's campaign posters were said to bear a picture of Mrs Gandhi.[63] Amrik Singh was also apparently killed in the Golden Temple in June 1984.

Badal optimistically claimed that the results represented the 'defeat of the forces of fanaticism' and showed widespread Sikh support for 'the policies of moderation, secularism and communal harmony'. He condemned 'the unholy alliance between the Congress (I) and the extremist forces'. Outsiders, however, felt that the elections 'considerably weakened' the Akali Dal by showing up its divisions. Its opponents, after all, had taken more than a third of the vote, even though the Akalis had all the advantages of being in power.[64]

Badal, however, could take comfort from the fact that there were also deep splits among Sikhs attached to the Congress (I). Zail Singh and his rival, Darbara Singh, blamed each other for the failure of a civil-disobedience campaign to support Mrs Gandhi against alleged government persecution. In a parliamentary by-election, which the Congress (I) lost, Zail Singh's supporters were 'indifferent if not hostile' towards their party's candidate because he was associated with Darbara Singh.[65] Though Zail Singh and Darbara Singh had been in the Congress since at least Kairon's time, they had been rivals since Kairon's fall. Caste may have sharpened the edge: Zail Singh is a Ramgarhia (artisan); Darbara Singh, a Jat.

Mrs Gandhi's methods of dealing with the state branches of her party throve on such antagonisms. Tension between two powerful local leaders kept them both beholden to her. When she returned to power in January 1980, Zail Singh came to Delhi as Home Minister, but she made Darbara Singh the Chief Minister of Punjab after the state elections in May. From these key positions, they sought to embarrass each other for the next two years, encouraging, yet misunderstanding, the powerful emotions that were pervading Punjab.

In a sense, Bhindranwale was the major winner of the SGPC elections. The victory of four of his followers showed his appeal to significant numbers of Sikhs. Furthermore, though his friend Amrik Singh lost to the Akali minister, it was a close fight in which both Badal and Tohra, the president of the SGPC, had to campaign heavily. 'Bhindranwale a crowd-puller', the *Tribune* headlined an account of his speech to a crowd in Ludhiana estimated at 10 000. The story pointed out that none of the Akali stalwarts drew so many people.

He delighted the Ludhiana meeting with the remark that he could not offer his candidates cars or financial help because he was 'neither a Minister nor an opium smuggler'. Here was someone who called politicians to account and vowed a return to older, purer ways. For the literate, underemployed young, the message was exciting and romantic; for the old, it was reassuring: the way things once were was better. Bhindranwale, it appears, began to feed off the adulation.[66]

POLITICS: NEW-STYLE SANTS, OLD-TIME FILM STARS

The Janata Party government in New Delhi tore itself apart in July and August 1979. Bitter factional rivalry, similar in many ways to Punjab's, brought down Morarji Desai's ministry and led the President, N. Sanjeeva Reddy, to dissolve parliament on 21 August and call general elections for January 1980.

The rows within the Akali Dal prevented it from mounting a coherent campaign for the parliamentary elections. Congress (I) supporters, who had been wiped out in 1977, won twelve of Punjab's thirteen seats. The Akalis were reduced from nine to one.

After it came to power in March 1977, the Janata Party took less than six weeks to impose President's Rule on nine Congress-controlled states and to hold new elections. After her victory in January 1980, Mrs Gandhi therefore had a precedent which allowed her to oblige her office-hungry supporters. Nine state legislatures, including Punjab's, were dissolved in February and elections called for the end of May.

For Badal, the dismissal must have come almost as a relief, for he and his ministers had a precarious majority in the legislature and were preoccupied with internal battles. The election of the Akali Dal president in March 1980 generated so much rancour that the chief *granthi* (custodian and reader) of the Golden Temple asked for police protection.[67]

Another religious leader lacked such protection when he needed it: on 24 April, as the Punjab election campaign was beginning, Gurbachan Singh, the leader of the Sant Nirankari Mission, whose followers were held responsible (though acquitted by the courts in January) for the killings of 13 April 1978, was shot and killed in New Delhi. This was the man whom Bhindranwale had promised to see punished, and the Nirankari Mission immediately accused Bhindranwale of instigating the murder. His name was included in what the Indian police call the 'First Information Report', a statement taken at the time of a crime. In at least one town in Punjab, fifty Sikhs took out a procession and distributed sweets to celebrate.[68] It was a gesture that engrained bitterness, cried out for retaliation – and was to become all too common during the next four years.

The Punjab election campaign and the hunt for the murderers went on simultaneously. Bhindranwale was involved in both. Central-government police questioned him in Amritsar on 11 May. By the end of the month, he was seeking 'anticipatory bail' in expectation of being arrested once the assembly elections were out of the way.[69]

This raises the question of his relations with the Congress (I). Later, various sources claimed that Bhindranwale campaigned for the party.[70] To be sure, he attempted to avenge Amrik Singh's defeat in the SGPC elections. Bhindranwale and friends backed a candidate of their own against their old Akali foe, and this was expected to help the Congress by snatching votes from the Akalis. It did not work; the Akali won. And though at least one Congress (I) candidate was a Bhindranwale supporter, this scarcely represented full-scale Bhindranwale participation in the Congress (I) campaign.[71]

Had Bhindranwale been closely associated with the Congress (I), he might have expected to be left alone after their victory. Rather, the central police in September got warrants for the arrest of one of his brothers in the Sant Nirankari Mission murder case, and in November, rumours flew that Bhindranwale himself was to be arrested.[72] By that time, the president of the SGPC was assuring him of full support. No Sikh wanted to be against him.

Indeed, the evidence suggests that Bhindranwale exercised a cunning independence, playing the factional antagonisms of Punjab politics with knowledge and skill. In August, for example, he praised the new Congress (I) Chief Minister, Darbara Singh, 'for strictly following the Sikh norms', unlike the politicians of the Akali Dal.[73]

In this independence lay much of Bhindranwale's appeal. It left him untainted by close association with any of the older political leaders, yet at the same time suggested that he knew how to handle them. For a younger generation, nurturing a romanticism that only literacy, leisure and constant exposure to the past can breed, the older politicians, immersed in their endless factional wars, exercise little appeal. What many youths look for is a dashing figure who confirms what they want to believe about their history and holds out promises about a brave, exciting future. This Bhindranwale did.

In all-India terms, the Bhindranwale phenomenon is not unique. The film star, N. T. Rama Rao, who founded a political party and won elections in Andhra Pradesh in the space of a few months in 1982–3, represents a similar process. His party, the Telugu Desam, stresses the worth and the glorious history of the Telugu-speaking people and points to the indignities they experience from callous, inept governments in New Delhi. The revolution in communications – the striking increases in literacy and vernacular press readership together with the powerful impact of the booming film industry – allowed Rama Rao to lay his interpretation of the past and vision of the future before millions of Telugus.[74] In both Punjab and Andhra Pradesh, the process at work is similar. The form differs because regional cultures differ. Rama Rao started a political party which exploits his film-star, 'good-guy' fame in a state where people have long flocked to the cinemas. Bhindranwale, a Jat Sikh sant from Punjab, evoked folk memories of the stormy eighteenth century and ended up surrounded by killer gangs.

ROMANTICS OVERSEAS: ARE SIKHS A NATION?

As one might have expected, the narrow Congress victory (sixty-three out of 117 seats) in the Punjab legislative elections in May 1980 brought no tranquillity. Within the Congress, two old foes – Darbara Singh, the Jat, as Chief Minister, and Zail Singh, the Ramgarhia, as Home Minister of the Government of India – squared off as Kairon and Rarewala had done twenty years before. Though both faithful acolytes of Mrs Gandhi, they harboured for each other an 'unconcealed animosity', which constituted 'an open scandal'. Reports quoted Darbara Singh as saying: 'My biggest problem is the Union Home Minister'.[75]

Within the Akali Dal, the fall from power and reduction to thirty-seven seats in the assembly intensified factional battles. In August, the party split formally into two groups. The former party president, Jagdev Singh Talwandi, was expelled and took with him his allies to form an Akali Dal (Talwandi). A new president for the main group was installed: another, older sant, Harchand Singh Longowal (1934–85).

In these circumstances of narrow majorities, deep divisions and devious old-style plots, the role of Sikh romantics overseas grew in importance. Although some of these men had not lived in the Punjab for thirty years or more, they continued to wear the Five Ks in Britain, the USA, Canada and elsewhere; they cherished visions of Guru Gobind Singh and long-lost glories. In this, they are no different from other migrant communities. Scots overseas still talk readily about Bonnie Prince Charlie (1720–87) and listen faithfully to the sentimental songs of Robert Burns (1759–96). For Sikhs, romantic notions help to enliven mundane yet tolerable jobs in Yorkshire, British Columbia or California and to deflect the taunts of non-Sikhs about the Five Ks. Yet unlike Scots, who showed no great enthusiasm for Bonnie Prince Charlie's cause, even when he returned to 'liberate' them in 1745, Sikhs have a near-at-hand legacy of active support for revolutionary movements in India. People alive in the 1980s can remember the Ghadr movement of 1915. Romantic notions can inspire concrete actions.

On 16 June 1980, Jagjit Singh Chauhan's supporters (he was back in Britain by this time) proclaimed 'Khalistan' at the Golden Temple in Amritsar. Chauhan himself was named the president of what was to be a 'purely Sikh State'. The proclamation, its organisers claimed, was made simultaneously in the USA, West Germany, Britain, Canada, and France. The Government of India dismissed the proclamation as 'a mad man's dream'. By August 'Khalistan' postage stamps, apparently printed in Canada, were being sent to newspapers and colleges.[76]

The dabbling of overseas Sikhs suggested useful ploys to the rival Akali Dal groups. By April 1981, each group had passed resolutions announcing that the Anandpur Sahib Resolution would be revived and declaring that 'Sikhs are a nation'.[77] More important, a conference in March was attended by a wealthy American-based Sikh, Ganga Singh Dhillon, who shocked the Indian government by his repeated statements that 'Sikhs are a nation'. Dhillon later claimed that he was not advocating, at that stage, a separate Sikh state, simply genuine autonomy for Punjab within India.

But perhaps what was most revealing was his bearing. The tough US correspondent of *India Today*, who interviewed him in his 'modest house' near Washington, DC, found a man capable of 'gushing sentimentality' who 'can weep openly and unabashedly when moved by a thought or remembrance'. Overseas romantics now were far more capable of influencing politics in Punjab than in the days when the *Komagata Maru* steamed at 10 miles an hour from Hong Kong to Vancouver.[78]

There was growing evidence that cultural appeals evoked more response from more Sikhs than those based on constitutional points or economics. Although the profits from agriculture had undoubtedly fallen since the mid-1970s, and a credible case could be made about the lack of central-government investments in Punjab, such issues were for the conference table, not the public platform. An attempt to build an Akali agitation around better terms for farmers 'did not find much enthusiasm' in December 1980.[79]

The revivalism of Bhindranwale and the romanticism of overseas Sikhs blended with the anxieties of ordinary people in a time of rapid change. This generated enthusiasm for symbolic acts. In May 1981, for example, the All-India Sikh Students' Federation, led by Bhindranwale's confidant, Amrik Singh, began a campaign to ban the sale of tobacco within the walled city of Amritsar. Hindu traders objected. A Hindu-led pro-cigarette procession of 10 000, some carrying swords, marched through Amritsar on 29 May. On 31 May, 20 000 Sikhs, many brought in from the countryside by appeals from Bhindranwale and 'almost all . . . armed', paraded through the city.[80]

As a means of dramatically dividing Sikhs from Hindus, the issue was ideal. Hindus knew Sikhs spurned tobacco; Sikhs knew Hindus smoked. In the past, this rarely caused problems, but now crowds of thousands were provoked into the streets. Sikh and Hindu newspapers in Jullundur exchanged biting attacks. These contributed to the hatred which Sikh extremists harboured for the Hindu newspaper editor, Lala Jagat Narain, and which led to his sten gun killing on 9 September.

September 1981 marks a turning point. Until then, violence was scattered, Akali demands were almost ritualistic, and the mood was one of 'we've seen it all before'. The rival Akali factions, to be sure, were raising their rhetorical bets. Sant Harchand Singh Longowal, new president of the Akali Dal, told a 'world Sikh convention' in Amritsar on 26 July that Sikhs would 'resort to direct action' to achieve their goals, which included recapturing 'their glorious past ... enshrined in the words "*Raj Karega Khalsa*" '.[81] More concretely, he listed forty-five examples of wrongs to Sikhs that must be remedied. These included demands for Amritsar to be declared a holy city and for a top-grade train to be called the Golden Temple Express. However, he explained that the cry 'Sikhs are a nation' did not mean a demand for secession from India. Though an Akali demonstration in New Delhi on 7 September drew an estimated 100 000 Sikh marchers, it was orderly and peaceful.[82] Two days later, however, the murder of Jagat Narain shattered the illusion that the old nationalist-style political customs still held sway.

Warrants for Bhindranwale's arrest in connection with the killing were issued on 13 September. He was in neighbouring Haryana state, and the police attempt to capture him early on the morning of 14 September ended in a spasmodic gun-battle and Bhindranwale's escape in a truck. He and his associates managed to travel 250 kilometres through Punjab and cross the Sutlej River without being spotted by police. He arrived at his headquarters of Chowk Mehta at daybreak on 14 September and announced that he would surrender to police at a time of his choosing.[83]

Giving his followers four days' notice, he named his day – a Sunday, 20 September 1981. His followers streamed to Chowk Mehta from all over Punjab, along with the presidents of the Akali Dal and the SGPC. Of the top three Akali leaders, only Badal, the ex-Chief Minister, absented himself from Bhindranwale's surrender. After speeches, Bhindranwale gave himself up in front of a crowd of 50 000 people. Then the rioting began; before it was over the police had opened fire and eight people were dead.[84] Twenty-five days later, the police admitted they had no evidence worth presenting to a court; Bhindranwale was released. He was never again in police custody.

The aftermath of his arrest produced a string of firsts which emphasised the novelty of what was happening in Punjab. The Jullundur market was sten-gunned on 22 September (pp. 94–95). An Indian Airlines plane was hijacked to Lahore on the 29th. Two people were killed in a shoot-out at the Secretariat in Chandigarh in an attempt to murder a leading Nirankari official on 16 October. A Hindu politician and another Nirankari were murdered on 24 October and 17 November respectively. On 19 November the first two policemen were killed and their weapons stolen. On 29 November a bomb exploded in Bhindranwale's own headquarters, killing three. The police were not allowed to investigate, and whether it was an attempt on Bhindranwale's life or an accident with explosives was never clear. And on 21 December, Santokh Singh, the most powerful Sikh in New Delhi, closely connected to the Congress (I) and a regular associate of Bhindranwale, was shot and killed. His murderer, a former colleague, was himself killed on the spot. The motive was said to be frustrated ambition and wounded pride. However, another controversial story circulated that the man had in fact joined the Akali Dal and the Akalis saw dangers for themselves in a possible alliance between Santokh Singh in New Delhi and Bhindranwale in Punjab.[85] The range of possibilities for factional alignments seemed endless.

Yet something was different. In part, it was Bhindranwale's astuteness in keeping all factions chasing his favour. This aloofness itself contributed to the fact that he was now 'extremely popular among the Sikh masses', his short spell in jail having made his 'influence ... greater than when he was a free man'.[86] By the end of the year, the Punjab police, long known for their rough ways, were writing meekly to Bhindranwale 'with a request that in case' any wanted criminals were seen near his headquarters, 'they should be handed over to the police'. Bhindranwale cheekily replied that the police might like to surrender their guns to his *gurdwara* for safe-keeping. It was announced at the same time that he and his followers would now do their religious tours in a new 48-seat bus, costing US \$45 000 and donated by Sikh admirers in Bombay and Calcutta.[87] For the next two and a half years, no faction made a move in Punjab without considering the response it would draw from Bhindranwale. Punjab, never more prosperous, literate or widely read, looked constantly to a man who went to school for only five years.

Thus Parkash Singh Badal, university graduate, landlord, faction leader, twice Chief Minister, stood in jacket and tie on 27 February 1984, pages of the Indian constitution smouldering in his hand. He was to spend most of the year in detention. Bhindranwale, white-smocked, blue-turbaned, iron arrow in hand, was dead before the year was half over. The ensuing chain of events led to the assassination of Mrs Gandhi herself on 31 October. Punjab's factional struggles, time-honoured, long deadly, yet held in check by the narrow horizons of peasant life, were swept into an open sea of mass politics. The innovations accompanying the 'green revolution' brought a keen sensitivity to outside economic forces. They brought, as well, increased travel to foreign places and regular mobility within Punjab. They brought buses, motor cycles and modern weapons. They brought schools and history books and newspapers – and produced youths who had not just the ability, but the time, to read them. They also brought a need to explain what was happening – what the transformations meant for hallowed customs and beliefs. Overseas romantics had their own ideas, which could now be broadcast as never before, and, like any mass appeal, found some response. Against this background, the old-style factional struggles went on, one side raising the bets against another, only dimly aware that their former ability to influence behaviour was fast diminishing – as the rise of Bhindranwale, the leader who communicated directly with 'the people', suggested.

7 Explosion

On the morning of 2 November 1984, as organised mobs continued their attacks on Sikhs in New Delhi and elsewhere, the story on the front page of *The Statesman* drove home the fact that India was plunged into its gravest crisis since independence. The newspaper, perhaps the most respected daily in India, reported that a serving Sikh major-general had been arrested for his part in Mrs Gandhi's assassination two days earlier.

Officials denied that a senior officer had been arrested. But a veteran journalist in New Delhi, who thought the story probably true, pointed out: 'What else could they do? They couldn't confirm it in the present conditions'.[1]

The army represents the last resort of the Indian state. Since its revival after the humiliating defeat in the war against China in 1962, it has been one of the country's most successful institutions: efficient, reliable and largely free from political meddling. In spite of recent signs of hardening arteries,[2] it still commands the confidence and admiration of large numbers of Indians. Indeed, 'call out the army' has become too common a remedy for natural disasters and public disorder. The point is this: if the army were to dissolve, the state could not survive. And in November 1984, a shadow of doubt hung over the army for the first time since independence.

The doubt concerned the dependability of Sikh military men, who compose at least 10 per cent of the country's million-strong armed forces. The precise proportion is unclear. Although Jagjit Singh Aurora, the retired Lieutenant-General, estimated Sikhs to be as many as 30 per cent, Sikhs in recent years have often complained that their proportion was falling. An article in the *Sikh Review* in 1984 asserted that it was 'less than 12 per cent'. In any case, at least 100 000 – and probably closer to 150 000 – serving military personnel are Sikhs, who are, moreover, concentrated in the officer corps and the fighting

148

branches.[3] In June 1984, after the army stormed the Golden Temple, young Sikh enlisted-men at the regimental centre of the Sikh Regiment in Bihar mutinied, killed their commanding officer and set out to reach Punjab. At the time, well-informed journalists estimated that 1000 Sikh soldiers in camps from Bombay to Calcutta had mutinied and that fifty or more had been killed as they were rounded up by other troops.

Later, however, *India Today* reported that 'nearly 2000 Sikh soldiers' were to be brought before courts martial. The story of the arrested major-general seemed to die out, though it was reported that a brigadier would be charged with 'dereliction of duty'.[4] The legacy of the June 1984 mutinies will remain with the army, and Punjab politics, for years.

During British rule, Sikhs may have constituted as much as a quarter of the Indian Army. Today, there are more than 100 000 Sikh servicemen. There are, as well, tens of thousands of retired Sikh soldiers living in Punjab and other parts of India. Since the Indian Army has always been entirely composed of volunteers, these men served for fairly long periods and were thoroughly trained. Most of them, too, saw active service in the wars with China (1962) or Pakistan (1965, 1971). Punjab has the makings of a formidable people's army.

This depth of military experience, the dependence of the army on Sikhs and the dispersal of Sikhs throughout India recalled a parallel from recent world history which reinforced the feeling of gravest-crisis in the days after Mrs Gandhi's murder. This was the so-called 'Biafra scenario'.

More than 20 per cent of Sikhs in India, roughly 3 million people, live outside Punjab. Following Mrs Gandhi's assassination, as Sikhs throughout the country were attacked by mobs, there were increasing reports of Sikhs fleeing to Punjab. If a mass migration were to occur – if 3 million people, each with a tale of suffering and bitterness were to arrive in Punjab – the chances of reprisals against Punjabi Hindus would increase immeasurably. So, too, would a 'fortress Punjab' mentality among Sikhs and the possibility of secessionist civil war.[5]

Most Punjabis have heard about (if they did not experience) the events of 1947. In March 1947, Muslims attacked Sikhs in the Rawalpindi area of western Punjab, and many victims of these attacks carried tales of horror with them when they fled to eastern Punjab. Then at partition in August 1947, Sikhs in eastern Punjab attacked and expelled Muslims. Scenes in the Golden Temple in late November 1984 bear a frightening resemblance to this sequence of events. Victims of anti-Sikh riots, 'a majority of them with their hair and beards shaven, were presented before large [and obviously outraged] ... audiences. These were Sikhs who reached the relative safety of Punjab, surviving the deathly steeplechase as mobs attacked them in their houses [and] shops and besieged rail and roads'.[6]

The possibility of a general migration of Sikhs to Punjab raises the chilling comparison with Nigeria. In 1966, a military coup and counter-coup in Nigeria led to attacks on Ibo people in the Muslim-dominated north of the country. Though most Ibo remained in their adopted localities after the first wave of rioting in May, renewed attacks on Ibo in September and October sent them streaming towards their 'homeland' in eastern Nigeria. By May 1967 there were estimated to be 1.5 million refugees in eastern Nigeria. In the same month, 'Biafra' proclaimed its independence, and the $2\frac{1}{2}$-year Nigerian civil war began in which millions were killed by bullets, starvation or disease.[7]

For India, the 'Biafra scenario' holds out the prospect of appalling ramifications. Unlike eastern Nigeria, Punjab shares a border with a powerful neighbour hostile to India, which harbours a grudge going back at least to the war of 1971, the victory of the Indian Army and the emergence of Bangladesh. There is a line of thought in Pakistan which says: 'India dismembered our country in 1971; we should welcome the opportunity to dismember India'.

Moreover, unlike Biafra, the high proportion of Sikh soldiers in the Indian Army (or retired from it) means that Punjab already has tens of thousands of men experienced, not merely in the use of weapons, but in battlefield tactics. The skilful resistance at the Golden Temple in June 1984 showed that. In certain circumstances, Pakistan could allow military supplies to flow across the border into Punjab to arm such men.

Finally, the 'Biafra scenario' has an alarming international dimension. Amritsar is 300 miles (480 kilometres) from New Delhi, and only 400 miles (640 kilometres) from Kabul in Afghanistan, where the Soviet army is in occupation. The USA keeps its toehold in the region by sending military aid to Pakistan. Because Punjab is in the superpower cock-pit as

Biafra never was, India has grounds for fearing foreign involvement in Punjab.

This chapter carries the story of the ferment in Punjab down to the storming of the Golden Temple in June 1984. By moving from the widest focus to the narrowest, it attempts to identify various ingredients in the brew: the role of 'foreign involvement'; the significance of the continual, but unsuccessful rounds of negotiations between the central government and Sikh politicians; the contest in Punjab itself for the allegiance of large numbers of people; the accelerating slide into violence; and the destruction of the Punjab police as an effective institution. Each aspect raises more general questions: about the nature of India's central government under Mrs Gandhi; about the behaviour of people caught up in the head-spinning dilemmas of rapid 'modernisation'; and about the fragility and decay of Indian institutions in the years since about 1970.

FOREIGN HANDS

The White Paper published by the Government of India in July 1984 hints darkly about 'the terrorists ... receiving different types of active support from certain foreign sources'. To say more, however, the report goes on, 'would not be in the public interest'. Newspapers reported that the government wanted to name the CIA but was warned off by the USA.[8]

Others, including a former Indian High Commissioner to Canada, have claimed that 'CIA money was at work and senior US senators' were involved.[9] Soviet sympathisers in India have accused the USA of starting 'a tough battle for destabilising India, if possible balkanising her'. In evidence, they refer to a speech which Jean Kirkpatrick, former US ambassador to the United Nations, is alleged to have given to a conservative policy group in Washington in February 1982, in which she discussed the possibility of the 'balkanisation of India'. The document, however, has been fairly convincingly exposed as a forgery.[10] Although Ganga Singh Dhillon and Jagjit Singh Chauhan may well have received hospitality from a few politicans in the USA,[11] this is a long way from official US support for 'Khalistan'.

The foreign triumphs of the 'Khalistanis' have in fact been

meagre. When they managed to sneak an entry for 'Khalistan' into the national listings of a trade directory published by the government of the Canadian province of British Columbia, they crowed about 'recognition'. In fact, of course, the only recognition the entry represented was that clerks in minor offices in British Columbia are not particularly concerned with political geography.[12] If, as has been claimed, millions of rupees have been collected overseas for Khalistan activities in India, they do not seem to have bought a great deal.[13] In any event, the equipment – the weapons and the motor cycles – that the gunmen used in Punjab was easily within the reach of country and city youths. If large sums were involved, they were going elsewhere.

There is, however, a more subtle and important foreign influence at work in Punjab. It represents another aspect of the revolution in communications that made possible the old-but-new phenomenon of Bhindranwale. A leading Indian political scientist partially identified it when he spoke of an 'invisible presence' in India: the Western media which had focused on Bhindranwale and thereby enhanced his prestige.[14] The speed with which ideas and reports were transmitted out of India, reacted to by Sikhs (and others) overseas, and those reactions then fed back to India, meant that this foreign audience itself now played a part in Punjab's politics. Reports that a man had been noticed in the foreign media made him seem more influential in his own place. Once the pendulum of international media reporting began to swing, it was difficult to stop. It added a new consideration to every political problem.

The foreign consideration was particularly important for Mrs Gandhi who planned 1982 and 1983 as years of personal and international triumph. One of her first acts on regaining power in 1980 was to revive the Indian offer to stage the Asian Games in November 1982. These were to be followed in March 1983 by a full meeting of the 97-member Non-Aligned Movement, of which she was to assume the chairmanship. And in November 1983, the Commonwealth Heads of Government were to meet in India.

All these were international media events, intended to project both India and Indira Gandhi. All were scheduled for New Delhi, with half a million Sikh residents and only a few hours' drive from Punjab itself. Concern to impress the international audience affected timing, negotiations and decisions about Punjab, and in this sense, the 'foreign hand' – more correctly, the foreign eye – was often present.

INDIAN TALKS

Consideration of the foreign audience and the international events planned for India led to protracted rounds of talks between the central government and representatives of the Akali Dal from October 1982 to May 1984. Indeed, the government White Paper reported nine secret meetings alone, plus three publicly announced meetings involving Mrs Gandhi, four involving members of the central cabinet and ten including members of the opposition as well.[15]

Why did this apparent readiness to negotiate culminate in a full-scale battle at the Golden Temple and the murder of Mrs Gandhi? The answer, it seems to me, captures the essence of Mrs Gandhi's failure – the suspicion she both harboured and engendered and the centralisation she pursued at every opportunity. I try to explore these aspects in more detail in Chapter 8. For now, let us look at the two common explanations of why the seemingly endless talks brought no results.

From Mrs Gandhi's side, the story is very much that of Mr Gladstone and the Irish Question according to *1066 and All That*: every time Mr Gladstone got close to the answer, the Irish changed the question. On 2 June 1984, the day Mrs Gandhi announced the deployment of the army in Punjab, she 'regretted that the Akali leaders added new demands and adopted a harder attitude whenever a settlement appeared in sight'.[16] As evidence, she cited the Akali call, made only in 1984, for amendment of the constitution to remove an apparently innocuous phrase that bracketed Sikhs and Hindus.

Mrs Gandhi's admirers would have it that she and her helpers were up against slippery, desperate men who would say or do anything on the spur of the moment if it seemed likely to relieve them of a political dilemma in Punjab. Thus they could never be relied upon to hold firm to a set of demands or an agreement.

There is, however, another side to the story of the fruitless talking. This version, which is not simply Akali propaganda, emphasises the duplicity of the central government, Mrs Gandhi's unwillingness to delegate authority and the constant attempts to manipulate Punjab events either to serve Congress (I) electoral interests or Mrs Gandhi's international reputation.

One example, whose consequences had widespread effects, illustrates this version well. In August 1982, the Akali Dal and Bhindranwale had united in a civil-disobedience movement which put more than 30 000 men into Punjab's 7000-capacity prisons by October. The Asian Games, the first of the prestige ventures, were to begin in New Delhi on 19 November, and a number of intermediaries were carrying messages between the central government and the Akalis to try to get the agitation stopped. One of these was Swaran Singh, a Congress politician of long standing and a former Foreign Minister.

In the space of two weeks in early November, Mrs Gandhi's representatives and the Akalis twice appeared to have reached agreements which would have transferred Chandigarh to Punjab and simply referred the dispute over the sharing of river water to a Supreme Court judge. On the first occasion, however, the agreement fell apart the following day when the announcement in parliament did not square with the terms the Akali representatives believed they had accepted the previous night.[17]

On the second occasion, on the night of 18 November, Akali negotiators and central-government officials met at the house of Mrs Gandhi's principal secretary, Dr P. C. Alexander, in a leafy New Delhi suburb, less than ten minutes' walk from Mrs Gandhi's own residence. Again, an agreement seemed to be reached, but the Akali representatives called in a Sikh member of the Communist Party of India (Marxist), Harkishan Singh Surjit, and asked that the national opposition parties be included in the settlement of the territorial disputes. Mrs Gandhi, informed by her bureaucrats, was 'infuriated' and refused.[18] She is said to have consulted the Congress (I) Chief Minister of Haryana, whose state stood to lose territory under the proposals. He assured her that his government would prevent any Sikhs reaching New Delhi to disrupt the Asian Games.[19]

The immediate result was that thousands of Sikhs from all walks of life were humiliated on the roads and in the railway stations of Haryana in November and December 1982. The

Haryana government used all the police at its disposal to block roads, search cars and prevent Sikhs from travelling to the national capital. The retired major-general, J. S. Bhullar, who by 1985 had become secretary-general of a newly-founded World Sikh Organisation operating out of Washington, DC, recalled how he was stopped by police who 'searched me'. His army identity card did no good. 'They said, "We don't bother with these identity cards." It was quite insulting. I was very hurt. I got damn mad.' By the end of 1982, Bhullar was working with the Akali Dal and had become a devotee of Bhindranwale. The story of Shabeg Singh, the retired major-general who was killed leading the resistance inside the Golden Temple in June 1984, is similar. He went 'on record as saying that after the humiliation meted out to him in Haryana, he decided to join Bhindranwale'.[20] Shabeg Singh, to be sure, had other grievances against the central government (he left the army under a corruption cloud), but the insults of the Asian Games (which passed off without disruption) soured the attitude of thousands of Sikhs towards the national government.

The abortive talks of November 1982 have an even wider significance. First, they demonstrate Mrs Gandhi's need to turn every subordinate into a message-boy and to make all major decisions herself. Second, they show the electoral and international considerations that influenced the prime minister's conduct of the talks with the Akalis.

Her attitude towards her negotiator, Swaran Singh, is revealing. He appears to have believed in early November that he had built a genuine agreement with the Akalis, but this was scuttled by the changes that appeared in the statement to parliament. Journalists at the time wrote that Mrs Gandhi 'developed cold feet' and 'reduced Swaran Singh to a messenger'. He later told Kuldip Nayar that he 'swore to himself not to get involved [again] in the talks'.[21] Mrs Gandhi may have had fears about Swaran Singh's negotiations, but these had little to do with the substance of the talks. Swaran Singh had deserted her after her fall from power in 1977. If he were to get the credit for successful negotiations, how would her loyalists in Punjab react?

Her second misgiving related to elections and grand occasions. First, she had to ensure the success of the Asian Games, and by keeping talks going in November, she was preventing Akali politicians from preparing demonstrations. But she also had to consider elections in various Indian states. In May 1982, the Congress (I) had narrowly won elections in Haryana state, and the prospect of these elections had influenced talks with the Akalis earlier in the year. Table 7.1 sets out the various major events which the Congress (I) Party had to take into account from 1982 to 1985.

TABLE 7.1   *Congress (I) party-considerations, 1982–5*

May 1982	elections in Haryana
November	Asian Games; elections in Nagaland
January 1983	elections in Andhra Pradesh, Karnataka and Tripura
February	elections in New Delhi
March	elections in Assam and Meghalaya; Non-Aligned Movement conference in New Delhi
June	elections in Jammu and Kashmir
November	Commonwealth Heads of Government Meeting in New Delhi
Before January 1985	national general elections

Elections imposed limits on Mrs Gandhi's readiness to negotiate with Akali politicians – especially elections in Punjab's neighbours (Haryana, New Delhi and Jammu and Kashmir). She could offer no concession to Punjab that might anger voters, or inspire politicians, in other states.

There was a further, more sinister element. She appears to have grown increasingly aware of the possibility that in north Indian states, where Sikhs were a noticeable, somewhat resented minority, she could gain electoral advantage by taking a tough line with the Akali Dal. In New Delhi in February 1983 the Congress (I) won an outright majority in both the metropolitan council and municipal corporation. Elsewhere, however (except in the bloody, bungled elections in Assam) it received major setbacks. In January, it was overthrown in two long-established strongholds, Andhra Pradesh and Karnataka, and in June, it failed to dent the hold of the National Conference in Jammu and Kashmir.

As the results of the 1982–3 state elections came in, it appears that Mrs Gandhi herself sensed not only the changing political climate but a way of dealing with it. The new anti-Congress regional forces could be portrayed as greedy and 'anti-national' because they demanded more powers and criticised the central government. 'No community', she told journalists after another round of talks with the Akalis broke down in January 1983, 'could hope to become strong by weakening the Centre.'[22]

By standing up to those who tried to 'weaken the Centre', the Congress (I) could portray itself as the protector of long-suffering Hindu India living on the Gangetic Plain. People in these areas were also experiencing (though less intensely) the effects of the communications revolution that was crackling through Punjab and other regions. Might not, therefore, large masses of voters in the Hindu, Hindi-language heartland be rallied by appeals to *their* language or *their* religion?

The electoral arithmetic is attractive. The area contains 41 per cent of the seats in the national parliament (222 out of 542). If Gujarat (26 seats) and Maharashtra (48) are added – and they have more in common with the Gangetic core than with the Dravidian south or the brittle northern and eastern edges – the percentage rises to 55. With national general elections due by January 1985, Mrs Gandhi had rational political reasons for not being particularly sorry if the 'Punjab talks' constantly stalled over something that could be portrayed as 'Sikh intransigence'.

And stall the talks did. A further round collapsed in January 1983, and Akali legislators (four MPs and thirty-six MLAs) submitted their resignations, to take effect from 21 February. On 5 February, the Congress (I) won the elections in New Delhi.

In November 1982, Mrs Gandhi ruled out the participation of the opposition in discussions aimed at a settlement. In February, however, the inclusion of the opposition parties in a new series of negotiations lent weight to the contention that her objections in November had been for purely tactical reasons.[23]

At the same time, however, heavy external considerations also weighed on the Akali politicians. They did indeed change their demands and emphases. A journal unsympathetic to both sides condemned 'the lack of honesty of purpose on the part of either party'.[24] Yet Akali politicians hungered for a settlement that would get them back within reach of power and that they could defend against the inevitable charges that they had betrayed Sikh interests.

The 'forty-five demands' of 1981, which stressed religious discrimination against Sikhs, had shifted by April 1982 to a heavy emphasis on the injustice of the way in which river waters were shared among Punjab, Haryana, Rajasthan and New Delhi.[25] By the end of the year, the ownership of Chandigarh and boundary disputes with neighbouring states were to the fore. River-sharing remained a preoccupation in 1983, but in January 1984 two new demands surfaced: deletion of an explanation in the Indian constitution which clubbed together Hindus, Jains, Sikhs and Buddhists. and the call for a separate code of Sikh personal law.[26]

In the background of these changes in emphasis loomed the various versions and interpretations of the Anandpur Sahib Resolution and the debate over whether Sikhs were a *qaum*. This Persian word dated from an age when there were no nation-states, and its most appropriate translation into English seems to be 'community'. Such a translation poses no problems. But it is sometimes translated as 'nation'. Indeed, Jawaharlal Nehru called his English newspaper the *National Herald* and its Urdu equivalent *Qaumi Awaz* (*awaz* means voice). Sikhs are certainly justified in referring to themselves as a *qaum*, but when the word is then translated into English as 'nation', the ramifications for the Indian state are considerable. Discussion of what is a *qaum* and how the word should be translated into English is almost certain to sidetrack talks on more concrete issues.[27]

As sympathy for gunmen and Khalistanis slowly spread, as a result of incidents like the Asian Games humiliations, Akali politicians felt greater difficulty in agreeing to central-government proposals. Yet as late as November 1983, after two incidents of random slaughter of Hindu bus passengers, the Akalis supported a day's reconciliation strike throughout Punjab, Haryana and Himachal Pradesh called by other parties.[28] And in February 1984, they went to New Delhi for a further round of three-way talks including the opposition. On 14 February, however, the day talks began, rioting between Hindus and Sikhs in towns of Haryana and Punjab resulted in the burning of a *gurdwara* in Panipat and fifteen deaths, the worst day's killing for ten months. The Akalis walked out of the talks in protest.[29] But as late as May, less than a month before the battle at the Golden Temple, Badal and others showed sufficient readiness to negotiate for the central government to think it worthwhile to release them from prison (where they had been since their burning of the constitution).[30]

Though they shifted their ground and constantly looked over their shoulders to see what the gunmen were doing, the Akali politicians were schooled in legislative factional politics and wanted to get back to them. The reason that so many rounds of talks failed had at least as much to do with the compulsions and advantages perceived by Mrs Gandhi as with the tendency of the Akalis to 'change the question'. Indeed, two of India's most distinguished political scientists contend that 'the Punjab problem' was essentially 'Mrs Gandhi's war against the Akali Party'. Once Bhindranwale had been used to destroy 'the political threat from the Akali Party', then he 'would be handled appropriately'.[31]

These are grave charges, yet the men who make them have notable records of scholarship and are not politicians themselves. They underline the fact that the Akali politicians did not comprehend the fast-moving transformation of individual behaviour that had overtaken Punjab and was spreading throughout India. Mrs Gandhi, on the other hand, sensed this change, even in the Hindu north, and this determined her tactics against the Akalis and her strategy for national elections. Her error – if this interpretation is correct – lay in believing that the growing violence in Punjab could be easily contained later.

SYMBOLS AND VIOLENCE

After Bhindranwale's release from custody in October 1981 when the police were unable to find sufficient evidence to charge him in connection with either the murder of the Sant Nirankari Mission chief or Jagat Narain, the struggle in Punjab became a struggle over symbols. What political symbols did the Indian state consider legitimate? What symbols were legitimate in the eyes of large numbers of Sikhs? What themes would arouse enthusiasm and support? In the past, when Sikh leaders like Master Tara Singh and Sant Fateh Singh went on fasts, they were accepting a technique of protest that the 'father of the nation', M. K. Gandhi, had made legitimate. By the 1980s, however, much of the official rhetoric of the Indian state provoked cynicism, not just in Punjab but in many parts of India. Both the old-style factional leaders, eager to hold constitutional power, and the men with grandiose visions wanted to win support. It was a question of deciding which symbols would achieve desired ends.

This clash shows up clearly as Bhindranwale's star rose throughout 1982. It began as a contest between river water on one side and cows' heads on the other. It led to violence that could only benefit the Khalistan visionaries (and perhaps the Congress).

When the fourth round of talks between Akalis and the central government ended unsuccessfully in April 1982, leading Akali participants contended that the issue was not so much discrimination against Sikhs as against Punjab: unjust attempts to steal its lifeblood, river water. The Ravi, Beas and Sutlej Rivers all flow through Punjab, but an elaborate canal system channels off surplus water, sending it south to irrigate dry areas in Haryana and Rajasthan. Additional dams and canals would allow more land to be irrigated.

The highest priorities are for the Thein Dam on the Ravi just north of Pathankot, and a canal to carry Sutlej water across Punjab and Haryana to the Jamuna River, which forms Haryana's eastern boundary (see Map 2.3). Mrs Gandhi awarded shares of river water among Punjab, Haryana and Rajasthan in 1976 during the 'emergency' when most Akalis were in jail and Zail Singh's deferential Congress government ruled in Punjab. Many Punjabis, especially Sikh agriculturalists, regarded the award as unfair. At the end of 1981, Mrs Gandhi revised the award, but this too, Akali leaders held, did not give Punjab its due. In April 1982, however, the Prime Minister announced that construction of both the Thein Dam on the Ravi and the Sutlej–Jamuna canal would begin at once. There was good reason for her timing: the state election in Haryana on 19 May.

April, however, is the beginning of the hot season when every drop of water in north India is precious and when people yearn for the monsoon but know it will not come until late June. 'Quarrels over [water] often led to murder', wrote

Prakash Tandon, 'almost as commonly as quarrels over women.' The suggestion that water was about to be taken from them appeared likely to arouse a large section of Punjabi cultivators.[32]

For Akali politicians, already sensing that they had formidable rivals in the glistening-eyed young men who talked of Guru Gobind Singh and carried guns, a campaign against the central government based on water had two advantages. It stirred emotions and it was a 'Punjab', not a 'Sikh' demand. For politicians like Badal, who saw an alliance between urban Hindus and prosperous Jat Sikh agriculturalists like himself as the way to gain legislative power, the 'theft' of Punjab's precious water promised to unite people rather than divide them. Badal's own ancestral lands in Ferozepur district, moreover, lie in dry country at the south-eastern extremity of the present canal system. When Mrs Gandhi inaugurated work on the Sutlej–Jamuna canal on 8 April, Akalis, supported by the Communist Party of India (Marxist), held a conference nearby to resolve their readiness to make 'supreme sacrifices to safeguard Punjab's interests'.[33] Such a resolution contrasted strikingly with customary Akali statements about the honour of the Sikh community.

The civil-disobedience movement to prevent the digging of the canal, however, did not elicit much enthusiasm. The work was going on in a corner of Patiala district, too far away from centres of population to capture attention. Furthermore, the campaign suggested too much of the discredited, nationalist-Gandhian style of political action. Having seen it all before, people took little notice.

The visionaries, on the other hand, eager for conflict, succeeded far better in the hunt for emotive symbols which would shock large numbers of people and force them to take sides. Just before dawn on the hot morning of 26 April, the bleeding heads of two cows were found in front of a Hindu temple in Amritsar.[34]

To Hindus throughout India, the cow is sacred, and though cow slaughter is not totally banned it is strongly discouraged in most states. Less than 1 per cent of India's estimated 180 million cattle are slaughtered each year, compared with 30–40 per cent in meat-eating Western countries.[35] Though Sikh religious teaching does not forbid it, Sikhs do not slaughter cattle or eat beef. In abstaining from beef, some Sikhs have argued that they help to justify the annoying claim that they are simply a sect of Hindus. Indeed, a Sikh businessman suggested to Joyce Pettigrew in the early 1970s that to underline Sikh separateness Sikhs should start eating beef.[36] Many Punjabi Hindus, moreover, are strict vegetarians. A senior public servant once confessed to a colleague in tones of state-secret confidentiality: 'Once, I ate an egg'. To such people, even the thought of killing cattle is outrageous and the possibility of eating beef, nauseating.

The rioting in Amritsar following the discovery of the cows' heads resulted in one death and a 24-hour curfew. In retaliation, packets of cigarettes were tossed into Sikh *gurdwaras* to defile them, and rioting spread to twenty Punjab towns. The Dal Khalsa, founded in August 1978 allegedly with the support of Congress (I) members, was said to be responsible for planting the cows' heads, in retaliation for the failure to ban tobacco in Amritsar. On 1 May 1982 the Government of India banned the Dal Khalsa and the National Council for Khalistan. Active members – the government claimed there were only seventy – took refuge in the Golden Temple and other *gurdwaras*, where they were still granting interviews to the press two years later.[37]

Comparison between the incident of the cows' heads and the campaign to defend river water underlies the fact that the old-style political techniques were jaded. Punjabis showed that increasingly in future they would respond to the novel and the outrageous. Bhindranwale combined both qualities, for though in some respects he was simply an old-fashioned sant, his theatricality, his call to a renewed purity and his exploitation of every means of communication made him a man to match film stars. By August 1982, Akali politicians were forced to go to him.

On 19 July, Bhindranwale's confidant, Amrik Singh, president of the All-India Sikh Students' Federation, was arrested on charges involving illegal arms and attacks on members of the Sant Nirankari Mission. The timing of the arrest appears to have owed a good deal to the battles within the Congress (I) between the factions of Zail Singh and Darbara Singh, whose 'feud', wrote an Indian journalist, 'is a major factor behind the present difficult situation'.[38]

Zail Singh left the Home Ministry in July to become President of India, but he and his supporters in Punjab were still intent on getting rid of Darbara Singh. 'We were all out for his exit', recalled Amarindar Singh, a former Congress (I) Member of Parliament (who would have been Maharaja of Patiala if the old princely states had still existed).[39] One possibility was a coalition between the Zail Singh forces and a section of Akalis, whose MPs and MLAs lent credibility to this picture by voting unitedly for Zail Singh for President (an election in which all Indian legislators vote).[40]

To protect himself – according to this version – Darbara Singh struck hard at a hornets' nest by arresting Amrik Singh. 'He felt', according to Amarindar Singh, 'that if some kind of controlled destabilisation took place in Punjab, Mrs Gandhi would not change horses in mid-stream.'[41] When news of the arrest reached Bhindranwale, the angry sant and his followers hastened to Amritsar by bus from their headquarters at Chowk Mehta 40 kilometres away and paraded the streets fully armed, defying bans against carrying weapons. Bhindranwale announced that groups of fifty-one volunteers would each day dare the police to arrest them until Amrik Singh and others were released. The whole Sikh community, Bhindranwale claimed, was being harassed and threatened.

The crackdown on Bhindranwale's friends destroyed the possibility of a section of Akalis joining with Zail Singh's followers to form a new government in Punjab. How could true Sikhs unite with the Congress (I) when the dynamic young sant said the whole community was in danger?

Indeed, in early August, the beginning of a powerful new movement signalled the fact that Bhindranwale was winning the war of symbols. The Akalis ended their desultory protest against the canal-digging in Patiala district and merged their campaign with Bhindranwale's in Amritsar. The aim was to put him in his place by taking over his agitation. In fact, Bhindranwale took over theirs.[42]

August proved a momentous month. Bhindranwale moved from his headquarters at Chowk Mehta to the Golden Temple complex, where he was immune from arrest since no Chief Minister seemed likely to repeat the disaster of 1955 and send in the police. He never made another public appearance outside the complex. August also produced two bungled hijacks of Indian Airlines planes, an unsuccessful attempt to murder the

Chief Minister and 10 000 arrests in the Bhindranwale–Akali Dal civil-disobedience campaign.[43] Close to 30 000 prisoners were in Punjab's overtaxed jails in October when Mrs Gandhi ordered their release to encourage talks and protect the Asian Games.

The campaign also produced 'martyrs' and further 'evidence' that Sikhs were 'second-class citizens'. On 11 September, a bus carrying prisoners collided with a train and more than thirty people were killed.[44] Four more were killed in New Delhi on 11 October when a procession carrying the ashes of those who died in the bus crash attempted to march to parliament. According to Akali leaders, it was a peaceful demonstration. According to the police, Sikh youths broke through a police cordon, 'their naked swords and daggers gleaming in the afternoon sun', reported the *Hindustan Times*.[45] To Sikh youths, such an account may well have suggested excitement and romance; even if four died, had not Bhindranwale said that the cause was just?

Bhindranwale himself had become a symbol whom everyone wanted to control. His appeal now reached not only idealistic youths but aggrieved elders as well. Bhullar, the retired major-general, humiliated on his way to New Delhi during the Asian Games, helped the Akalis to organise a conference of ex-servicemen in Amritsar in December 1982. Between 5000 and 10 000 participants pledged their support to the Anandpur Sahib Resolution. Bhullar was reported to regard Bhindranwale as 'a saviour of the Sikhs'.[46]

For the next eighteen months, while the gunmen and police killed and were killed, the politicians talked in public and manoeuvred behind the scenes. Each death, each set of failed talks and each too-clever-by-half ploy contributed to the mistrust and bitterness. Let us briefly trace the landmarks before we see how the morale of the Punjab police disintegrated.

SLIPPERY SLOPES

On 27 February 1983, one year to the day before Parkash Singh Badal burned the constitution in front of the Bangla Sahib Gurdwara in New Delhi, Mrs Gandhi herself made a public appearance at the same *gurdwara*. She announced to a cheering crowd that the central government was formally accepting the religious demands that the Akalis had been making for the past two years. All-India Radio would carry live broadcasts of hymns from the Golden Temple and parliament would pass an act to bring all *gurdwaras* in the country under a single management. Sikhs would also be allowed to carry *kirpans* up to nine inches long on Indian Airlines flights, and tobacco and meat shops near the Golden Temple would be moved.[47]

New Delhi's non-Jat Sikhs appeared to have supported the Congress (I) in the just-completed local elections. In part, the announcement was Mrs Gandhi's reward to them. But it was also a tactic to aid her supporters in Punjab. A journalist concluded that the announcement 'deprived [Akali] leaders of an opportunity to claim credit'.[48] The gesture said in effect: 'The Congress (I) will look after Sikh interests if only Sikhs will reject Akali politicians'. But undermining legislative politicians did not necessarily strengthen the Congress (I) in the long term. Indeed, in Punjab it was far more likely to turn younger Sikhs even more sharply towards the violent, glory-seeking alternatives. True political sagacity would have allowed the Akali legislative politicians some crumbs of credit which they could have used to bolster their own faltering position. Instead, they were driven to search for dramatic confrontations that would prevent Bhindranwale and those like him from denouncing them as spineless time-servers with no sense of honour or adventure.

The next stage in this seemingly inexorable march came on 4 April 1983 when the Akali Dal declared that it would block all traffic on Punjab's roads as part of its campaign to have the Anandpur Sahib Resolution accepted. In the violence on that day, armed central police trying to clear roads opened fire on demonstrators; twenty people were killed. It was the highest death toll for a single day – excluding the bus–train collision the previous August – since the shoot-out between the Sant Nirankari Mission and orthodox Sikhs (including Bhindranwale's followers) in April 1978.[49]

The deaths in the demonstrations on 4 April marked a significant break. Although Akalis claimed that more than a hundred Sikhs had already died in the campaign against the central government, no single day had been as dramatic as this one. The police claimed demonstrators had come armed, that primitive bombs had been thrown, and that there had been arson and firing from *gurdwaras*.[50] To the demonstrators, it was purely police oppression, another example of the excesses committed against 'peaceful agitators', further proof that Sikhs were second-class citizens.

This creation of new martyrs provided (in some minds, at least) legitimate targets for the men with the guns: the police, both Hindu and Sikh. Indeed, the picture that began to emerge in April 1983 was reminiscent of Ireland during 'the troubles' of 1918–21: police were murdered in the streets by gunmen who came 'on foot ... and then moved out of the bloody scenes with ease'.[51] Disintegrating police morale allowed the gunmen to become bolder. On 4 April, they raided a paramilitary armoury in Ferozepur and, apparently with the connivance of guards, escaped with fourteen sten guns, twenty-eight rifles and 350 rounds of ammunition. Gunmen looted two armouries in April (one of them in the adjoining state of Rajasthan) and escaped with more than 150 weapons and hundreds of rounds of ammunition. The guards appeared to have co-operated with the raiders.[52]

On 25 April the gunmen demonstrated that all police were potential targets when they murdered Avtar Singh Atwal, a Sikh Deputy Inspector-General, as he emerged from the main clock-tower entrance of the Golden Temple where he had gone to worship. Later, reports circulated that Atwal had been on some sort of special mission; whether spying or negotiating was unclear. What was perfectly clear, however, was the fact of his death: a devout Sikh cut down in front of the faith's holiest shrine. 'Littered a few paces away', wrote a journalist, 'was the "prasad" [consecrated food] tinged with . . . blood. The shots shattered Mr Atwal's head.'[53] First reports said that Atwal was shot from the balcony of the temple gate; later, it was said that his killer followed him outside, shot him as he was retrieving his shoes and turned the body over to make sure he was dead before going back into the temple.[54] Police posted nearby simply disappeared, a further indication of their demoralisation and fear. A 9-year-old boy was also killed by stray bullets. Atwal's major 'crime' had been his role in planning the ambush of a group of Bhindranwale's followers in March in which one person died and two returned wounded to the Golden Temple. Bhindranwale condemned Atwal's murder but blamed the Congress (I) state government.[55]

The murder of policemen went on unabated thereafter: a detective inspector on 18 June; four drowsy Sikh policemen on an illicit liquor stake-out on 14 July; a senior superintendent wounded and his guard killed on 21 September; then five constables in a week between 22 and 29 September.[56] The random slaughter of six Hindu bus passengers followed on 5 October, and the next day President's Rule was declared in Punjab. It made little difference. On 21 October 1983, a passenger train was derailed and nineteen people, most of them agricultural labourers, killed. Another bus was hijacked and four Hindu passengers murdered on 18 November.

At the same time, the central police forces deployed in Punjab began searches for weapons and gunmen. They staged more than 300 raids in Amritsar district alone by the end of October. 'Residents . . . were fast asleep', reported the *Tribune* about a typical swoop, 'when two companies of the B.S.F. [Border Security Force] and C.R.P. [Central Reserve Police] descended' at 3 a.m.[57] Such actions had a deadly inevitability about them. They were all that central police officers, ordered to get results, could think of. Yet each raid seemed to confirm what had previously been only vaguely considered: that Sikhs were 'slaves' even in their own birthplaces. By mid-November, there were said to have been more than 4000 arrests since early October.[58]

The rioting in the towns of Punjab and Haryana on 14 February 1984, which took more than a dozen lives, destroyed the hopeful talks in New Delhi and began the last swift slide into seemingly uncontrollable violence. The riots also gave bloody evidence of an organised Hindu counter-thrust to Sikh terrorists. The Hindu Suraksha Samiti (self-defence association) had been formed in Patiala at the end of 1982, and by February 1984 similar organisations were active in many of Punjab's towns.[59]

The catalogue of murders and sabotage shown in Table 7.2 emphasises the growing confidence of the gunmen and demoralisation of the police. It records simply the murders of prominent figures. Official statistics state that more than 130 people were killed between the imposition of President's Rule on 6 October and the end of March.[60]

TABLE 7.2   *Violence in Punjab, February–May 1984*

- 22 February, Sumit Singh, 30-year-old shaven-Sikh editor of a left-wing Punjabi magazine, near Amritsar
- 28 March, Harbans Singh Manchanda, president of the New Delhi *gurdwara* management committee, in New Delhi. (His predecessor, Santokh Singh, was murdered in December 1981.)
- 2 April, a Bharatiya Janata Party leader, Harbans Lal Khanna, in Amritsar
- 3 April, V. N. Tewari, university professor and Congress (I) member of the upper house of parliament, in Chandigarh
- 15 April, more than thirty railway stations in Punjab set on fire in co-ordinated raids on a Sunday morning
- 17 April, Surindar Singh Sodhi, close associate of Bhindranwale, in Amritsar
- c. 20 April, Baljit Kaur, allegedly responsible for the murder of Sodhi, in Amritsar
- c. 24 April, Squadron-Leader Paramjit Singh Walia, uncle of Sumit Singh (murdered on 22 February), near Amritsar
- 10 May, Giani Partap Singh, 85, former chief custodian of the Golden Temple, in Amritsar
- 12 May, Ramesh Chandar, son of Lala Jagat Narain (murdered 9 September 1981), in Jullundur

---

Some members of the Congress (I) may once have plotted to use Bhindranwale as a cat's paw. The bitter irony of such schemes was clear to all by the beginning of 1984. 'They wanted me to go to Delhi', he told an interviewer, 'but I refused. It is not fitting for a man to go to a woman. I said she should come to me.'[61] He now ran his own court from the Akal Takht, one of the inner buildings of the Golden Temple complex, to which he had moved in December 1983. Villagers came to him with their problems, Bhindranwale pronounced judgements and called frightened policemen on the telephone to instruct them on how a matter was to be settled. Journalists from all over the world sought interviews. The rough-hewn young sant – whose performances were 'like an extract from a bad comic show', according to M. J. Akbar – clearly enjoyed combining the roles of eighteenth-century princeling and twentieth-century media star.

He had also established his ascendancy over the other prominent sant, Harchand Singh Longowal, president of the Akali Dal. Longowal, Bhindranwale and Sant Fateh Singh came from remarkably similar backgrounds which reveal the strengths and limitations of sants as political leaders. All three were from the southern Punjab, and all three were sent off at an early age (10 years or younger) to live with Sikh religious teachers. Bhindranwale was the youngest of seven sons; Longowal the youngest of four; while Fateh Singh, it is simply said, was 'neglected' by 'his own parents'. For a superfluous son of none-too-wealthy peasant parents, the religious life is an honourable one. All three men had little formal education, but became accomplished in the skills required in *gurdwaras*.

Longowal, like Bhindranwale and Fateh Singh, acquired popularity among worshippers for his polished presentation of religious discourses and songs in praise of God. Like Fateh Singh, he did not marry, but based himself successively in a number of *gurdwaras* until the early 1950s when he settled at Longowal village near Sangrur. He acquired a reputation as an organiser and fund-raiser. He also became involved, as must anyone living in the *gurdwaras*, with Akali Dal and SGPC politics and was elected an MLA in 1969.

In April 1976, with the Akalis' civil-disobedience campaign against Mrs Gandhi's 'emergency' flagging, Longowal became the chief organiser and put new life into the movement. It ended only in January 1977 after Mrs Gandhi announced elections and began releasing prisoners. By 1979, Longowal had become president of the major faction of the Akali Dal.

It is plausible to interpret Longowal's rise after 1977 as part of an attempt to check Bhindranwale. Though already 'highly respected for his saintly bearing', simple habits and work during the 'emergency', Longowal 'shot into the limelight' in the middle of 1978, almost immediately after Bhindranwale's first notoriety – the gun-battle of 13 April. Bhindranwale was initially said to trust him, though by 1984 they had bitterly fallen out and 'Sant Bhindranwale', Longowal said, 'did not speak to me'.

In 1978, it is possible that Akali ministers, particularly Badal, the Chief Minister, aimed to use Longowal to thwart any attempt by the Congress (I) to manipulate Bhindranwale. A respected, older sant – such reasoning would have held – would surpass any attraction that Bhindranwale might exercise over Sikhs.

Longowal had a sound militant record: even in 1978, he was known 'for his advocacy of the "Anandpur Sahib Resolution"', though he also stressed that 'I do not make any distinction between the Hindus, the Sikhs and the Muslims'. He seemed an ideal figurehead, willing to appeal to both 'extremists' and moderates.

Bhindranwale, however, increasingly overshadowed him. Longowal had neither Bhindranwale's theatrical fire, nor the sophistication necessary to deal with complicated negotiations and persistent journalists. He sometimes found himself forced embarrassingly to change stories in mid-stream, and by 1982 newspapers were reporting that 'his credibility is in serious danger'. He was, another report concluded, 'courteous and good-intentioned but not as effective in party affairs as were the veterans of the past'. After the battle of the Golden Temple in June 1984, a foreign correspondent dubbed him 'the sorriest figure of all' because, though aware of the fortifying of the Golden Temple and Bhindranwale's growing armed power, his impotence had compelled him to feign ignorance of both.

Training from childhood in singing, harmonium-playing, Sikh scriptures and *gurdwara* politics enabled 'the veterans of the past' to build reputations and wield influence in Sikh institutions. But it was poor preparation for the fast-moving complexities of Indian politics in the 1980s. Indeed, Longowal himself seems once to have felt this. 'Only such graduates as can speak English', he told a reporter, 'should be sent to the [national parliament].' He became perhaps the outstanding example of an old-style politician tragically out of his depth in new conditions.[62] On 20 August 1985, less than a month after signing an agreement with Prime Minister Rajiv Gandhi, he was shot and killed during a religious service in a *gurdwara* near Sangrur (see 'Postscript').

DESTROYING AN INSTITUTION: THE POLICE

The murder of A. S. Atwal, the senior police officer, at the Golden Temple in April 1983 emphasised the disintegration of the Punjab police as a reliable institution. Proceeding side-by-side with the rise of the gunmen, the collapse of the police was closely linked to the same political rivalries. Indeed, the collapse stands as a case-study both of the destruction of institutions under Mrs Gandhi and of the 'green-revolution' changes in society.

Throughout India, divisions of rank within the police reflect class divisions in society as a whole. Holding the very top posts, and often moving from state to state, are members of the Indian Police Service (IPS), a nationally recruited body. To many ambitious young Indians, a career in the IPS is only slightly inferior to one in the civil service. Beneath the IPS are state cadres of middle-ranking officers, few of whom can hope to be promoted to the top, high-paying posts usually held by the IPS. And at the bottom are tens of thousands of constables and head constables, poorly paid and many barely literate. The system could be India in microcosm: a tiny, well-off national elite; comfortable, regional middle classes; and a vast mass of poor people who live from day to day.

Poor constables survive by exploiting their poor fellow citizens. It would be rare, for example, to find a traffic policeman attempting to charge a well-dressed businessman or official for a driving offence. A constable would only act against such people under direction of senior officers also belonging to the upper classes.[63]

That such a force is usually able to prevent widespread disorder testifies to the deference that still prevails among most of India's population, particularly the poor. But in Punjab in 1983 the morale of the police had collapsed, as is evident from their failure to go to Atwal's aid at the time of his murder.

There were two reasons, one largely technical, the other relating to widespread political interference. The technical problem was relatively simple, yet it well illustrates an argument of this book: that old-style leaders (police as well as politicians) only slowly began to realise that the game was different from the one that had been played for the past hundred years. Put simply, the gunmen were better equipped than the police. Mobility was the most obvious example. The gunmen rode motor cycles and drove cars. Most policemen had nothing more than a bicycle. Cars and motor cycles were intended for transporting officers not for chasing criminals. When the motor cycling gunmen sprayed the Jullundur market in 1981, none of the available police was capable of chasing them. In May 1984, the police were reported to have a thousand radios and sten guns – on order.[64] 'The criminal today is far ahead of the police', said a senior policeman in Punjab in December 1983. Though the police were barely in the bicycle age, they were expected to regulate and protect – and this is simply one example – 800 passenger buses a day that passed in and out of Amritsar.[65] The police were as overwhelmed by the new criminal as the old faction leaders were by the new style of mass politician.

The availability of automatic weapons, either procured through well-established smuggling channels into Pakistan or from Indian police or military sources, meant that the gunmen had far more fire-power than most policemen. A majority of the police were unarmed, and many of the armed police had nothing better than .303 rifles, a poor match at close quarters for a sten gun. If the police showed little enthusiasm for engaging, for example, the killers of Atwal, it may well have been because they feared they would draw more fire than they could return.

Political interference with the police is nothing new in Punjab or India. Joyce Pettigew recounts a bizarre and fascinating tale which contributed to the downfall of Kairon. It began with two factions fighting the elections for the headship of a village. The losers challenged the result in the courts. The winners replied by murdering members of the losing candidate's family. A new district superintendent of police, sympathetic to the losing candidate, planned the murder of the winning candidate. The latter, who knew Kairon, appealed to him for protection, but the police superintendent carried out the murder anyway, disguising it as 'an armed encounter with the police', a favourite police tactic for doing away with the troublesome. Unable to prove murder, Kairon demoted the police superintendent who thereby became a bitter enemy, 'fabricated evidence against the CM [Chief Minister]' and eventually embroiled the whole Kairon family in court cases and inquiries.[66]

It was well understood, therefore, that Punjab governments tried to appoint district superintendents who were tough 'but also susceptible to political control'. During the police strike of 1979, the *Tribune* pointed out that 'there are instances of local legislators practically commanding police stations in their areas'.[67]

The police strike, which began in Punjab but spread to other states in north India, was yet another indication of social changes outstripping the ability of the political and administrative system to cope. The strike, moreover, warned of the fragility of the Punjab police.

In May 1979, with the Janata government still in power in New Delhi and the Badal ministry in Chandigarh, drunken supporters of an Akali MLA beat up a police constable in Patiala. This was followed by other alleged insults to constables by MLAs. Though it was widely recognised that 'a new educated class' – even graduates – had come 'into the force down to the constable level', MLAs and senior police officers continued to treat their inferiors like servants. Such indignities, coupled with poor service conditions and constant political interference, led to a strike which ran for six weeks.[68]

The striking policemen won support from the out-of-power Congress (I) leaders, Zail Singh and Darbara Singh. The government raised salaries (from Rs. 396 to Rs. 420 a month as the starting salary for a constable – that is, from US \$40 to US \$42) and promised to hasten the construction of improved accommodation for policemen and their families. It also dismissed 900 militant policemen, said to have links with communist parties. Congress (I) leaders promised to reinstate them, and a year later, once Mrs Gandhi was back in power and Punjab under President's Rule, Zail Singh as Home Minister did reinstate a majority of them. Dismissed constables, however, gravitated towards the gangs of gunmen. Zail Singh also instituted cases against police officers who investigated Congress (I) supporters under the Akali-led government.[69]

Changes in the character of the lowest levels of the police force mirrored changes in society as a whole. Just as police officers expected the mass of constables to do what they were told and not to try to understand the subtleties of higher police work and politics, so had local faction leaders expected obedience from their lesser followers. The police strike of 1979, however, showed that the effects of schooling and literacy had spread even into the lowest ranks of police. Not only were many young constables literate and even graduates; there was also, wrote the *Tribune*, 'a new class of politically oriented recruits', even at this level.[70] Able to read the rule book for themselves, such men simply could not be controlled in the old ways. They would look for support from within the police force or from outside, from communists or sants; but what was new was the fact that they were looking.

As far as higher-ranking police officers were concerned, their connection with formal politics was as well known as their role in factional struggles. The first Education Minister in the 1977–80 Akali-led government, Sukhjinder Singh, for example, was both a strong advocate of greater autonomy for Punjab (even, it seemed, to the point of 'Khalistan') and a former police superintendent. B. S. Danewalia, the Inspector-General, the state's top officer at the time of the 1979 strike, resigned in April 1980 to enter politics, initially with Akali backing.[71]

Consider the example of P. S. Bhindar, the senior Sikh officer whom Mrs Gandhi sent to Punjab in June 1983. Bhindar had a reputation for toughness, though not independence. A member of the late Sanjay Gandhi's circle, he headed the New Delhi police during the 1975–7 'emergency'. In 1980, his wife was elected as the Congress (I) Member of Parliament for Gurdaspur, a constituency which includes the town of Chowk Mehta, Bhindranwale's headquarters.[72] Having a number of loyalties to consider, police officers – and increasingly their men – showed more enthusiasm for some cases than others.

By February 1982, Darbara Singh's government claimed to have discovered that ten policemen of various ranks were working with the promoters of Khalistan. The police, according to one report, were 'personally ambitious men who think that the shoes in which they stand [are] too small for them'. A district superintendent was even said to have helped extremists to get arms and training.[73]

The police were thus contorted by the same pressures working on the wider society. In controlling those pressures, the police therefore were of little use. 'The force is so demoralised today', a senior officer said in June 1983 after the murder of Atwal, 'that it takes no notice of these incidents – it is as if the communal outbursts and killings were happening in another world.'[74]

The imposition of President's Rule on 6 October 1983 recognised the fact that the Punjab police were now as deeply divided as the society itself. The remedy was Mrs Gandhi's panacea: central control. The Border Security Force (BSF) and Central Reserve Police (CRP), both maintained by the central government, were assigned the major anti-terrorist duties in Punjab. On 2 June 1984, she raised the bets still higher by deploying the Indian Army, the central government's last resort.

WHO ARE 'THE EXTREMISTS'?

A number of segments made up what appeared to be – but was not – the monolith of 'Sikh extremists' who had helped to tear to tatters the fabric of the Punjab police. The two most prominent were the Dal Khalsa, whose founding in 1978, with the alleged backing of Zail Singh, seemed almost a media stunt, and the All-India Sikh Students' Federation (AISSF), in existence since 1944, but since the late 1970s under the control of Bhindranwale's associate, Amrik Singh.

In addition to these groups was the Babbar Khalsa, said to comprise only a few score youths operating from the Golden Temple precincts, who, though committed to terrorism and a Sikh state, were sworn enemies of Bhindranwale.[75] Harchand Singh Longowal, the Akali Dal president, was protected by an Akali Youth wing, also armed and opposed to Bhindranwale. The wife of one of the men killed on 13 April 1978, Bibi Amarjit Kaur, led the Akhand Kirtani Jatha, an armed group that at first supported Bhindranwale but later clashed with him. And by the beginning of 1984, a group called the Dashmesh Regiment, loyal to Bhindranwale, was claiming responsibility for individual murders.[76] Later, however, some sources held that the 'Dashmesh Regiment' existed only as a catch-phrase thrown to journalists wanting to assign responsibility for a killing to some named group.[77]

Questions about the origins – and, indeed, the number – of 'extremists' will tax officials and historians for years. From the information now available, two points are notable. The first is predictable: the large majority of those who were named in the press were under 30 years old. Second, and more surprising, their educational and economic backgrounds were diverse. Many, it appears, were like Bhindranwale: rural Jats, from none-too-prosperous families, yet having had four or five years of primary school. Beside them were young men like Amrik Singh, who had a Master of Arts degree, and Harmindar Singh Sandhu, general secretary of the AISSF. The latter, who was captured after the storming of the Golden Temple, studied law and is said to be the son of an education official.[78]

On the other hand, non-Jat Sikhs were also attracted to the vision embodied in Bhindranwale. The five men involved in the first plane hijacking, after Bhindranwale's arrest in

September 1981, were all non-Jats.[79] One of them, Gajindar Singh, a graduate, born in 1954, came from a refugee family from the North-West Frontier Province in what is now Pakistan. His father ran a small general store in Chandigarh. One brother worked for the government; the other helped in the store. Gajindar Singh tried a government job briefly but was dismissed for publishing 'a seditious booklet' called 'Five More Arrows', a fairly obvious allusion to Guru Gobind Singh. A sister had won a court case to allow Sikh women to ride motor scooters without helmets, a right already enjoyed by Sikh men. Gajindar Singh was imprisoned for a time during the 1975–7 'emergency', unsuccessfully contested the SGPC elections in 1979 and eventually joined the Dal Khalsa. He had married in 1980 and had a baby daughter, but he paid little attention to family affairs, and his wife lived with her parents.[80]

A single profile cannot explain a movement, but Gajindar Singh seems to typify at least one strand. Indeed, one writer suggests that non-Jat Sikhs have been particularly influential because they have seen terrorism as a way of making up for their loss of influence within the Akali Dal.[81] Involvement in acts of derring-do also allows non-Jats to demonstrate that they too can measure up to the standards of physical courage that the dominant Jat-Sikh ethos values so highly. There is evidence that Mazhbi (ex-Untouchable) Sikhs are also attracted, probably for similar reasons.[82]

Trying to discern a pattern of explanation in what we know about the backgrounds of the 'extremists' recalls the Janatha Vimukti Peramuna (JVP) [people's liberation front] revolt in Sri Lanka in 1971. Its ideology was taken heavily from Lenin, Mao and Che Guevara, but its leaders and participants were overwhelmingly rural youths from the dominant social category – Singhalese-speaking Buddhists. They were very often the first in their families to have had a high-school education, and they lacked satisfying occupations in their villages or elsewhere. Five years later, they might have gone to the Persian/Arabian Gulf as migrant workers, but in 1971 that prospect had not yet arisen. Like Sikh youths in the 1980s, they had ideas, aspirations and leisure unknown to their parents.[83]

Ideas were crucial to both the young Sri Lankans and young Sikhs, but while the former thumbed the pages of Marx and his disciplines, the latter took their inspiration from the Gurus and Sikh history. If Marx promised the ultimate triumph of the oppressed, traditional Sikh history could be construed to teach that every tyrant received retribution from the community.

If this comparison between Marxist-motivated rebels and the Sikh 'extremists' seems far-fetched, it is worth drawing attention to another South Asian example of a similar phenomenon. Since the 1970s the Communist Party of India (Marxist), once the strongest single party in the south-western state of Kerala, has experienced a drift of young members into an aggressive Hindu revivalist organisation, the Rashtriya Swayamsevak Sangh (RSS). One explanation contends that the CPI(M) has become so habituated to legislative manoeuvring and made such a feeble protest against the 'emergency' in 1975–7 that it no longer promises excitement or grand visions of the future. The RSS, on the other hand, still does. What is important to the literate, leisured young is not so much the details of an ideology as the promise of a glorious goal and the chance to participate in the struggle to achieve it.[84] One of Bhindranwale's devotees put this well. The old Akali leaders, he told Tavleen Singh, 'had adjusted to the democratic system. To be a Sikh and to be young necessarily means to be adventurous. Sant Bhindranwale offered us the adventure'.[85]

The 'emergency' also played a part in initiating Sikh youths into the excitement of political agitation. Thousands of Akali demonstrators, like Gajindar Singh, were detained. The fact that the Akali Dal was one of the few political parties in India to put up a sustained resistance fostered pride and reinforced ideas about the unique readiness of Sikhs to suffer for a cause. Indeed, just as the civil-disobedience movement against the British in 1930–4 blooded a whole generation of youths who only now are passing from the top levels of politics (Morarji Desai, the ex-Prime Minister, and E. M. S. Namboodiripad, general secretary of the CPI(M) are two examples), so the events of 1975–7 formed bonds and changed lives, particularly among the Akalis in Punjab.

It has been suggested that criminals also sought the protection of Bhindranwale inside the Golden Temple and formed the nucleus of the killer gangs.[86] There can be little doubt that such refuge would have attracted toughs, smugglers and other 'anti-social elements', as they are known in India. But this kind of labelling is fraught with dangers if one is trying to understand and not simply to condemn.

From 1968 to 1972, Calcutta was the scene of a deadly war between so-called 'Naxalites' (revolutionary terrorists originally inspired by Mao) the police and gangs of toughs working for political parties. Every petty criminal became a Naxalite for purposes of police 'body counts', and, indeed, if there were sometimes advantages to being a political prisoner rather than a mere criminal, no doubt some ordinary criminals claimed to be Naxalites.[87] Today's criminal can be tomorrow's political hero.

One of Punjab's most distinguished retired police officers claims that Naxalites 'infiltrated Bhindranwale's rank, . . . Longowal's group and . . . to quite an extent, the Punjab police'.[88] Such a charge, however, seems unlikely, in spite of the distinction of the man making it. In Punjab, given the violent factions of the countryside and the porous smuggler-ridden border with Pakistan, smugglers and bandits are likely to attach themselves to – and be recruited by – groups which can offer protection (through the *gurdwaras*, for example) and which, in return, look for arms and funds. To suggest that they represent an organised, ideological group is, I think, to assign far too much cohesion and influence to India's minuscule, fragmented revolutionary movement.

There is also little doubt that the police themselves killed troublesome and uninfluential activists. Before the storming of the Golden Temple, estimates ranged from 150 to about 300 deaths in such ambushes and 'encounters'.[89] In the final attack on the Golden Temple itself, it appears that about 700 defenders and about 100 soldiers died.[90] How many 'extremists' then were there?

The largest group, the All-India Sikh Students' Federation, banned in March 1984, is said to have had 40 000 members.[91] Membership of the AISSF, however, did not necessarily make someone a gunman. One suspects that a large majority of the members sympathised, shared a thrill of participation but did not take part in bank robberies, bombings or murders.

Other groups, it appears, numbered only in hundreds. The Babbar Khalsa, for example, was thought to have a few score members, divided into three- or four-man squads, some of them led by former police constables.[92] The Dal Khalsa was estimated to have between 500 and 1000 members. Other groups, it appears, number fewer still.[93]

Such estimates, however, can be of only the roughest kind, sometimes perhaps pulled out of the air by a desperate journalist or intelligence chief to satisfy a superior. Memberships fluctuate with political fortunes, as the example of Naxalites who became Sikh-state activists well shows. At times, it is a great advantage to be able to disown all connections with an organisation. Members of the Babbar Khalsa, who were said to have come to a reconciliation with Bhindranwale during the last days in the Golden Temple, are supposed to have slipped out of the Golden Temple through neighbouring houses and down back-lanes before the army's final assault.[94]

At most, it appears that the 'extremists' numbered close to 10 000 at the beginning of June 1984. Much, of course, depends on how one defines an 'extremist'.[95] It is impossible to estimate how many 'anti-social elements' who became 'extremists' out of convenience will not quickly return to being merely 'anti-social'.

At the core, however, were the true-believers. They were – are, those of them still alive – young, they came from all Sikh castes and they had been to school, even if only for a few years. Their families were often – if Bhindranwale's is any criterion – peasants who managed to live adequately but who were far from being 'green revolution' capitalist farmers. If they were from urban families, their fathers were likely to be in petty commerce or government service. What all seem to share, however, is a vision of Sikh history that fits poorly with their own demoralised present. The world as it is seems to offer them no stimulating opportunities. Their task in such a world therefore becomes – as it is also for people with Marxist visions – to change it.

STORMING THE GOLDEN TEMPLE

On 23 May 1984, Harchand Singh Longowal, the Akali Dal president, announced that the next phase of the agitation would include attempts to stop the sale of food-grain to the Food Corporation of India. Since Punjab provides half of the central reserves of grain, which are used to sustain the government distribution system and thus keep prices down, a successful grain blockade would have had inflationary consequences for the whole country. It was a suggestion that Bhindranwale had made more than a year earlier.[96]

As matters stood in May, the imposition of President's Rule, the use of thousands of central police, the banning of the AISSF in March and the attempt to embroil Longowal in a sedition case in April were not bringing peace to Punjab. Indeed, as the list of killings shows, terrorists in May were able to murder enough prominent people to spread a sense of fear and mistrust into virtually every corner of Punjab. On 18 April, for example, Corbusier's Chandigarh, cosseted and antiseptic, was placed under curfew for the first time in its thirty-year history.[97]

Mrs Gandhi went on radio and television on the evening of 2 June to announce that the army was now taking charge of Punjab. A 36-hour curfew on the whole state was imposed from 9 p.m. on 3 June and all motor traffic banned. All trains in Punjab were cancelled; all newspapers in Chandigarh and Punjab were instructed not to publish reports of the army action.

The fighting began on the night of Sunday, 3 June, and it was early morning on Thursday, 7 June, before the army controlled the Golden Temple. The story of that sad battle will be constantly disputed in the future. Among Sikhs, it stands a chance of occupying a place alongside the exploits and martyrdoms associated with Guru Gobind Singh.

There seems little doubt that the army was poorly informed about the strength and ability of the men inside the Golden Temple. Officials must have hoped that once Bhindranwale and his followers saw that a full-scale army assault was imminent, they would surrender. In fact, it appears to have taken a commando raid on the night of 5/6 June to capture Longowal, Tohra and other Akalis from outer buildings of the Golden Temple complex.[98] They were taken away from the fighting and held in detention. Badal, who was not in Amritsar, was detained a few days later.

Bhindranwale appears to have believed that the army would not attack. A journalist who interviewed him on Sunday evening, 3 June, just a few hours before the fighting began, wrote: 'I don't think he really felt that the army would actually enter the temple'. Bhindranwale told the reporter to come the next day for another interview. However, when the reporter pressed him with the question, 'Are you afraid of death?', Bhindranwale replied: 'Don't try to scare me with death. If I was afraid of death, I would not be a Sikh'.[99]

The bravado helps to explain why the men inside the Golden Temple fought so well. The army grudgingly admitted that their preparations, tactics and resolution were remarkable; but then the commander inside the Golden Temple was an old Indian Army man – Major-General (retired) Shabeg Singh, who had led guerrillas against the Pakistani army in Bangladesh in 1971. His commander in the 1971 war recalled that he was 'rather good at his job'. He had clipped his hair and 'played the part' of a guerrilla leader by wearing 'lungis [the cloth worn by men in Bangladesh] and balaclava caps'.[100]

How many died will remain a burning question for years to come. The official version puts the number killed defending the Golden Temple at about 500.[101] A well-connected Indian journalist writing in a foreign publication put the figure at 712 defenders and 90 soldiers.[102] The chief *granthi* of the Harmandir Sahib, the actual golden temple from which the complex takes its name, thought the number of dead was between 1000 and 1200.[103] Amarindar Singh, Congress (I) Member of Parliament (until he resigned in dismay in June 1984), thought at least 2000 people had been killed throughout Punjab during the army operation.[104]

The army did not completely succeed in stamping out opposition. Soon after the battle in Amritsar, insurgents twice breached the broad, fast-flowing Bhakra Main Line Canal near the town of Rupar, north of Chandigarh. It took more than a month each time to repair, and deprived farmers as far south as Rajasthan of irrigation during the hottest month of the year. Another plane was hijacked in July, the fourth since the Punjab 'troubles' began. Occasional bank robberies, shootings and sabotage continued. Eight bus passengers were murdered in the all-too-familiar, random way near Amritsar on 12 September.[105] No one could feel completely secure, least of all the Prime Minister whose calculations and style had contributed so much to making the 'Punjab crisis'.

8 What's Happening to India? The Test for Federalism

Late October and November wrap north India in balmy nights and blue-skied, bone-warming days. The finest weather of the year is made all the better by the thought – if you have a quilt for your bed – that it will get steadily cooler and the brick-kiln dust and heat of May and June are half a year away. On such an exhilarating morning, Wednesday, 31 October 1984, Mrs Gandhi was assassinated.

Shortly after 9 a.m. she and her aides left her residential bungalow to walk a few dozen metres to the office bungalow next door where she was to videotape an interview with the British actor, Peter Ustinov. As her group approached the gate in the wall separating the two compounds, the senior of the two Sikh police guards on duty there drew his revolver and fired at her from point-blank range. His younger companion then fired a long burst from his automatic weapon into her collapsing body. It is likely that she died within moments.

The two assassins are said to have thrown down their weapons and been led off to a guard room, where a few minutes later they scuffled with their captors. The senior man, Beant Singh, an ex-Untouchable Sikh, was shot and killed. The younger, Satwant Singh, was wounded but survived and was to become the initial focus for inquiries about the extent of the plot to kill Mrs Gandhi.[1]

It was ironic that Mrs Gandhi, the suspicious centraliser, should have been murdered in her own garden. Her style so often said: 'I am only comfortable when the decisions pass through my hands and when people come to me'. There can be little doubt that the abject slogan of the 1975–7 'emergency' – 'Indira is India and India is Indira' – had her approval. Chief

Ministers of most states became her creatures, forced to come frequently to New Delhi as humble petitioners. No matter how constitutionally correct the decision of a Chief Minister might be, he could still be called on to defend or reverse it at No. 1 Safdarjang Road. Even assassins had to seek Mrs Gandhi there.

The other notable assassinations in India in this century have occurred in front of crowds or in public places. The 'father of the nation', M. K. Gandhi, was murdered at a prayer meeting attended by a large crowd in New Delhi on 30 January 1948. Partap Singh Kairon, as we have seen, was killed on the Grand Trunk Road in 1964. L. N. Mishra, a minister in Mrs Gandhi's government, was killed by a bomb at a public meeting in Bihar in January 1975. Indeed, even Sir Michael O'Dwyer (1864–1940), though long retired, was attending a public meeting in London on 13 March 1940 when Udham Singh, a shaven Sikh, shot and killed him. O'Dwyer, Governor of the Punjab in 1919, had given his full support to the slaughter ordered by Brigadier-General Reginald Dyer at Jallianwalla Bagh, where Udham Singh is said to have been one of the wounded.[2] The fact that his rage burned hot for twenty-one years must be a constant source of anxiety to soldiers and officials involved in the battle at the Golden Temple in June 1984.

In a sense, Mrs Gandhi's need to centralise – to hold all the reins in her hands – led to her death. There is a good case to be made that if Parkash Singh Badal's government had been left alone in 1980 to survive or fall on the basis of its own merits, the spread of ethnic violence, and the raising of the political stakes, would not have occurred. This argument is closely bound up with the hypothesis that political decisions, rather than inevitable social processes, determine the forms ethnic groups assume and whether violence breaks out between them.

This final chapter argues that heedless attempts at centralisation worsen the problems that accompany modernisation in a state with as many potential ethnic divisions as India. It attempts to assess both the forces in the Indian state that foster such attempts and Mrs Gandhi's own peculiar contribution to them. In conclusion, the chapter tries to identify some of India's possible futures. It suggests that the same forces of modernisation that underlay the explosion in Punjab are also producing scores of grass-roots organisations committed to humanitarian change. If the central government adheres to the federal and democratic provisions of the present constitution, the expansion of such movements offers possibilities for improvement in the lives of large numbers of people, improvement that can only come through their own efforts and organisations. In the long term, such developments would transform the Indian state.

CENTRALISATION: PRESSURES AND APPEARANCES

The constitution of 1950 reposes far greater powers in the central government than do the federal constitutions of the United States, Canada or Australia. There were both 'defensive' and constructive reasons for doing this.

Let us look first at the 'defensive' reasons, some of which relate to the way in which Indian society has crystalised in the past hundred years.

Most of the nationalists who came to high office in 1947 were from the upper castes and educated in English. Their backgrounds were similar to those of the officials who had simultaneously replaced the British in the bureaucracy. Together, these officials and politicians – and the industrialists who supported the national movement – constituted a national elite. Such people drafted, worked and defended the constitution in the first thirty years of independence. They saw themselves as creators and sustainers of a national identity that only a strong central government, of which they would be in charge, could foster. State governments, increasingly showing the influence of less educated and urbane people, often from rugged peasant castes (consider Sikh Jats), were slightly suspect and in need of guidance.[3] Only a dominant central government could educate the masses in nationalism.

An example may help to dramatise the way in which this elite, regardless of the region of its origins, dominated national life in the first thirty years after independence. P. Subbarayan (1889–1962) came from a landlord family in Tamilnad. Educated in the law in Britain, he was Chief Minister of the old Madras Presidency from 1926–30. Later, he was a member of the Constituent Assembly and a minister in the central government from 1959–62 before briefly becoming Governor of

Maharashtra until his death. His career aptly illustrates the type of person who laid the foundations of the Indian state. The careers of his children, however, are even more revealing. One son, P. P. Kumaramangalam (b. 1913), entered the Indian Army in 1933 and retired as its chief in 1969. His brother, Mohan Kumaramangalam (1916–73), was educated in Britain, joined the Communist Party of India in the early 1940s, later became a member of the Congress Party and was a minister in Mrs Gandhi's cabinet when he died in a plane crash. A sister, Mrs Parvati Krishnan, remained in the Communist Party of India and was a Member of Parliament until 1980. Though Tamils by origin, they were committed to the idea of an Indian state. Mixing confidently and freely with Indians like themselves from the other regions, such people developed a sense of understanding – perhaps even trust. They were willing to see large powers consolidated in a central government which they and their like controlled.[4]

Some observers suggest that Nehru's mixed-economy socialism was also well suited to the post-1947 national elite. Government ownership of major industrial projects meant control by central officials, not by upstart capitalists or technocrats. Similarly, the old capitalist families like Birla and Tata, having smooth channels to politicians and officials, were able to cope with government requirements about licences and quotas. Such requirements allowed officials (and established capitalists) to keep new entrepreneurs in line and under control. In recent years, too, there is the suggestion that bureaucrats like government controls because of the opportunity for bribery they afford.

Most of the politicians contending for power in New Delhi seem to agree on how power is to be exercised once it has been won. Morarji Desai (Prime Minister, 1977–9), himself a good example of the old national elite, was no less imperious than Mrs Gandhi. In his behaviour towards Akali leaders, he perhaps embodied a widespread (though not unanimous) belief about how a Prime Minister should behave towards the states.

Though the Akali Dal were partners in the central coalition, when the party in Punjab raised demands for greater powers for the states, they found Morarji Desai 'the toughest Prime Minister to deal with'. He dismissed all their proposals in a 'brusque manner', and, wrote the *Tribune*'s well-informed

'Analyst', 'the Akali leaders are scared of a face-to-face meeting with him'.[5] If there was little to choose between Morarji and Mrs Gandhi, this suggests that pressures and expectations within the Indian state prompt Prime Ministers to assert their own dignity and the powers of the central government.

This is the place to correct one popularly-held but demonstrably-wrong notion about the 1977–80 Akali Dal-led government in Punjab: that it 'did not make a squeak' about the rights of states and 'discovered' the issue only after it lost office. Mrs Gandhi was fond of repeating this charge, and by 1984, even her sternest critics, like the *Economic and Political Weekly*, were prepared to accept it. 'She could not', said an *EPW* editorial, 'have been more right.'[6] In fact, she could not have been more wrong. As their bitter experiences with Morarji Desai indicated, the Akalis pressed claims on the central government only to have them rejected out of hand. The grievances were primarily those of Punjab – sharing of river waters, for example – not of Sikhs. The *Tribune*'s 'Analyst' contended that Jayaprakash Narayan had supported the Akalis' claims, but Jayaprakash had been 'rendered politically inoperative' almost as soon as the Janata government was formed. In mid-1978, moreover, the newspaper commended Badal, the Chief Minister, for his 'persuasive persistence' with New Delhi, though it regretted that Akali Members of Parliament did little to put Punjab's case.[7] It is simply not true, however, to claim that the Akali Dal discovered an emotional commitment to federalism and the rights of Punjab as a cynical ploy after it had been turned out of office in February 1980. I shall return to this question of sentiment and centralisation later, but now let us go back to the constructive reasons that the framers of the 1950 constitution had for vesting wide powers in the central government.

First, Nehru's belief in Fabian socialism and economic planning is well known. State-planned industrialisation and economic development, to which the Congress Party had been committed since the 1930s, made a strong central government vital. If, too, the poorest parts of the country were to get special attention, the required finances would have to come from a central government able to channel investment from richer areas to poorer. Similarly, social justice and reform – the abolition of untouchability, for example – seemed likely to progress more steadily if an 'enlightened' central government were able to overcome 'parochial' vested interests in the states. (But when does 'decentralisation' become 'parochialism'?)

Like the Government of India Act of 1935, the constitution of 1950 vests the most important powers of taxation in the central government: customs and most excise duties, income tax and corporation tax are the most obvious.[8] The major state source of revenue tends to be from sales tax. Indeed, two Indian scholars conclude that the constitution is in fact 'only semi-federal in character' since so much revenue-raising power lies with the centre.[9] Of all the revenue collected by both the states and central government, the states get only about 37 per cent. Moreover, of the funds they receive as transfers from the central government, only about 40 per cent comes as a formal entitlement. Roughly 60 per cent of the transferred funds come in one way or another, only at the central government's discretion.[10]

This raises the possibility that the party in power at the centre may reward state governments it controls or punish those run by its opponents. In recent years, the Communist Party of India (Marxist) government in West Bengal has made such charges.[11] It is also conceivable that a government could seek to 'sweeten' electorally important states by giving them more money than economic logic or justice entitled them to.

In fact, however, the distribution of the revenue collected by the central government seems to be largely determined by different considerations. The American political scientist Paul Brass argues that central control over state expenditure 'has been reduced' since 1947 and that the proportion of funds transferred to the states in reliable, formula-based ways has risen.[12] Critics of the present system would no doubt dispute any suggestion that the states receive a sufficiently large proportion of transferred funds in reliable ways. But critics also contend that the present arrangements have failed to help the poorest states. The central government has not been particularly successful in directing funds from rich states to poor ones.[13]

The idea of 'sweetening' electorally-important states for political reasons does not seem to stand up. Uttar Pradesh, the largest state, with eighty-five seats in the national parliament, 'has perhaps got the rawest deal of all'.[14] Its per capita share of budget transfers over twenty-five years is the lowest of all the states.[15] Those that have done best are the delicate border states: Jammu and Kashmir and those of the north-east. Similarly, the relatively developed states have been able to prevent resources being diverted away from them. The central government's financial powers seem to be used more to try to oil squeaky wheels than to reward friends or punish enemies.

For our purposes, it is important to point out that perceptions are more important than accurate arithmetic in influencing political behaviour. Jammu and Kashmir, Assam, the smaller north-eastern states and Punjab have all throbbed with grievances against the central government in the 1980s. Uttar Pradesh, on the other hand, gave the Congress (I) eighty-three out of eighty-five seats in the parliamentary elections of December 1984, and more than 260 out of 425 assembly seats in the state elections in March 1985.

This is not to rule out the possibility that one day a 'fairness for UP' (or some such) movement might sweep the state and confront the central government with similar demands to those it has faced elsewhere. The point is that the immediate problems of Indian federalism are not so much financial as political and emotional. People of UP can bask in the fact that men and women speaking their language, coming from their towns and villages, play a prominent role in the governing of India. Four out of five of India's Prime Ministers have been from the UP, and every central government contains a large contingent of UP ministers. In a sense, the UP can – and Indians from other regions sometimes argue that it does – equate itself with the nation. So far, this basic fact has been far more important for popular politics than the terms of UP's financial relations with the central government. Federations falter or fail, I suspect, more on their ability to satisfy sentiments than accountants.

Shortly, we shall turn to more obvious and galling forms of centralisation to get a picture of the tests that federalism faces from the innovation-induced ferment bubbling throughout India. But in addition to federal financial powers, we need to be aware of a further centralising pressure.

CENTRALISATION: THE NEEDS OF PARTY

A ruling party in New Delhi has good reason to want to have its nominees in control of state governments: the need to keep a political party alive. What do state or provincial politicians do in the USA, Canada or Australia when they lose an election? Most often, it appears they go back to their former jobs or use their connections acquired in politics to find new ones. At worst, they may have to rely on working spouses or register for unemployment benefits. In India, however, few of these expedients exist.[16] A rural politician – recall our Punjab examples – can go back to his land; but his standing in his neighbourhood may also depend on his political connections.

The national politician in New Delhi knows that factions are more difficult to manage when they do not have the trough of office from which to feed. Moreover, the Congress party no longer maintains any pretence about having a 'constructive programme' of the kind that Gandhi gave it in the 1920s and 1930s. In those days, members of the Congress were expected to work for rural reconstruction when they were not involved in confrontations with the British or campaigns to elect Congressmen to legislatures. Indeed, for M. K. Gandhi, the 'constructive programme' would have ranked as the most important aspect of Congress membership.

Today, however, adherents of the Congress (I) – and most Indian political parties – have little concern for ideology. Their aim is to be close to power, because that proximity brings status and reward. The task of national leaders striving to hold a party together is to get it within sight of office as quickly as possible. Otherwise, how can one hope to find allies and helpers for national elections?

Though these suggestions may seem fanciful, there is evidence to support them. Consider, for example, the efforts of the Congress (I) to bring down the Janata government in Karnataka in 1983, the overthrow of the Sikkim and Jammu and Kashmir governments in 1984 and the comic-opera attempt to get rid of N. T. Rama Rao's government in Andhra Pradesh in August and September 1984.[17] If a party lacks a substantial programme and ideology, and if the workers and leaders on whom it depends depend themselves on proximity to power for their status and livelihood, then the need exists to use all means to keep them in power. That may well involve the exercise of the central government's prerogatives.

PRESIDENT'S RULE AND THE CONSTITUTION

In August 1979, the Janata Party withdrew from the coalition with the Akali Dal in Punjab. However, after Mrs Gandhi's huge victory in the national elections in January 1980, it vowed to support Badal's government in the Punjab legislature and thus prevent its defeat.[18] Since the Congress had fewer than twenty seats in a house of 117, it would have taken major defections to have brought down Badal in the legislature. Although there was plenty of evidence of plots and dissension, Badal and his faction had coped with such things in the past.[19] There was, moreover, no sign of organised, violent protest against his government, in spite of the fact that the Congress had won twelve of Punjab's thirteen seats in parliament in the January elections. (It had not won a single seat in 1977.) On 17 February 1980, however, the president of India, acting on the instructions of the central government, dismissed the governments and imposed President's Rule in ten non-Congress (I) states, including Punjab.

To people familiar with the US, Canadian or Australian federal systems, the idea of the national government dismissing a state or provincial ministry is outlandish. The provision of such powers in the Indian constitution dramatically illustrates the legacy of imperial rule and the heavy central bias of Indian federalism. Article 356 empowers the President to impose central rule on the basis of a report from the Governor 'or otherwise' that 'the government of the State cannot be carried on in accordance with the provisions of this Constitution'. The central government may either dissolve the legislature and eventually call elections or simply suspend the legislature until a new government can be formed.

That the foreign rulers in 1935, reluctantly handing over some measure of responsible government to elected Indian politicians, should have wanted such powers for their Viceroy is not surprising. But why should the Constituent Assembly of free India have retained them in the constitution of 1950? The explanation relates to the 'defensive' aspects of the constitution, some of which we have already touched on.

First, when the constitution was drafted in 1948 and 1949, India was threatened from both within and without. The creation of Pakistan suggested that further fragmentation of the subcontinent was possible. A communist insurgency from 1948 to 1950, which was strong enough to establish 'liberated villages' in parts of the Telengana area of what is now Andhra Pradesh, reinforced the sense of vulnerability. 'We have to deal', Nehru said, 'with a situation in which ... if we do not try our utmost the whole of India will be a cauldron within six months.'[20]

The second reason for the President's Rule provision lay in the character of the Constituent Assembly itself. The most influential members, as we have seen, tended to be highly educated lawyers who were happy to have a document they understood and had seen work (in the shape of the 1935 Act). Moreover, since the provinces of British India – unlike the colonies of eighteenth and nineteenth-century North America or Australia – had never been independent entities, India's constituent assembly felt few of the compulsions about 'states' rights' that had taxed Americans, Canadians and Australians.

In the fourteen years between the inauguration of the constitution in 1950 and Nehru's death in May 1964, President's Rule was imposed six times: in Punjab in 1951, PEPSU 1953, Andhra 1954, Travancore–Cochin 1956, Kerala 1959 and Orissa 1961. In the examples of Punjab, PEPSU and Kerala, the decision was controversial: viable governments had not been defeated in the legislatures. In the other three cases, state government did appear to have reached an impasse. The point is that Nehru himself occasionally used President's Rule for partisan ends.

However, the contrast with Mrs Gandhi's years is striking. Between 1966 when she became Prime Minister and her death in 1984, President's Rule was imposed more than fifty times.[21] To be sure, the Janata Party, which governed from 1977–9, was responsible for the dismissal of nine Congress governments in April 1977. This in turn provided Mrs Gandhi with justification for her removal of non-Congress governments in February 1980. In mitigation of the Janata's actions, however, it is worth pointing out that some of the state governments in 1977 had completed their five-year terms. In its nation-wide authoritarianism, moreover, the 1975–7 'emergency' was unique in the country's history. It may be possible therefore to justify the 1977 dismissals. For 1980, however, such a task is much more difficult. The explanation offered by Mrs Gandhi's lieutenants simply stated that because states had returned Congress (I) candidates in the national elections, their non-Congress (I) governments were no longer legitimate. If such an extraordinary 'convention' were possible in Canada, a number of its provinces would have spent the 1970s and 1980s under 'President's Rule' since the Liberal Party, which held power nationally, was seldom able to win provincial elections.

Paul Brass argues that the frequent use of President's Rule is 'more appropriately seen as a failure of the government of India to exercise effective central control over state affairs than as an index of centralisation'.[22] The destruction of a living, district-based Congress Party, according to this argument, drove Mrs Gandhi and her successors to use constitutional machinery to try to assert central authority in the states. Brass is probably right in suggesting that the Congress Party under Nehru exercised more *effective* control in the states. Though no doubt a sign of desperation, the flagrant use of President's Rule fuels a sense of local grievance. The central government *appears* powerful – and unjust – when it attempts to use its powers to overthrow popular state governments. As with the financial aspects of federalism, the appearance may be more important than the underlying reality.

Two sets of reasons explain why attempts to centralise have steadily continued. The first involves the peculiarities of Mrs Gandhi's own personality and the circumstances of her coming to power. The second concerns far wider, more diffuse pressures resulting from India's class structure and the rule that democratic politics play within it.

THE DECLINE OF THE CHIEF MINISTER

Mrs Gandhi's need to centralise stemmed partly from personal experience. A lonely, insecure only-child, she changed schools frequently, saw her parents imprisoned and yet received doting attention from servants and politicians keen for the favour of her father and grandfather. Her marriage in 1942 to Feroze Gandhi (a Parsi by religious background and not related to M. K. Gandhi) came apart within five or six years, and she moved into the house of her father, Jawaharlal Nehru, to become the Prime Minister's hostess. Her two sons, Rajiv (b. 1944) and Sanjay (1946–80), were raised there.[23] As the Prime Minister's daughter-in-residence and confidante, her influence grew.

She seems rarely, however, to have seen projects through to a successful conclusion. Her visions were wispy and romantic – witness her celebrated childhood fascination with Joan of Arc – rather than concrete and practical. Her studies at Somerville College, Oxford, petered out in 1939–40. Her presidency of the Congress Party in 1959–60 lasted little more than a year (though in that time she is said to have convinced her father to dismiss the Communist government and impose President's Rule in Kerala in July 1959). In 1973, during her 'socialist period', her own government nationalised the wholesale trade in wheat, only to abandon it the following year.[24] Her strengths emerged in short-term crises, whether scuttling her rivals in the Congress in 1969–71 or navigating the dangerous international seas produced by the secessionist movement in East Pakistan (Bangladesh) in 1971. This ability to deal confidently with crises led her, I suspect, to look for them – problems that could be 'solved' with a few swift, decisive strokes ending in popular acclaim. If this analysis is correct, it helps to explain the disdain with which she treated political institutions and politicians who did not fall at her feet.

When Nehru died in 1964, the states were producing powerful politicians who fought their way to the top by putting together a vigorous team of supporters and allies.

We have seen how Kairon worked in Punjab. In Madras (today's Tamilnad), K. Kamaraj (1903–75; CM, 1954–63) was 'so secure that he can defy New Delhi on important matters', while Dr B. C. Roy (1882–1962; CM, 1948–62) of West Bengal was confident enough of his position to 'wage a running war with the central government'.[25] On Nehru's death, it was a group centred on powerful Chief Ministers, (the so-called 'syndicate') who were responsible for the nomination of Lal Bahadur Shastri (1904–66) as his successor.

In his dealings with Chief Ministers, Nehru, to be sure, usually got his way. Indeed, one study suggests that in seventeen years as Prime Minister, there were 'only three . . . instances where the outcome of crises [in states] did not conform to Nehru's wishes'.[26] However, in day-to-day affairs he left Chief

Ministers alone. And even in their selection, he often took no part and simply allowed the rival forces in a state party to work it out for themselves. The Punjab example is worth emphasising. Nehru was indeed responsible for the choice of Kairon as Chief Minister in January 1956 and for consistently supporting him thereafter. When opponents accused Kairon of corruption in 1962, Nehru is said to have protected him: 'I want Partap Singh Kairon to be the Chief Minister of the Punjab'.[27] Kairon was forced to resign within three weeks of Nehru's death on 28 May 1964. Kairon, however, was an ally of Nehru, not a supplicant, and their relationship had advantages for both men.

Nehru backed Kairon because he saw him as a strong man capable of getting on with the business of running Punjab. In Nehru's eyes, an effective Chief Minister won time and energy for the Prime Minister who was freed from the necessity of involving himself in the state. Kairon's confident independence is reflected in his boast just before the Punjabi Suba agitation of 1960: 'I shall not let a single leaf stir in the Punjab'. Contrast this with Mrs Gandhi's nominee as Chief Minister, Zail Singh: 'if someone wants to survive in politics he must have some godfathers, and I admit that Indira ji [Mrs Gandhi] is my . . . patron'.[28] It is not a public statement that Kairon would have felt constrained to make.

When Shastri died on a diplomatic mission to Tashkent in 1966, it was again the leading Chief Ministers who were instrumental in the choice of Mrs Gandhi to succeed him. Their calculations appear to have been that she would be an easily controlled – and dispensable – candidate who would serve in the meantime to block the ambitious Morarji Desai (b. 1896). The power of the states and their Chief Ministers seemed firmly established.[29] Indeed, in 1969, just as Mrs Gandhi began her battle for complete dominance of her party, the political scientist Rajni Kothari wrote that:

> the general trend is for the states ... to consolidate their power ... and to assert their rights ... The most important fact here is the critical importance occupied by the office of the chief minister ... The chief minister is not only the most powerful person in his state ... ; he is also slowly becoming an important figure in national affairs. In important political

decisions such as the succession to the office of the prime minister . . . , the chief ministers have been consulted as if they were national leaders.[30]

The decision to instal Mrs Gandhi as Prime Minister proved a monumental misreading of character, for she developed into the most ruthless cut-and-thrust politician in India. To free herself from 'the syndicate', she split the party in 1969. In February 1971, showing a keen sense both of the prevailing mood of the people and of her own ability to reach them with the message they wanted to hear, she won an overwhelming election victory on the platform of *'garibi hatao'* – 'banish poverty'. She skilfully managed India's involvement in the East Pakistan (Bangladesh) crisis as it developed throughout the year and culminated in the Indian Army's victories over Pakistan in December. In March 1972, her Congress Party won assembly elections in most of the states. This triumph marked a severe setback for the office of Chief Minister. 'Mrs Gandhi sought to impose . . . nominees whose prime qualifications', wrote the doyen of British students of Indian politics, 'was loyalty to her, believing that her approval should suffice to build support at state level. But not so: one after another the retainers failed and every local difficulty became a central headache.'[31]

Something in Mrs Gandhi's lonely, suspicious character made her, I believe, seek dependents and sycophants as Chief Ministers. But there was also something in her experience: elevated to the prime ministership by powerful regional bosses who intended to exploit her, she was determined not to let such powerful rivals arise again. In future, the Prime Minister would create Chief Ministers, not the other way round.[32]

In the 1980s, Chief Ministers trooped to New Delhi to see her off on overseas trips and welcome her on return. She spelled out the essentials of Indian federalism, Indira-style, to a group of dissident MLAs in 1981: 'If you can't support your chief minister, who was selected by me, then let me dissolve the Assembly. Let me go back to the people again'. *India Today* kept a scorecard of the first hundred days of the new state governments formed in 1980: the Chief Minister of Rajasthan spent forty-eight days in New Delhi and the rest averaged about thirty days each.[33]

Many of these lacklustre men were bewildered about what was expected of them. T. Anjiah, the Chief Minister of Andhra Pradesh, was said to have been reduced to tears by the snub he received for arranging too lavish a welcome to Hyderabad for Rajiv Gandhi in February 1982. Yet under Sanjay Gandhi during the 'emergency', such welcomes were expected and Chief Ministers who incurred Sanjay's displeasure were replaced.[34] The example of Anjiah also shows how humble dependents can survive and prosper. He was back in office in Rajiv Gandhi's cabinet in January 1985 as Minister of State for Labour, still telling reporters about his complete devotion to Indira Gandhi and her family. 'Madam made me minister of state. Madam made me chief minister. Now I'm back. I never wanted to go back to the state. All their decision.'[35]

Anjiah's humiliation in 1982 (he lost the Chief Ministership soon after) illustrates the way in which such apparently remote clashes on Olympus now communicate themselves to the masses below. When N. T. Rama Rao launched his Telugu Desam Party and contested the state elections in Andhra Pradesh at the end of the year, he and his supporters portrayed the humbling of Anjiah as an affront to all Telugus, a further example of New Delhi's disregard for Telugu pride. Rama Rao of course won a crushing victory with 202 seats in a house of 294.[36]

Thus Mrs Gandhi's centralising reflex increasingly collided with populations better equipped than ever before to hear political messages and to act on them. Ironically, she herself had taken advantage of the early manifestations of this very quality in the elections of 1971. Once securely in power, however, she was unwilling to tolerate either old-style machine bosses or the idea that there could be political figures, besides herself, who could appeal directly to the hopes and sentiments of the masses.

THE NEED FOR FEDERALISM

This book is based on two premises. The first is that though Punjab's turmoil since 1980 has been dramatic, the conditions that produced it are not unique to Punjab. The heightened sense of ethnic identity that we have seen there will repeat itself constantly in other areas of India as 'modernisation' –

schooling, communications, ideas of competition, etc. – gradually affects ever larger numbers in ever more remote areas. Different local cultures will respond in different ways, and those responses will heavily depend on decisions made by political leaders. Violence and secession are *not* the inevitable products.

The second premise is that the meddlesome attempts at central control, which characterised Mrs Gandhi's time in power, are not the surest way to try to govern a country of 730 million people. No doubt a balance has to be struck. If the Indian nation-state is worth preserving – and few Indians today would argue that it is not – then it must have a central government capable of co-ordinating enormous plans for economic and social change. It must also have the powers to defend itself and to prevent secession. But Mrs Gandhi's brand of centralisation is more likely to increase regional tensions and secessionist pressures than to overcome them.

India's own experience supports the contention that it is in the long-term interests of the country to allow state governments to run their full terms. In Tamilnad, for example, the Dravida Munnetra Kazhagam (DMK) party which came to power in 1967 had a long history of secessionist rhetoric and attacks on 'north Indian domination'. The DMK, and its offshoot, the All-India Anna DMK (AIADMK), have governed Tamilnad since 1967. Their rule has many critics, but it has been no worse than that of other state governments in India. More important, the DMK and AIADMK long ago gave up secessionist slanging against the domination of north India.

An international comparison may also be instructive. In 1976, the Parti Quebecois won the provincial elections in Canada's French-speaking province of Quebec. The platform of the party called for separation from Canada and the creation of a sovereign state. Nationally, the Liberal Prime Minister from 1968 until 1984 (with a break of a few months in 1979) was Pierre Trudeau, a French Canadian, committed to policies of bilingualism throughout the federal government. These policies opened up a wide range of opportunities for French Canadians. From 1976, the Parti Quebecois in Quebec also aggressively pursued policies aimed at promoting French language and culture and the interests of Quebec. When the party held its long-promised referendum in 1980 to ask the people of Quebec whether they wished to separate from Canada, the proposition (even in a watered-down form) was rejected by about two-thirds of the voters. Yet in the same year, the Parti Quebecois was re-elected. In Janaury 1985, the party abandoned separation as a plank of its platform for coming elections.[37]

All this is not to argue that Quebec separatism or Tamil separatism are forever dead. On the contrary, the evidence suggests that each generation will consider the option of separation. Indeed, Tamil unrest may grow quickly if the Indian government proves unable to intercede effectively on behalf of Tamil citizens of Sri Lanka who have been involved in riots and guerrilla war since 1983.

The point of the Tamilnad and Quebec examples, however, is to argue that office sobers and domesticates political parties. Once in government, narrow programmes are difficult to pursue. Indeed, to reach government, it is often necessary to dilute the purity of the doctrine. No doubt, there will be occasions when politicians unprepared for such compromises may gain power. But from a central government's viewpoint, it seems wiser to gamble on the system's ability to deal with them than to attempt to overthrow all but the most docile, slavish state government.

Nothing that Parkash Singh Badal's government could have done in 1980 would have posed such a crisis for the Indian state as the repercussions of his dismissal have done. Similarly, the kind of revivalism – the sharpening of ethnic dividing lines – that Bhindranwale represented would have been neutralised more easily by a ruling party which itself claimed a religious endorsement. To be sure, there was a possibility that the whole Akali Dal might have been swept away in a wave of revivalist enthusiasm. But given the power-oriented realism of most Akali Dal politicians at that time, this seems unlikely. They were interested in office, not Khalistans-in-the-sky. They were also entitled to enjoy office until defeated in the legislature or their five-year term expired.

NEW RULES?

In 1973, the magazine *Seminar* published an essay in political geography by Rasheeduddin Khan. It enthralled anyone who loved maps and India because it put forward a proposal to redraw state boundaries in a more rational, decentralised way. It argued for 'a harmonious federal polity . . . built on . . . the socio-cultural regions of India' and proposed the creation of fifty-seven states.[38] If the USA with 250 million people could have fifty, fifty-seven seemed none too many for India's (then) population of about 550 million. The UP, (1981 population: 110 million) for example, would have been divided into six states, each with a cultural, geographic unity. The advantages of such subdivision would have been to allow closer local control and decision-making than is now possible and to reduce the secessionist potential of single-language states. Under the proposal, for example, there would have been two Punjabi-speaking states, three Telugu, close to twenty Hindi, etc. So far as I know, Rasheeduddin Khan's scheme has never been seriously considered by any political party, but it raises the question of whether new rules would make India more efficient or humane.

During Mrs Gandhi's last ministry, the constitutional changes proposed by her followers flowed in precisely the opposite direction: towards a presidential system with still greater powers concentrated in the president. There were no prizes for guessing who that would have been.[39]

If applied honestly, however, the present constitution can still contribute to the balance between regional ambitions and a central government able to hold the ring in times of unusual strain. A correct, even-handed working of the constitution – appointing independent people instead of political hacks as Governors, for example – would go a long way towards revitalising Indian federalism. As an American scholar remarks: 'the most destructive aspect of the 1970s lay in the fact that [India's] constitutional democratic institutions . . . were eroded rather than nurtured and maintained by those best in a position to understand them'.[40] Constitutions work because people make them work. A study of the factors contributing to the effective functioning of multi-ethnic states in North America and Europe suggests that 'the most vital area of concern . . . is the capacity and good will of the elites'.[41] That capacity and goodwill was evident among the national elite that came to power in India in 1947, but it is wanting in the 1980s. Today's regional elites, powerful in their own areas, lack the shared experience of struggle and the commitment to the ideals of M. K. Gandhi that the national elite of 1947 felt compelled to honour. In the mid-1980s, the Indian state appears to have few symbols that evoke genuine, nation-wide reverence or respect.

1984, however, was a bad year for the constitution, as the dismissal of the governments in Jammu and Kashmir and Sikkim and the farce in Andhra Pradesh indicate. Rajiv Gandhi must have been aware of these exercises, though one can only guess about whether he approved or encouraged them. However, after his party's victory in December, when the Karnataka state government of R. K. Hegde resigned to call new elections, the centre asked Hegde to remain as caretaker Chief Minister. In the recent past, President's Rule would probably have been imposed, and the state's administration would have been used to promote Congress (I) candidates. Instead, the advantage of controlling the administration at election time was left to Hegde. He and his Janata Party secured an absolute majority (139 seats out of 200) in their own right in March 1985 and ought to be able to complete a full five-year term.[42] The willingness in this instance of the new Congress (I) central government to abide by the generally accepted conventions of responsible government provides modest grounds for optimism.

REASONS FOR HOPE

The story so far has emphasised the dangers of modernisation and the destruction of institutions. It has suggested the possibility of increasingly violent rivalries between newer, larger ethnic categories – the possibility, as one writer has put it, that ultimately India might 'end up with a social formation similar to Khomeni's [*sic*] Iran'.[43] The social forces that made Bhindranwale an attractive voice, and later appear to have produced a 'Hindu wave' in the national elections in north India, lend some support to such a proposition.

But more humane and (to me) optimistic possibilities exist. It is important for people outside of India to be aware of them, because so often, the accounts of Indian events in their newspapers or on their televisions dwell on misery, violence or duplicity. Yet the 'churning at the bottom of society'[44] that produced the clientele for Bhindranwale and the 'Hindu wave' has also thrown up dozens of 'voluntary associations' or 'non-government organisations', independent of political parties but deeply and impressively committed to social justice and change. Most people who live in India for even a short time discover 'countless acts of heroism, both great and small'. It is a familiar experience to witness a scene of shocking callousness or disparity and within hours to encounter by chance an individual or a group working impressively to stamp out just such inhumanities. Mother Teresa's Missionaries of Charity are India's most internationally famed 'voluntary association', but throughout the country scores of 'non-government organis-ations' also do remarkable work. Many of them, too, display a keen awareness of the political implications of what they do.

These organisations are so effectively attracting the attention and commitment of large numbers of people, stirred to social action, that the Communist Party of India (Marxist) has begun to attack them. The people involved in these action groups would once have been regarded as obvious candidates for membership of a communist party. Today, however, the country's communist parties are weighed down with reputations that make them little different (and little more attractive) than any other political party. An old leftist writes of the 'progressive decline in the relevance of the communist parties' and of their 'major ailment': 'an unbelievable preoccupation – bordering on obsession – with election politics'. That preoccupation prevents the communists from taking strong stands on social issues: their first concern is the electoral arithmetic. How many people will be offended? How many pleased?[45] The Missionaries of Charity, on the other hand (and I use them simply because they are the best-known example of an Indian action-group), do not contest elections.

Prakash Karat, an able scholar from Kerala and an important member of the CPI(M), has attacked such action-groups as being part of 'a sophisticated and comprehensive strategy worked out in imperialist quarters ... to penetrate Indian society and influence its course of development'.[46] To win the compliment of a stinging attack from a sophisticated communist, these organisations must be making some impact.

The growth of the action-group phenomenon is, I believe, the result of the same innovations and ferment that gave rise to Bhindranwale and the bitter ethnic conflict of Punjab. The action-groups suggest, however, that alternatives are possible. Modernisation may lead to greater concern for humanity rather than to narrow ethnic chauvinism. Let us look at two voluntary associations, from opposite ends of the country, to try to get an idea of how they originate, what they do, whom they involve – and why they give reason for hope. The two examples are the Chipko environmental movement which began in the Tehri Garhwal district of UP in 1973 and the Kerala Sastra Sahithya Parishat (KSSP), one of the most inventive of the 'people's science movements', founded in 1962 but a widely active organisation only since 1972.

In Hindi, the word *chipko* means to hug or embrace. It began literally as a movement to 'hug the trees'. In the hill areas of western UP, men are often forced to migrate to cities to look for work, and women are left to look after barely economic holdings. State governments have leased out areas of forest to be felled by contractors, and insufficient attention has been paid to problems of erosion, appropriate reafforestation or the needs of local people for constant tree cover. In 1973, village women began to resist the felling operations by clutching the trees to prevent loggers from cutting them down. The method harked back to a fabled episode in eighteenth-century Rajasthan when more than 300 women are said to have been killed, trying to prevent loggers sent by a local raja from felling trees on the edge of the desert. The modern Chipko movement has used the story to lend appeal to the organisation. The blending of legend and activism recalls Bhindranwale and his iron arrow.

Chipko has become a vehicle for taking scientific ideas to the villages, as well as pressing home villagers' demands to governments. It has brought together peasants and college students; women have spearheaded many of its campaigns. By 1982, when some of its most prominent organisers were in the midst of a twenty-month propaganda march along the foothills of the Himalayas from Kashmir to Nagaland, the organisation was well-enough known to elicit a message of support from Mrs Gandhi herself.[47] By the mid-1980s, it was working, particularly among forest-dwelling people, not only in the UP but in Maharashtra and in Karnataka in south India. 'It's only the common people who can do something real', its leading figure, Sunderlal Bahuguna told journalists. His aim, he said, was to bring together social activists, 'humanitarian scientists' and journalists all over India. Together, he argued, 'they can bring a change'. The combination, it seems to me, is telling: modernisation (the scientists) and communications (the journalists) blend with the glaring need to reorganise society. The ingredients are the same as we have seen at work in Punjab, but a different set of chefs strive for a more palatable outcome.[48]

The KSSP has similar goals and works in similar ways. Its entertainment troupes travel into Kerala's most isolated villages to perform music, dance and theatre dedicated to the fulfilment of its motto, 'science for social revolution'. Its monthly science magazines have a circulation of more than 35 000. It has successfully lobbied the Kerala government on various environmental issues, while at the same time priding itself on the manner in which it brings together people of various social classes, religions and castes. It snipes not only at 'political parties avowedly based on religion' but also at 'so-called radicals' leaning on 'a crutch of borrowed phraseology'.[49] Neither the KSSP nor Chipko contests elections or is in league with a political party.

Organisations like them, however, are to be found throughout the country. In a brief article not purporting to be a survey, Harsh Sethi referred to a dozen examples. They ranged from rural health-co-operatives in Bihar, to worker-improvement associations in Madhya Pradesh, and land-rights organisations in Maharashtra. Nor did the list include groups associated with the slowly growing women's movement, of which the magazine *Manushi*, published from New Delhi, has acquired a reputation as the voice. 'One needs to recognise', writes Rajni Kothari, 'that something is on, it is serious, it is genuine and it is taking place at so many places.'[50]

The future of such action-groups is uncertain. Attempts in some regions to unite various groups have not been particularly successful.[51] The difficulties, for example, of Chipko and the KSSP doing anything more than exchanging information and visits are obvious. Their bases lie nearly 1000 miles apart. Their strengths lie in the fact that they are products of local conditions and that they work in local languages. However, there is already a widespread recognition of the power that a coalition of various action-groups could wield.[52]

The phenomenon of the action-groups is simply another response to the forces of modernisation working on India. In Punjab in recent years, these forces mixed with the unique traditions of Punjabis generally and Sikhs particularly to produce an explosion that rivetted international attention. Yet even in Punjab, other outcomes were – and are – possible. Sumit Singh, the 30-year-old shaven-Sikh editor of *Preet Lari*, murdered in February 1984, though more closely connected to leftist parties than many members of action-groups elsewhere, propagated ideas with which the KSSP would have felt at home. In addition to his writing and journalism, he too was involved in popular entertainment and theatre, attempting to use them, like the KSSP, for spreading ideas of social change among large numbers of people.[53] Growing ethnic conflict is only one possibility for India's future.

Mrs Gandhi and her circle often argued that to preserve the Indian state, they as the central government needed overwhelming power. Indeed, during the 'emergency' of 1975–7, they decreed that democracy and federalism had to be curtailed to save the state. A similar undercurrent ran through the national election campaign of 1984.

Yet it seems to me that the opposite proposition is closer to the truth: if the Indian state is to survive, federalism and democracy are essential. In no other way can the state adjust to the tensions of steady modernisation; in no other way – except in explosions – can such tensions be responded to and released.

To rectify the galling yet ineffectual centralisation that was at the root of the turmoil in Punjab does not necessarily require major constitutional change. Adherence to the commonly accepted norms of responsible government would mark a beginning. Beyond that, institutions – police, judiciary, etc. – need to be revived and reformed. At the same time, new institutions need to be encouraged; the action-groups point to the potential. Perhaps institution-building in India in the next twenty years will take place from the bottom up. That would be appropriate, since institution-destruction in the past twenty years has often worked from the top down. Mrs Gandhi's death holds out the possibility of new starts.

Few would dispute the glaring shortcomings and immense problems of the Indian state. Heartless exploitation and heartrending poverty are the lot of nearly half the population. Yet the destruction of the present state – or, indeed, political revolution – will not necessarily bring liberation and prosperity. The evidence of Biafra, Ethiopia, Kampuchea or Uganda suggests that the lot of the poor can become still worse: to poverty, can be added terror and starvation. The hope of the poor lies in their own burgeoning political awareness, the product of the modernising ferment that penetrates even remote corners of India. From one region to another, that process goes on at varying speeds and with different effects. In Punjab, the innovations of the past twenty years were already reacting with a proud, violent culture when a series of unwise political decisions, aimed at short-term gains, set off the explosions of the 1980s.

The ferment of modernisation is capable of generating religious revival, ethnic conflict and secession. Events in Punjab illustrate the dangers. But these new energies also make it possible for the poor to organise. For the first time, they have the potential to unite over wide areas, to co-operate with sympathetic sections of the elite and to create or capture institutions which they can turn to their own needs. Ultimately, the possibility exists for them to transform the Indian state and make it work for them.

Postscript: November 1985

In the time since the typescript of this book went to the publishers, events have highlighted a number of its themes. Perhaps the most important – the agreement between Prime Minister Rajiv Gandhi and Harchand Singh Longowal, announced on 24 July 1985[1] – emphasised a basic argument of the book: that political decisions, rather than inexorable social forces, determine the form and intensity of ethnic conflict.

On the face of it, Punjab's problems should have been more intractable by July 1985 than ever before. The mood of Sikhs, for example, should have been more intransigent. The army had been deployed in Punjab for more than a year, the Sikhs there complained of violations of civil rights. In addition, Sikhs everywhere shared the anger and humiliation, if not the loss and death, of those who suffered in the rioting following Mrs Gandhi's murder.

'National opinion', too, might have been expected to have hardened against Sikhs. The death of more than 80 people in terrorist bombings in New Delhi and other parts of north India on 11 and 12 May ought to have embittered feelings further, as should the mysterious crash of an Air India jumbo jet off the coast of Ireland on 23 June which killed more than 320 people.

Furthermore, the 'Memorandum of Settlement' of July 1985 between the central government and Longowal's Akali Dal appeared to contain nothing new. Indeed, wrote *The Tribune*, it ran 'along lines known and agreed upon almost two years ago'.[2] The 'Indian Talks' section of this book (pp. 153–9) makes that point clear. However, different people were doing the talking for the central government, and the perceptions of other participants (notably Longowal) about how to prosper (or, at least, survive) had also changed. Politicians do not simply speak *for* their followers. They speak *to* them as well; they can choose to incite or placate. To be sure, they must constantly take account of what they can 'sell' to their supporters – what their social base expects of them. But the decisions they make at particular times result from complex calculations involving personal conviction, the mood of followers, the position of rivals and judgements about the likelihood of gain or success. Such calculations led to the July agreement.

Within a month, Longowal paid for it with his life. Young Sikh assassins, outraged at his 'treachery', shot and killed him in a *gurdwara* near Sangrur on 20 August. But Longowal became more powerful dead than alive.

The creation of symbols and their use in politics has been a theme throughout this book (e.g. pp. 159–64), and Longowal became such a symbol. Journalists claimed that 'there were as many Hindus as Sikhs' in the crowd of tens of thousands at his funeral.[3] Even among the most militant overseas Sikhs, few acclaimed his assassination, while in India, it was universally condemned. The Akali Dal built its campaign for the elections, called for 25 September, around Longowal the martyr. 'Vote', an advertisement implored, 'so that he may live forever in thought and in deed . . . A man of God . . . A man of peace . . . Sant Longowal died for the rebirth of Punjab. Vote for a Government that would keep alive his ideals.'

Longowal provided a hero not merely for the Akali Dal. At last, the Indian state had a badly needed *Sikh* martyr to the cause of Indian unity. A newspaper editor caught this process of appropriation well: Longowal had become 'the second [Mahatma] Gandhi'.[4] Though Punjab remained under central-government rule during the campaign leading up to the elections of 25 September, the Punjab administration took the unusual step of buying newspaper advertisements to remind Punjabis that Longowal was 'a brave man who had the interest of the people and the country at heart. Punjab owes a lot to him.' With Longowal at the centre of the Akali Dal's campaign, it was as if the Congress (I) government in New Delhi were electioneering against its own members in Punjab.[5] Indeed, it was widely claimed that Prime Minister Rajiv Gandhi saw an Akali Dal victory as the best possible outcome and that his party had purposely chosen weak candidates in some constituencies.[6]

The desirability of an Akali Dal victory underlined a striking irony, which further emphasises the role of political decisions – rather than deeply etched social divisions – in the 'Punjab crisis' of the 1980s. In 1985, 'success' for the central government lay in getting Punjab back to the political position of January 1980 – with an Akali Dal government in power. Five years of deviousness and thousands of deaths emphasised the need for a more straightforward approach to federalism. Indeed, if the battle at the Golden Temple and the assassinations of Mrs Gandhi and Longowal achieved anything, it was to dramatise, even for the most old-fashioned, win-at-all-costs factional leader, the frailty of the very institutions that he struggled to control. An icy awareness grew that one's known enemies were no longer the only threat: mass hatreds could make stranger kill stranger for no reason of immediate gain or personal vengeance (see pp. 95–7). Politicians seemed sobered. The September election campaign was unusually muted and respectful.[7]

The elections brought a clear victory for the Akali Dal led by Surjit Singh Barnala (b. 1925), who had emerged as Longowal's English-speaking lieutenant. For Indian central governments, Barnala made a reassuring Chief Minister. A widely travelled lawyer, born in a Hindi-speaking area (now deep in Haryana) of the old princely state of Nabha, educated in Lucknow, Barnala was Minister of Education in Punjab in the Akali government of 1969–71 and Minister of Agriculture in the central government during the Janata Party ministry in 1977–9.[8] The correspondent of *India Today* noted that Barnala was a keen painter and that in his drawing room hung a portrait of his meeting with Pope Paul in Bombay in 1964.[9] So clearly a part of the national elite, Barnala seemed to pose no threat to the Indian state. The question, however, was whether these very characteristics would make it impossible for him to deal with new challenges in Punjab. How many youthful imaginations was such a man likely to fire?

In spite of an attempted boycott of the elections by Sikh opponents of the July agreement, who used Bhindranwale's elderly father as their titular leader, the turnout of nearly 68 per cent was higher than in 1977 or 1980.[10] The Akali Dal's 73 seats and 38.7 per cent of the vote were the best result in its history. (Compare the table below with Table 5.2 on p. 112). Among the successful Akali candidates were two Hindus and a Muslim, and two Hindus who won as independents had Akali backing.[11] The Bharatiya Janata Party, which in its former incarnations drew the votes of urban Hindus, retained some support. The communists, however, were reduced from a combined tally of

Punjab State Elections, September 1985

	Seats	Percentage of votes
Akali Dal	73	38.7
Congress (I)	32	37.7
Communist Party of India	1 ⎤	8.0
Communist Party of India (Marxist)	0 ⎦	
Bharatiya Janata Party	4 ⎤	
Janata Party	1 ⎬	15.6
Independents	4 ⎦	

NOTE   Voting in two seats postponed.
SOURCE   *HIE*, 12 October 1985, p. 14; *EPW*, 5 October 1985, p. 1681.

13 seats and 14 per cent of the vote in 1980 to one seat and eight per cent in 1985. Class division, as I wrote earlier (p. 33), is everywhere in Punjab, yet rarely in people's minds.

In the elections to the national parliament, the Congress (I) won six of the 13 seats; the Akali Dal, 7. Such a result again seemed promising for the central government. It could be interpreted as a readiness to separate local from national issues and to accept the legitimacy of the Indian state as embodied in Rajiv Gandhi's Congress (I) Party.

Throughout India, the frightening events of 1984 and 1985 seemed to moderate the judgement of politicians. In Assam, the central government negotiated a settlement in August with the leaders of the anti-'foreigner' agitation that convulsed the state from 1979. The leaders formed a new political party to contest state elections in December – no doubt with the examples of N. T. Rama Rao's Telugu Desam and other successful regional parties in mind.

This attempt to apply elastic bandages to the straining joints of bodies politic extended beyond India's borders. With 100 000 Sri Lankan Tamils as refugees in India, the Indian government sought to engineer an agreement between the unitary Sri Lankan government and Sri Lankan Tamil separatists. Such an agreement would involve the devolution of some powers to the northern, Tamil-majority areas of Sri Lanka. Indian governments must walk warily between two chasms. By appearing to disregard the plight of Tamils in Sri Lanka, they may enrage more than 50 million of their own citizens in Tamilnad. On the other hand, they cannot afford to be seen as appealing for international cooperation against violent 'Khalistanis' while encouraging secession in Sri Lanka.

What happened between April and November 1985 to some of the people who have figured in this book? Longowal was murdered. So, too, were Lalit Maken, MP (31 July) and Arjan Das (4 September), both New Delhi politicians named in one of the unofficial inquiries into the riots against Sikhs in November 1984.[12] The central government used the police to suppress a follow-up report in September 1985 which accused the security forces in Punjab of violent repression.[13]

Amarindar Singh, the Congress (I) MP from the Patiala princely family, who resigned from the party after the battle of the Golden Temple, joined the Akali Dal, was elected to the legislature and became Minister of Agriculture in Barnala's government. The wife of the policeman, P. S. Bhindar, retained her seat as the Congress (I) MP from Gurdaspur in the national parliament. Parkash Singh Badal at first opposed Longowal's agreement with the central government, was reconciled with him on the day he was assassinated, proposed Barnala's name as leader of the Akali Dal in the legislature, but did not join the new government. Zail Singh continued as president of India, his term not due to end until mid-1987, though Prime Minister Rajiv Gandhi was said to have little patience with him.[14]

The story of the destruction of the Punjab police (pp. 170–4) acquired further texture with allegations that the Congress (I) government of Punjab had instructed the police to kill 'extremists'. 'You kill the killers', the former Chief Minister, Darbara Singh, is said to have told BBC journalists, 'and I will take the responsibility'.[15] Such stories accord all too well with Joyce Pettigrew's accounts of politicians and police in Punjab (p. 172).

The official commission of inquiry into the riots of November 1985 under Supreme Court judge Ranganath Mishra, announced in April 1985, began work only in July. It seemed unlikely to report quickly. On the anniversary of the riots, widows of some of the victims demonstrated in front of the Prime Minister's residence. Though provided with places to live, they claimed they had no way of supporting their children. Jagjit Singh Aurora, retired Lieutenant-General and hero of the Bangladesh war in 1971, took up their cause and called for small pensions to be paid to them until their children were grown.[16]

The vision of 'Khalistan', or a sovereign Sikh state, shone most brightly from afar. The 'romantics overseas' (see pp. 142–7) nurtured it with a frantic passion. Stories circulated that the government of Ecuador had talked to 'Khalistan' advocates in Britain.[17] The crash of the Air India Boeing 707 on 23 June was suspected to have resulted from the explosion of a bomb planted on board in Canada. Later, wreckage salvaged from the sea bed began to confirm this initial theory.[18]

Arrests in Britain, the USA and Canada indicated either that the Indian government was becoming more successful in pressing foreign powers to crack down on violent proponents of 'Khalistan' or that these activities were becoming more troublesome and aggressive. The arrests involved alleged plots to assassinate Rajiv Gandhi during his visits to the USA in June and Britain in October.[19] In Canada, Talwindar Singh Parmar, a Canadian citizen since 1975, but said to be a founder of the Babbar Khalsa (see p. 175), was arrested on charges of illegal possession of explosives. Parmar had already spent 15 months in prisons in West Germany.[20] According to another report, regular collections of money in British *gurdwaras* were providing a steady flow of arms to Punjab.[21] The geographic sweep of the stories – from Germany to Vancouver to South America – recalled the days of the Ghadr movement and the voyage of the *Komagata Maru* (see p. 63). The romantics no doubt thought so too.

Images and sentiment move people to act in ways that may not seem to coincide with their immediate self-interest. Earlier in this book I tried to explain the struggles to appropriate desirable symbols for one's cause (pp. 87–92, 159–62). Subsequent events – the use of 'Longowal the martyr', for example – have emphasised the importance of such ceaseless contests. But there is still more intriguing evidence. A newsletter produced by *gurdwaras* in Malaysia carried a note entitled 'The Falcon Comes', which reported falcon-sightings at *gurdwaras* throughout north India at the end of 1984:

> Guru Gobind Singh came to the rescue of his suffering people
> . . . the Master's falcon is seen in almost every part of India. It
> is the same bird which was sighted by Sikhs in trouble from
> time to time. Whether it was a solitary Khalsa [Sikh] on horse
> back, in the wild forest, or hundreds of them being brutally

beaten by the tyrant authorities, it was the sight of the falcon that sustained this daring and devout race.[22]

One of Mrs Gandhi's accused assassins is said to have been inspired by 'a chance flight of a falcon [a symbol associated with Guru Gobind Singh]' into the grounds of the prime minister's residence. The man and his colleague allegedly 'agreed that it had brought the message of the Tenth Guru . . . that they should do something by way of revenge [for the assult on the Golden Temple]'.[23] The Akali Dal's election manifesto fused the old and new when it pledged the party to the 'secular, democratic and socialistic ideals of Guru Gobind Singh'.[24]

Another contention of this book is that Indian society is increasingly able to receive an array of messages and information that would have been unthinkable even to the grandparents of people alive today. Contests to appropriate symbols and win mass sentiment are one of the outcomes. In this connection, it is worth pointing out that Rajiv Gandhi's 'success' in the national and Punjab elections resulted in large measure from the skilful use of the emotions generated by two assassinations – his mother's and Longowal's. The future of India lies less with those who can manage its economy than with those who understand its sentiments.

The contrasts between Rajiv Gandhi and his mother (and younger brother Sanjay) became increasingly obvious during his first year in office. At first, veteran journalists joked about 'computer boys' in the prime minister's office. But the use of market-research and advertising techniques seemed to pay off in the 1984 elections, and within a year his emphasis on modern technology and scientific study became a matter for admiration rather than laughter. In contrast to the thoughtless bluster of the late Sanjay Gandhi, the new prime minister appeared to want to bring the best scientific information to bear on problems. The contrast with his late brother was most striking in the field of family planning where Sanjay Gandhi had terrified and alienated millions of poor people during the 'emergency'. Rajiv Gandhi, on the other hand, was said to have commissioned a major survey into attitudes towards family planning and its implementation. The accepted wisdom of contemporary social science informed his own views: 'One of the ways we are going to tackle [the high birth rate] is with education, and especially women's education.'[25]

No one who has read Punjab's modern history would predict that the agreement of July or the successful elections of September 1985 assure an era of reconciliation and peace. The murder in London in 1941 of Sir Michael O'Dwyer, Governor of Punjab at the time of the slaughter of Jallianwalla Bagh in 1919, is sufficient demonstration that the wounds of 1984 will probably torment the Indian body politic for years to come.

But having demonstrated the bloody cost of short-sighted central-government meddling in an age when communications foster burgeoning local pride, the 'Punjab crisis' may ultimately strengthen Indian democracy and federalism. Sobered politicians may be more inclined to strive for a balance between the prerogatives of regional leaders and the requirements of national integrity. Such a balance must lie at the heart of a democratic federation.

Notes

PREFACE

1. Moni Nag and Neeraj Kak, 'Population Control Is No Longer a Myth in Manupur, Punjab', paper presented to the seminar on Micro-Approaches to Demographic Research, Australian National University, Canberra, 3–7 September 1984, pp. 10, 14, 16. Marika Vicziany provided me with a copy of this paper.
2. P. R. Brass, 'Pluralism, Regionalism and Decentralization Tendencies in Contemporary Indian Politics', in A. Jeyaratnam Wilson and Dennis Dalton (eds) *The States of South Asia* (London: Hurst, 1982) p. 229; *OHT*, 19 May 1983, p. 4. *HIE*, 14 May 1983, p. 2; *Press in India, 1968*, p. 106; *Mass Media in India, 1980–1*, pp. 168–9.

3. *Army Action in Punjab. Prelude and Aftermath* (New Delhi: Samata Era, 1984) p. 52.
4. A Delhi High Court judge quoted in *EPW*, 9 March 1985, p. 392.

1 ETHNICITY

1. *SMH*, 13 November 1984 (Ranjan Gupta).
2. *Time Magazine*, 14 January 1985, p. 7.
3. *EPW*, 22–29 December 1984, p. 2153 and 5 January 1985, p. 2.
4. *T*, 13 August 1980, p. 4 (Satindra Singh).
5. V. D. Chopra, R. K. Misra, Nirmal Singh, *Agony of Punjab* (New Delhi: Patriot Publishers, 1984) p. 163. See also *EPW*, 1 January 1985, p. 131.
6. N. Glazer and D. P. Moynihan (eds) *Ethnicity: Theory and Experience* (Cambridge, Massachusetts: Harvard UP, 1975) spell out some of this in their introduction, pp. 1–26. See also D. Bell, 'Ethnicity and Social Change', in ibid, pp. 141–74; C. F. Keyes, 'The Dialectics of Ethnic Change', in Keyes (ed.) *Ethnic Change* (Seattle: University of Washington Press, 1981) pp. 3–30; P. R. Brass, 'Ethnicity and Nationality Formation', *Ethnicity*, III, 3 (1976) pp. 225–41. The literature on the subject is vast.
7. R. G. Fox, C. H. Aull and L. F. Cimino, 'Ethnic Nationalism and the Welfare State', in Keyes (ed.) *Ethnic Change*, p. 202.
8. E. J. Hobsbawm, *Age of Revolution, 1789–1848* (London: Weidenfeld & Nicholson, 1962) p. 135.
9. Dipesh Chakrabarty, 'Communal Riots and Labour: Bengal's Jute Mill-hands in the 1890s', *Past and Present*, no. 91 (May 1981) pp. 140–69.
10. *London Journal*, 13 November 1858, p. 200.
11. M. F. Katzenstein, *Ethnicity and Equality* (Ithaca: Cornell UP, 1979) especially pp. 37–66.
12. For background on Assam and ethnic theory generally, see M. Weiner, *Sons of the Soil* (PUP, 1978); also *HIE*, 3 and 10 July 1982, both p. 9. For Andhra Pradesh, *IT*, 31 December 1982, p. 46.
13. P. R. Brass, *Language, Religion and Politics in North India* (CUP, 1974) pp. 27–47.
14. Weiner, *Sons*, ch. 5, pp. 219–54.
15. *IT*, 15 February 1985, p. 76.
16. Brass, *Language*, p. 45.
17. *T*, 4 September 1978, p. 4; *OHT*, 14 April 1983, p. 7 (Khushwant Singh).
18. *EPW*, 24 November 1984, p. 1985 for the official figure. The early report *Who Are the Guilty?* (New Delhi: People's Union for Democratic Rights and People's Union for Civil Liberties, 1984) p. 1, estimated 'more than a thousand' deaths. A condensation of this report is in the *EPW*, 24 November 1984, pp. 1979–85. Madhu Kishwar's impressive report in *Manushi*, no. 25 (November–December 1984) p. 13, estimated 2500 deaths. *Report of the Citizen's Commission* (New Delhi: Citizens' Commission, 1985) p. 35, estimated 'well over two thousand were murdered'. See also *IT*, 31 January 1985, p. 50.

19. *Sunday*, 17–23 February 1985, p. 65.
20. *Manushi*, no. 25 (November–December 1984) p. 32.
21. The following account is based on the three non-official accounts cited in note 18 above.
22. *Manushi*, no. 25 (November–December 1984) p. 18.
23. *EPW*, 24 November 1984, p. 1985; *Who Are the Guilty?*, p. 26.
24. *EPW*, 24 November 1984, p. 1985 and 8 December 1984, p. 2066; *Manushi*, no. 25 (November–December 1984) p. 19; *Report of the Citizens' Commission*, p. 12.
25. *EPW*, 8 December 1984, p. 2068.
26. *India Magazine* (January 1985) p. 73.
27. *HIE*, 2 March 1985, p. 4. *OHT*, 2 March 1985, p. 3.
28. *Who Are the Guilty?*, Annexure IV.
29. J. R. Wood in *Asia Pacific Report*, University of British Columbia (January 1985) p. 7.
30. *IT*, 31 December 1984, pp. 36–7. *Business India*, 17–30 December 1984, p. 87.
31. *IT*, 15 January 1985, p. 24.
32. *IT*, 31 December 1984, p. 36.
33. I am grateful to Dipesh Chakrabarty for this example.
34. *EPW*, 8 December 1984, p. 2066 (Amiya Rao).
35. *IWI*, 23 December 1984, p. 15 (Ivan Fera).
36. *EPW*, 12 January 1985, p. 80.
37. *EPW*, 26 January 1985, p. 150 (Balraj Puri).
38. *Guardian Weekly*, 6 January 1985, p. 7.
39. For background, see *EPW*, 1 September 1984, p. 1509 (Kashmir); *IT*, 15 June 1984, p. 22 (Sikkim); *EPW*, 15 September 1984, p. 1623 (Karnataka); *IT*, 15 September 1984, p. 7 (Andhra Pradesh).

2 PUNJAB

1. *IT*, 1–15 March 1979, p. 33.
2. G. D. Khosla, *The Murder of the Mahatma* (Bombay: Jaico, 1968) p. 188.
3. Prem Bhatia, *All My Yesterdays* (New Delhi: Hind Pocket Books, 1977) pp. 87–92.
4. Rajaram Dasgupta, 'Nutritional Situation in India: A Statistical Analysis', *EPW*, 25 August 1984, p. 1492.
5. W. H. McLeod, *Guru Nanak and the Sikh Religion* (Oxford: Clarendon, 1968) p. 228.
6. M. S. Randhawa, *Out of the Ashes* (Chandigarh: Public Relations Department, Punjab, 1954) p. 221.
7. Prakash Tandon, *Punjabi Century, 1857–1947* (New Delhi: Orient Paperbacks, 1961) p. 55.
8. Khushwant Singh, *Train*, p. 37.
9. J. Pettigrew, *Robber Noblemen* (New Delhi: Ambika, 1978) p. 59; Tandon, *Punjabi*, p. 71.

10. *Times of India Yearbook 1979*, p. 198; *Quick Canadian Facts*, 1983, 36th ed, p. 201; *T*, 19 June 1979, p. 4; J. Pettigrew, 'Conflict Escalation in the Punjab', in M. J. Aronoff (ed.) *Freedom and Constraint* (Amsterdam: Van Gorcum, 1976) p. 44; M. Juergensmeyer, 'Cultures of Deprivation', *EPW*, Annual Number (February 1979) p. 257.

11. Mahmood Mamdani, *The Myth of Population Control* (New York: Monthly Review Press, 1972) p. 135. As with so much else in Punjab, things have changed in Manupur since 1970, and acceptance of contraception has become far more common, partly a result, it seems, of the spread of female education. Moni Nag and Neeraj Kak, 'Population Control Is No Longer a Myth in Manupur, Punjab', paper presented at Seminar on Micro-Approaches to Demographic Research, Australian National University, Canberra, 3–7 September 1984.

12. Mamdani, *Myth*, p. 138.

13. Ibid, p. 141.

14. *IT*, 15 August 1982, pp. 46–7; *EPW*, 23 October 1982, p. 1725 and 15 January 1983, pp. 61–4.

15. *IT*, 1–15 March 1979, p. 1.

16. *EPW*, 18 April 1984, p. 1224. The figures are for 1979–80 and exclude Sikkim.

17. *T*, 7 August 1980, p. 12; *FEER*, 10 December 1982, p. 27.

18. *EPW*, 11 April 1981, p. 643.

19. *IT*, 1–15 March 1979, p. 33; *HIE*, 12 January 1985, p. 6.

20. *FEER*, 10 December 1982, p. 27; *IT*, 1–15 March 1979, p. 36.

21. B. L C. Johnson, *Development in South Asia* (Harmondsworth: Penguin, 1983) pp. 75–7, 85–7.

22. Sucha Singh Gill and K. C. Singhal, 'Punjabi Farmers' Agitation: Response to Development Crisis in Agriculture', *EPW*, 6 October 1984, p. 1729.

23. Ibid.

24. M. S. Randhawa (ed.) *Green Revolution* (New Delhi: Vikas, 1974) p. 181.

25. Dalip Singh, *Dynamics of Punjab Politics* (New Delhi: Macmillan, 1981) p. 50.

26. Johnson, *Development*, p. 86.

27. M. Darling, *The Punjab Peasant in Prosperity and Debt* (New Delhi: Manohar, 1977; 1st pub. 1925) p. 35.

28. K. Davis, *The Population of India and Pakistan* (PUP, 1951) p. 197; S. L. Keller, *Uprooting and Social Change* (New Delhi: Manohar, 1975) p. 37.

29. Randhawa, *Out*, p. 93. The 4.7 million acres constituted about 15 per cent of the total area of eastern Punjab.

30. Ibid, p. 97.

31. Darling, *Punjab Peasant*, pp. 240–1.

32. Randhawa, *Out*, p. 184.

33. Dalip Singh, *Dynamics*, p. 59.

34. Ibid, pp. 49, 77.

35. Randhawa, *Green Revolution*, p. 179.

36. Sucha Singh Gill, 'Agrarian Transformation in a Punjab Village', *Mainstream*, 4 March 1978, p. 16.
37. Dalip Singh, *Dynamics*, pp. 248, 251.
38. Punjab: Rs. 2528; Kerala: Rs. 1334; Madhya Pradesh: Rs. 901; Bihar: Rs. 785. *EPW*, 28 July 1984, p. 1224.
39. *IT*, 1–15 March 1979, p. 36.
40. Ibid. Pramod Kumar *et al.*, *Punjab Crisis: Context and Trends* (Chandigarh: Centre for Research in Rural and Industrial Development, 1984) pp. 55–61.
41. See, for example, M. Weiner, *Sons of the Soil* (PUP, 1978) and M. Weiner and M. F. Katzenstein, *India's Preferential Policies* (University of Chicago Press, 1981).
42. *IT*, 1–15 March 1979, p. 35; *OHT*, 4 March 1982, p. 11. and 9 September 1982, p. 9, which estimates 500 000 Sikhs in Britain.
43. H. K. Trevaskis, *The Land of the Five Rivers* (OUP, 1928) p. 8n.
44. The Chenab rises in India.
45. Khushwant Singh, *A History of the Sikhs* (PUP, 1966) vol. I, p. 3.
46. J. B. Bury, *A History of Greece to the Death of Alexander the Great* (London: Macmillan, 1963) 3rd edn, pp. 807–8.
47. Tandon, *Punjabi*, p. 14.
48. Ibid.
49. Ibid, p. 116.
50. Darling, *Punjab Peasant*, p. 146.
51. Trevaskis, *Land*, p. 345.
52. Ibid, pp. 102, 131.
53. Randhawa, *Out*, pp. 34–5.
54. Darling, *Punjab Peasant*, pp. 260–1.
55. Ibid, p. 132.
56. Ibid, pp. 133–4.
57. Tandon, *Punjabi*, p. 254.
58. Davis, *Population*, p. 197; Keller, *Uprooting*, p. 370.
59. P. R. Brass, *Language, Religion and Politics in North India* (CUP, 1974) pp. 299, 301.
60. R. Jeffrey, 'The Punjab Boundary Force and the Problem of Order: August 1947', *MAS*, VIII, 4 (1974) pp. 491–520.
61. O. H. K. Spate, 'Partition of the Punjab and Bengal', *Geographical Journal*, vol. 110, 1948, p. 211.
62. Khushwant Singh, *History*, I, p. 200.
63. *OHT*, 15 October 1981, p. 10.
64. Lt.-Col. Manohar Singh, 'Sikh Way of Life', *Mainstream*, 1 May 1982, p. 31. Also W. O. Cole and Piara Singh Sambhi, *The Sikhs: Their Religious Beliefs and Practices* (London: Routledge & Kegan Paul, 1978) pp. 80–3. Manohar Singh's version of the *Ardas* is particularly grisly. Compare it with the more general version in W. H. McLeod (ed.) *Textual Sources for the Study of Sikhism* (Manchester UP, 1984) pp. 103–5.
65. See the reaction of Michael Richardson, *SMH*, 16 June 1984.
66. Tandon, *Punjabi*, p. 10.

67. B. Ramusack, 'The Princely States of the Punjab: A Bibliographic Essay', in W. E. Gustafson and K. W. Jones (eds) *Sources on Punjab History* (New Delhi: Manohar, 1975) pp. 374–5.
68. Brass, *Language*, p. 299.
69. P. R. Brass, 'Ethnic Cleavages and the Punjab Party System, 1952–72', in M. Weiner and J. O. Field (eds) *Electoral Politics in the Indian States: Party Systems and Cleavages* (New Delhi: Manohar, 1975) p. 10.
70. Indu Banga, *Agrarian System of the Sikhs* (New Delhi: Manohar 1978) pp. 141–2.

3 SIKHS

1. *IT*, 15 November 1983, pp. 19–20.
2. Since details of caste have not been collected at censuses since 1931, the figures can only be estimates. Ethna K. Marenco, *The Transformation of Sikh Society* (Portland, Oregon: The Ha Pi Press, 1974) pp. 151, 162–3; Pettigrew, *Robber*, pp. 35, 41; Satish Saberwal, *Mobile Men* (New Delhi: Vikas, 1976) pp. 96–102 for Ramgarhias.
3. H. Izmirlian, Jr, *Structure and Strategy in Sikh Society* (New Delhi: Manohar, 1979) p. 23.
4. For example, F. Conlon, *A Caste in a Changing World* (Berkeley: UCP, 1977) and K. Leonard, *Social History of an Indian Caste* (Berkeley: UCP, 1978).
5. Randhawa, *Out*, p. 41.
6. Marenco, *Transformation*, p. 296, says Sudras; Khushwant Singh, *History*, I, p. 14n says Vaisyas.
7. *Age* (Melbourne) 4 August 1979, p. 29.
8. D. Ibbetson, *Panjab Castes* (Delhi: B. R. Publishing Corporation, 1974; first published in this form 1916; based on census report, 1881) p. 103.
9. M. C. Pradhan, *The Political System of the Jats of Northern India* (Bombay: OUP, 1966) p. 2.
10. R. E. Parry, *The Sikhs of the Punjab* (London: Drane, 1921) p. 102; Marenco, *Transformation*, p. 113.
11. J. S. Grewal, 'A Perspective on Early Sikh History', in M. Juergensmeyer and N. G. Barrier (eds) *Sikh Studies* (Berkeley: Berkeley Religious Studies Series, 1979) p. 38.
12. Marian Smith, 'Synthesis and Other Processes in Sikhism', *American Anthropologist*, 3, Part 1 (1948) p. 457.
13. McLeod, *Guru*, pp. 3, 6.
14. For example, ibid, p. 222, and Irfan Habib, 'Evidence for Sixteenth-Century Agrarian Conditions in the Guru Granth Sahib', *Indian Economic and Social History Review*, I, 3 (January–March 1964) pp. 64–72.
15. *OHT*, 22 April 1982, p. 6.
16. McLeod, *Guru*, p. 161.
17. Ibid, p. 231. For fuller discussion of the Sikh religion, see the excellent entries in J. R. Hinnells (ed.) *The Penguin Dictionary of Religions* (Harmondsworth: Penguin, 1984).

18. Cole and Sambhi, *The Sikhs* (London: Routledge & Kegan Paul, 1978) pp. 15–18.
19. Nanak was a Khatri of the Bedi sub-group. Bishen Singh Bedi, the former Indian cricket captain, is a member of the same group.
20. Khushwant Singh, *The Sikhs Today* (Bombay: Sangam Books, 1976) p. 22; W. H. McLeod, *The Way of the Sikh* (Amersham: Hulton Educational Publications, 1975) p. 12.
21. Trevaskis, *Land*, p. 166.
22. Khushwant Singh, *History*, I, p. 58; W. H. McLeod (trans. and ed.) *Textual Sources for the Study of Sikhism* (Manchester UP, 1984) p. 1.
23. Khushwant Singh, *History*, I, p. 62.
24. Ibid, pp. 57–9.
25. W. H. McLeod, *Early Sikh Tradition* (Oxford: Clarendon, 1980) p. 4.
26. Ibid. Khushwant Singh, *History*, I, pp. 57, 89, 93; M. J. Leaf, *Information and Behaviour in a Sikh Village* (Berkeley: UCP, 1972) p. 219.
27. Grewal, 'Perspective', p. 37. McLeod, *Early*, pp. 4, 247.
28. Khushwant Singh, *History*, I, pp. 82–3. Cole and Sambhi, *Sikhs*, pp. 35–6. McLeod, *Way*, pp. 25–6.
29. Khushwant Singh, *History*, I, pp. 82–5.
30. Pettigrew, *Robber*, p. 25.
31. Cole and Sambhi, *Sikhs*, p. 37.
32. McLeod, *Early*, p. 4.
33. McLeod, *Textual*, p. 104.
34. Khushwant Singh, *History*, I, pp. 116–18, 127.
35. Ibid, p. 168.
36. Ibid, p. 127n.
37. Ibid, p. 128n.
38. Ibid, pp. 215, 250–3; McLeod, *Textual*, pp. 132–3.
39. *T*, 11 April 1978, p. 1.
40. *T*, 14 April 1978, p. 1.
41. Pettigrew, *Robber*, p. 27; Khushwant Singh, *History*, I, pp. 122–3.
42. *IT*, 31 May 1982, p. 13; *HIE*, 8 May 1982, pp. 1, 3.
43. Khushwant Singh, *History*, I, pp. 89, 120–1. The more precise distinction is between *amrit-dhari* Sikhs (those who have been initiated) and *sahaj-dhari*. See Hinnells (ed.) *Penguin Dictionary of Religions*, pp. 302–3. In theory, it is possible to be a follower of Guru Nanak but not a Khalsa-initiated Sikh wearing the Five Ks.
44. Khushwant Singh, *History*, II, p. 303.
45. 'Travellers' Tales', Australian Broadcasting Corporation, Radio 2, 5 January 1985.
46. Pettigrew, *Robber*, p. 27.
47. Ibid, pp. 27–8; Khushwant Singh, *History*, I, pp. 182–9.
48. Pettigrew, *Robber*, p. 202.
49. Ibid, p. 98; A. S. Narang, *Storm over the Sutlej* (New Delhi: Gitanjali, 1983) p. 128.
50. Khushwant Singh, *Sikhs Today*, p. 36.
51. Khushwant Singh, *History*, I, pp. 187–99.
52. Ibid, p. 289.

53. Criminal Investigations Department note, in N. G. Barrier (ed.) *The Sikhs and their Literature* (New Delhi: Manohar, 1970) p. xliv.
54. C. Aitchison, *Lord Lawrence* (Oxford: Clarendon, 1892) pp. 56–8; Satish Saberwal and Harjot Singh Oberoi, 'A Dialogue for Today', *Seminar*, no. 305 (January 1985) p. 5.
55. Letter, 7 May 1849, in Kushwant Singh, *History*, II, p. 96.
56. Secret Consultations, 28 February 1851, in Khushwant Singh, *History*, II, p. 113.
57. *HIE*, 22 September 1984, p. 8.
58. Parry, *Sikhs*, pp. 9, 122.
59. Khushwant Singh, *History*, II, p. 160.
60. Parry, *Sikhs*, p. 9.
61. For examples, see Marie M. de Lepervanche, *Indians in a White Australia* (Sydney: Allen & Unwin, 1984); A. W. Helweg, *Sikhs in England* (New Delhi: OUP, 1979); M. Juergensmeyer, 'The Ghadr Syndrome: Immigrant Sikhs and Nationalist Pride', in Juergensmeyer and Barrier (eds), *Sikh Studies*, pp. 173–90; T. G. Kessinger, *Vilyatpur, 1848–1968* (Berkeley: UCP, 1974); Sohan Singh Josh, *Tragedy of Komagata Maru* (New Delhi: People's Publishing House, 1975).
62. Khushwant Singh, *History*, II, pp. 178–81. Juergensmeyer, 'Ghadr', p. 173.
63. Juergensmeyer, 'Ghadr', pp. 173, 176.
64. Khushwant Singh, *History*, II, p. 160.
65. N. G. Barrier (ed.) *The Sikhs and their Literature* (New Delhi: Manohar, 1970) p. xli.
66. Helen Fein, *Imperial Crime and Punishment* (Honolulu: University of Hawaii Press, 1977) p. 21.
67. *Times* (London) 14 March 1940, p. 8.
68. Mohinder Singh, *The Akali Movement* (Delhi: Macmillan, 1978) pp. 4–5.
69. Ibid, pp. 88–92.
70. Khushwant Singh, *History*, II, pp. 198–200; Mohinder Singh, *Akali*, pp. 32–4.
71. Mohinder Singh, *Akali*, p. 97.
72. Harish K. Puri, 'Akali Politics: Emerging Compulsions', in P. Wallace and Surendra Chopra (eds) *Political Dynamics of Punjab* (Amritsar: Guru Nanak Dev University, 1981) p. 35.
73. Mohinder Singh, *Akali*, p. 138; Darbara Singh in *FEER*, 10 December 1982, p. 27.
74. Imran Ali, 'Relations between the Muslim League and the Punjab National Unionist Party, 1935–47', *South Asia*, no. 6 (December 1976) pp. 51–65.
75. Baldev Raj Nayar, 'Punjab', in M. Weiner (ed.) *State Politics in India* (PUP, 1968) p. 441.
76. Khushwant Singh, *History*, II, p. 217.
77. Uma Kaura, *Muslims and Indian Nationalism* (New Delhi: Manohar, 1977) p. 154.
78. See D. Gilmartin, 'Religious Leadership and the Pakistan Movement in the Punjab', *MAS*, XIII, 3 (1979) pp. 485–517.

79. O. H. K. Spate, 'Geographical Aspects of the Pakistan Scheme', *Geographical Journal*, CII (1943) pp. 125–36.
80. Khushwant Singh, *History*, II, pp. 239–45.
81. *Indian Annual Register*, 1944, II, p. 212.
82. Sadhu Swarup Singh, *The Sikhs Demand their Homeland* (Lahore: Lahore Book Shop, 1946) p. 72.
83. Ibid. See also L. Sarsfield, *Betrayal of the Sikhs* (Lahore: Lahore Book Shop, 1946) and Gurbachan Singh and Lal Singh Gyani, *The Idea of the Sikh State* (Lahore: Lahore Book Shop, 1946).
84. *Keesings Contemporary Archives*, vol IV (1946–8) p. 8634.
85. Jeffrey, 'Punjab', pp. 491–526.
86. Brass, *Language*, p. 319n.
87. Darling, *Punjab Peasant*, p. 47.
88. O. H. K. Spate, 'The Boundary Award in the Punjab', *Asiatic Review*, XLIV, (January 1948) p. 7; Ajit Singh Sarhadi, *Punjabi Suba* (Delhi: V. C. Kapur, 1970) p. 28. I. Stephens, *Pakistan* (London: Ernest Benn, revised edn, 1964; 1st pub. 1963) pp. 135–6; Kushwant Singh, *History*, II, p. 217.
89. Sarhadi, *Punjabi Suba*, p. 28.
90. E.g., note by Sir Evan Jenkins, 19 May 1947, in Mansergh and Moon (eds) *The Transfer of Power, 1942–7*, X (London: HMSO. 1981) p. 894.
91. Trevaskis, *Land*, p. 204.
92. Randhawa, *Out*, p. 40.
93. Pettigrew, *Robber*, p. 57.

4 INNOVATIONS

1. *T*, 13 November 1979, p. 1; 15 November, p. 3.
2. W. H. McLeod, 'Cohesive Ideals and Institutions in the History of the Sikh Panth', in W. H. McLeod, *The Evolution of the Sikh Community* (Oxford: Clarendon, 1976) p. 53.
3. Kapur Singh, 'The Golden Temple: Its Theo-Political Status', *Sikh Review*, XXXII (August 1984) p. 9.
4. A. Peterson, *Radio Broadcasting in South Asia* (Melbourne: Australian Radio DX Club, 1979) p. 2.
5. For example, *IT*, 31 August 1983, p. 69; *HIE*, 12 March 1983, p. 10; *EPW*, 5 March 1983, p. 319.
6. D. J. Smith, *Racial Discrimination in Britain* (Harmondsworth: Penguin, 1977) p. 32. A survey estimated 43 per cent of Indian migrants in Britain are from Sikh backgrounds, but since a proportion tend to abandon the Five Ks, the figure may be on the low side.
7. *T*, 26 May 1978, p. 7.
8. *T of I*, 29 November 1979, p. 8.
9. *T of I*, 4 September 1979, p. 1.
10. *Indian Express* (Chandigarh), 9 July 1984.
11. *New York Times*, 12 October 1971, p. 12.

12. *T*, 5 November 1979, p. 12. See also *OHT*, 5 November 1981, p. 13; *T*, 8 October 1980, p. 4; *FEER*, 10 December 1982, p. 28.
13. *T*, 5 November 1979, p. 12.
14. Ibid, p. 1.
15. *T*, 15 November 1979, p. 3; 13 November 1979, p. 1; 19 November 1979, p. 1.
16. *T*, 2 December 1979, p. 1.
17. Dalip Singh, *Dynamics*, p. 250.
18. *OHT*, 31 January 1980, p. 4.
19. *T*, 5 March 1980, p. 14; 4 March 1980, p. 1.
20. Dalip Singh, *Dynamics*, pp. 248, 251, for election results.
21. *T of I*, 16 November 1979, p. 15.
22. Pettigrew, *Robber*, p. 57.
23. M. J. Leaf, 'The Green Revolution in a Punjab Village', *Pacific Affairs*, LIII, 4 (Winter 1980–1) p. 625.
24. Ibid.
25. *HIE*, 12 January 1985, p. 6, predicted a record harvest.
26. Keller, *Uprooting*, p. 219.
27. Randhawa, *Green Revolution*, pp. 154–6.
28. Dalip Singh, *Dynamics*, p. 53; *Statistical Abstract: India, 1979*, p. 273; *Times of India Yearbook, 1979*, p. 212.
29. Randhawa, *Green Revolution*, pp. 153–4.
30. *IT*, 15 March 1979, p. 36; *Statistical Abstract: India, 1979*, p. 267. The proportion may be loser to one-quarter.
31. *T of I Yearbook, 1979*, p. 276.
32. *OHT*, 4 March 1982, p. 11.
33. I. K. Gujral, *Mainstream*, 14 August 1982, p. 13.
34. *OHT*, 4 March 1982, p. 11.
35. D. F. Barnes, F. C. Fliegel and R. D. Vanneman, 'Rural Literacy and Agricultural Development: Cause or Effect?', *Rural Sociology*, vol. XLVII, no. 2 (Summer 1982) p. 260, but see also D. P. Chaudhri, *Education, Innovations and Agricultural Development* (London: Croom Helm, 1979) p. 39.
36. Brij Pal Singh, *Educational Progress and Development in Punjab* (Patiala: Punjab Economy Research Unit, Punjabi University, 1974) p. ix.
37. Dalip Singh, *Dynamics*, p. 182.
38. *Third All-India Educational Survey* (New Delhi: National Council of Educational Research and Training, 1979) p. 367.
39. Brij Pal Singh, *Educational*, pp. 47, 49.
40. *Third All-India Educational Survey*, pp. 23, 53.
41. Brij Pal Singh, *Educational*, p. 54; *T of I Yearbook, 1979*, p. 185.
42. Sucha Singh Gill, 'Agrarian Transformation in a Punjab Village', *Mainstream*, 4 March 1978, p. 17.
43. Leaf, *Information*, p. 20.
44. *T*, 21 August 1978, p. 4.
45. *T*, 15 April 1978, p. 1.
46. *T*, 24 April 1978, p. 4.
47. *Link*, 8 October 1978, p. 20. *T*, 27 and 29 September 1978, both p. 1. Censorship ended on 1 October. *T*, 1 October 1978, p. 1.

48. E.g. S. Arasaratnam, *History, Nationalism and Nation-Building: The Asian Dilemma* (Armidale, NSW: University of New England, 1974).
49. *Mainstream*, 13 November 1982, p. 16.
50. *The Nirankari Mandal's Challenge to Sikhism* (Amritsar: SGPC, 1978). See also *They Massacre Sikhs* (Amritsar: SGPC, 1978).
51. *Nirankari Mandal's Challenge*, p. 14.
52. Pettigrew, *Robber*, p. 91.
53. K. K. Katyal in *HIE*, 10 October 1981, p. 4; Mohan Ram in *FEER*, 9 October 1981, p. 48; J. M. Sharma in *Newstime* (Hyderabad) 9 June 1984.
54. K. W. Jones, '*Ham Hindu Nahin*: Arya-Sikh Relations, 1877–1905', *JAS* XXXII, 3 (May 1973) pp. 458–9.
55. Ibid, p. 474.
56. J. C. B. Webster, 'Sikh Studies in the Punjab', in Juergensmeyer and Barrier (eds) *Sikh Studies*, p. 26.
57. Tegh Bahadur, *Hukumnamas*, ed. Fauja Singh (Patiala: Punjabi University, 1976).
58. K. S. Gill's remarks in J. S. Grewal and Indu Banga (eds) *Maharaja Ranjit Singh and His Times* (Amritsar: Department of History, Guru Nanak Dev University, 1980) p. xiii.
59. *The Immortal Story of Chamkaur Sahib* (Amritsar: SGPC, 1979) p. i.
60. *Supreme Sacrifice of Young Souls* (Amritsar: SGPC, 1977).
61. *T*, 25 May 1980, p. 12.
62. Surjit Singh Gandhi, *Struggle of the Sikhs for Sovereignty* (Delhi: GDK Publications, 1980) in the dedication.
63. *Immortal*, pp. 30, 37.
64. D. C. Pavate, *My Days as Governor* (Delhi: Vikas, 1974) p. 234.
65. Ibid; *T of I*, 11 April 1973, p. 11; Dalip Singh, *Dynamics*, p. 129; *Link*, 26 January 1974, p. 59; 26 January 1979, p. 67.
66. K. S. Gill in Grewal and Banga (eds) *Maharaja*, p. xii.
67. *OHT*, 11 June 1981, p. 3.
68. *Indian Express* (Cochin), 4 December 1983, p. 9.
69. *Sunday*, 11–17 March 1984, p. 15; *OHT*, 18 February 1984, p. 1.
70. *HIE*, 23 May 1981, p. 3, referring to Nalanda district in Bihar.
71. *HIE*, 13 September 1980, p. 5.
72. *IT*, 31 August 1982, p. 18.
73. *HIE*, 23 May 1981, p. 3.
74. *EPW*, 3–10 January 1981, p. 17.
75. *Indian Express* (Chandigarh) 20 July 1984; *Statesman*, 7 July 1984, quoted in *IWI*, 22 July 1984, p. 21.
76. A. Sampson, *The Arms Bazaar* (London: Hodder & Stoughton, 1977) p. 29.
77. Pettigrew, *Robber*, p. 32.
78. *T*, 30 May 1980, p. 12; 25 May 1980, p. 14.
79. *IT*, 31 May 1982, p. 11.
80. *Keesings Contemporary Archives*, 13–20 March 1965, p. 20632.
81. *T*, 10 September 1981, p. 1; *OHT*, 24 September 1981, pp. 3, 6.
82. *OHT*, 1 October 1981, pp. 1, 16; *T*, 25 September 1981, p. 9.
83. Pettigrew, *Robber*, p. 138.

84. Khosla, *Murder*, p. 189.
85. M. Bloch, *Feudal Society*, I, *The Growth of Ties of Dependence* (London: Routledge & Kegan Paul, 1965) pp. 224–5.
86. Keller, *Uprooting*, p. 155.
87. Pettigrew, *Robber*, p. 213.
88. Ibid, p. 215.

5 POLITICS, 1947–77

1. Mubarak Singh (ed.) *Kairon* (Ludhiana: Kairon Abhinandan Granth Committee, 1963) p. 95.
2. For example, S. S. Harrison, *India: The Most Dangerous Decades* (PUP, 1960).
3. Sarvepalli Gopal, *Jawaharlal Nehru*, II, *1947–56* (New Delhi: OUP, 1979) p. 122; Sarhadi, *Punjabi Suba*, pp. 173–5.
4. Baldev Raj Nayar, *Minority Politics in the Punjab* (PUP, 1966) p. 144.
5. Sarhadi, *Punjabi Suba*, p. 287.
6. Ibid; Mubarak Singh (ed.) *Kairon*, pp. 119–20; K. C. Gulati, *The Akalis Past and Present* (New Delhi: Ashajanak, 1974) pp. 75–7.
7. Sarhadi, *Punjabi Suba*, p. 287.
8. Pettigrew, *Robber*, p. 105; Sarhadi, *Punjabi Suba*, p. 281.
9. Sarhadi, *Punjabi Suba*, p. 288.
10. Ibid, p. 158.
11. Ibid, p. 160.
12. Tandon, *Punjabi*, p. 67.
13. Ibid.
14. Sarhadi, *Punjabi Suba*, p. 194, quoting Sir Gokal Chand Narang. For the complexities, Christopher Shackle, *An Introduction to the Sacred Language of the Sikhs* (London: School of Oriental and African Studies, 1983).
15. G. W. Leitner, *History of Indigenous Education in the Punjab since Annexation and in 1882* (New Delhi: Amar Prakashan, 1982; 1st pub. 1882) p. 37.
16. Sarhadi, *Punjabi Suba*, p. 179.
17. Ibid, pp. 193–4.
18. Brass, *Language*, p. 327.
19. Gopal, *Nehru*, II, pp. 256–71; Granville Austin, *The Indian Constitution* (Bombay: OUP, 1966) pp. 265–307.
20. Sant Fateh Singh, 'The Sikhs are Slaves', 27 August 1965, in *Two Talks*, cited in Brass, *language*, pp. 325–6.
21. Gopal, *Nehru*, II, pp. 132–3.
22. Brass, *Language*, p. 325.
23. W. H. Morris-Jones, 'India's Political Idioms', in C. H. Philips (ed.) *Politics and Society in India* (London: Allen & Unwin, 1963) pp. 133–54.
24. Harbans Singh, *The Heritage of the Sikhs* (New Delhi: Manohar, 1983) p. 363.

25. Dalip Singh, *Dynamics*, p. 16; Pandit Mohan Lal, *Disintegration of Punjab* (Chandigarh: Sameer Prakashan, 1984) pp. 20–5; Harbans Singh, *Heritage*, p. 353; Nayar, *Minority*, pp. 243–6.
26. M. Brecher, *Nehru* (London: OUP, 1959) pp. 486–7.
27. Nayar, *Minority*, p. 246.
28. Ibid.
29. Sarhadi, *Punjabi Suba*, pp. 322–3.
30. Akali estimates put the number arrested at 40 000. Mohan Lal, *Disintegration of Punjab* (Chandigarh: Sameer Prakashan, 1984) p. 93, says 26 000.
31. Sarhadi, *Punjabi Suba*, pp. 340–5.
32. Harbans Singh, *Heritage*, p. 365.
33. Ibid, pp. 366, 379. For the destruction of Master Tara Singh at this time, see J. Pettigrew, 'A Description of the Discrepancy between Sikh Political Ideals and Sikh Political Practice', in M. J. Aronoff (ed.) *Political Anthropology Yearbook I* (London: Transaction Books, 1980) pp. 168–79.
34. *T of I*, 31 October 1972, p. 7.
35. Sarhadi, *Punjabi Suba*, pp. 477–9.
36. Ibid, pp. 470–3.
37. J. Pettigrew, 'The Growth of Sikh Community Consciousness, 1947–66', *South Asia*, new series, III, 2 (December 1980) p. 45.
38. W. H. McLeod, 'Caste in the Sikh Panth', in McLeod, *Evolution*, p. 100; Pettigrew, *Robber*, p. 41.
39. Pettigrew, 'Growth', p. 52.
40. Ibid, p. 56.
41. P. K. Nijhawan in *Mainstream*, 29 May 1982, p. 24.
42. Nayar, *Minority*, p. 122; S. A. Oren, 'Religious Groups as Political Organizations: A Comparative Analysis of Three Indian States', Ph.D. thesis in political science, Columbia University, 1969, pp. 80–2.
43. Brass, *Language*, pp. 385–6.
44. *Kessings Contemporary Archives*, 8–15 May 1965, p. 20734.
45. Pavate, *My Days, passim*.
46. Harbans Singh, *Heritage*, p. 346.
47. Pavate, *My Days*, p. 22; A. S. Narang, *Storm over the Sutlej* (New Delhi: Gitanjali, 1983) p. 166; Sarhadi, *Punjabi Suba*, p. 379.
48. Pavate, *My Days*, pp. 22–3, 34, 89.
49. Ibid, p. 113.
50. *IT*, 31 May 1982, pp. 13, 15.
51. Dalip Singh, *Dynamics*, p. 250.
52. P. Wallace, 'Religious and Secular Politics in Punjab: The Sikh Dilemma in Competing Political Systems', in P. Wallace and Surendra Chopra (eds) *Political Dynamics of Punjab* (Amritsar: Guru Nanak Dev University, 1981) p. 20; *Link*, 21 October 1979, p. 15.
53. *IT*, 1–15 March 1979, p. 35; Narang, *Storm*, p. 192; Dalip Singh, *Dynamics*, p. 133.
54. Pavate, *My Days*, p. 139.

6 FACTION

1. *OHT*, 10 March 1984, p. 1; *HIE*, 10 March 1984, p. 4.
2. Pavate, *My Days*, p. 139; *T of I*, 28 March 1970, p. 9.
3. *OHT*, 10 March 1984, p. 16.
4. J. Malcolm, *Sketch of the Sikhs* (Chandigarh: Vinay Publishers, 1981; 1st pub. 1812) p. 83.
5. P. S. Bhindar in *IT*, 15 March 1983, p. 16.
6. E. Burke, *Works* I (London: George Bell & Sons, 1900) p. 376.
7. M. Juergensmeyer, 'Cultures of Deprivation', *EPW*, Annual Number (February 1979) p. 257.
8. Malcolm, *Sketch*, pp. 82–3; Pettigrew, *Robber*, p. 204; P. K. Nijhawan in *Mainstream*, 29 May 1982, p. 23.
9. P. Brass, *Factional Politics in an Indian State* (Berkeley: UCP, 1965) p. 237. For a critique of the literature on factions in India, see D. Hardiman, 'The Indian "Faction": a Political Theory Examined', in Ranajit Guha (ed.) *Subaltern Studies I* (New Delhi: OUP, 1982) pp. 198–231.
10. Satish Saberwal, *Mobile Men* (New Delhi: Vikas, 1976) pp. 173–6.
11. J. H. Plumb, *England in the Eighteenth Century* (Harmondsworth: Penguin, 1950) p. 41.
12. P. Loveday and A. W. Martin, *Parliament, Factions and Parties* (Melbourne: Melbourne UP, 1966) p. 1.
13. Saberwal, *Mobile*, p. 174.
14. S. A. Hoffmann, 'Faction Behaviour and Cultural Codes: India and Japan', *JAS*, XL, 2 (February 1981) p. 237, also p. 231, paraphrasing M. C. Carras, *The Dynamics of Indian Political Factions* (CUP, 1972).
15. Brass, *Factional*, p. 3.
16. Pettigrew, *Robber*, pp. 58, 56.
17. Ibid, pp. 145–67, *T*, 2 January 1980 and *Statesman*, 3 January 1980, for Rarewala's obituary.
18. *T*, 3 May 1977, p. 3 and 6 June 1977, p. 1.
19. Pettigrew, 'Growth', p. 57; *T*, 10 November 1978, p. 1.
20. *T*, 10 April 1978, p. 1; see also *T*, 12 April 1978, pp. 1, 10.
21. *T*, 7 November 1973, p. 3. A thorough search of both the *Tribune* and the *Times of India* (New Delhi) for October and November 1973 has failed to turn up a single reference to any resolutions passed at Anandpur Sahib.
22. Kuldip Nayar and Khushwant Singh, *Tragedy of Punjab* (New Delhi: Vision Books, 1984) p. 34.
23. Dalip Singh, *Dynamics*, p. 133.
24. *IT*, 15 November 1982, p. 45.
25. *T*, 30 October 1978, p. 11.
26. *T*, 28 October 1978, p. 7.
27. Three versions are to be found in *Army Action in Punjab* (New Delhi: Samata Era Publications, 1984) pp. 88–95, and Kumar *et al.*, *Punjab Crisis*, pp. 124–37. See also Nayar and Khushwant Singh, *Tragedy*, pp. 135–41; *OHT*, 23 November 1982, p. 10; *IT*, 15 November 1982, p. 45; *HIE*, 12 January 1985, p. 9.
28. *T*, 30 October 1978, p. 1.

29. *T*, 27 October 1978, p. 1.
30. *T*, 29 October 1978, p. 1 and 30 October, p. 11.
31. *T*, 3 November 1978, p. 3.
32. *T*, 10 November 1978, p. 1.
33. References are from the version in Nayar and Khushwant Singh, *Tragedy*, pp. 135–7.
34. *T*, 13 November 1978, p. 6.
35. Malcolm, *Sketch*, pp. 145–6.
36. *EPW*, 7 October 1978, p. 1697.
37. D. A. Swallow, 'Ashes and Powers: Myth, Rite and Miracle in an Indian God-Man's Cult', *MAS*, XVI, 1 (February 1982) p. 157.
38. Ibid, pp. 153, 156.
39. *T*, 8 June 1978, p. 9; 20 April 1978, p. 6.
40. *T*, 17 April 1978, p. 4.
41. *T*, 16 April 1978, p. 12; general secretary Hans Raj Sharma.
42. *T*, 15 April 1978, p. 1; 14 April, pp. 1, 12; 18 April, p. 1; 26 June, p. 3.
43. *T*, 16 April 1978, p. 1; 17 April 1978, p. 4.
44. *T*, 1 May 1978, p. 10; *OHT*, 3 July 1980, p. 11.
45. Chand Joshi, *Bhindranwale: Myth and Reality* (New Delhi: Vikas, 1984) p. 5.
46. *T*, 1 May 1978, p. 10.
47. Parry, *Sikhs*, p. 52; Barrier (ed.) *Sikhs*, p. xli.
48. Parry, *Sikhs*, p. 52.
49. *T*, 5 June 1978, p. 3; 1 May 1978, p. 10.
50. *T*, 5 June 1978, p. 3.
51. Joshi, *Bhindranwale*, p. 5.
52. Pettigrew, *Robber*, p. 156; Pavate, *My Days*, p. 214.
53. Tavleen Singh in the *Telegraph*, a Calcutta daily, quoting a friend of Sanjay, in Joshi, *Bhindranwale*, p. 1.
54. *T*, 17 April 1978, p. 4; Harish K. Puri, 'Akali Politics: Emerging Compulsions', in Wallace and Chopra (eds) *Political*, p. 35.
55. *IT*, 1–15 March 1979, p. 35.
56. *T*, 17 April 1978, p. 4.
57. *T*, 1 May 1978, p. 4.
58. *IT*, 31 May 1982, p. 13; *EPW*, 7 January 1984, p. 47; *T*, 15 August 1978, p. 7.
59. *T*, 19 March 1979, p. 4.
60. *T*, 24 March 1979, p. 9; 25 February 1979, pp. 10, 12; 24 March 1979, p. 9; 28 March 1979, p. 9.
61. *IT*, 15 August 1984.
62. *T*, 16 April 1979, p. 4; Surindar S. Suri and Narindra Dogra, 'A Study of the SGPC Elections, March 1979', in Wallace and Chopra (eds) *Political*, pp. 132–6.
63. *T*, 29 March 1979, p. 9; 2 April 1979, p. 1.
64. *T*, 3 April 1979, p. 12; 16 April 1979, p. 4.
65. *T*, 14 January 1979, p. 11; 22 May 1979, p. 1.
66. *T*, 26 March 1979, p. 3; 27 March 1979, p. 3.
67. *T of I*, 1 March 1980, p. 1.
68. *T*, 27 April 1980, p. 11.

69. *T*, 12 May 1980, p. 1; 30 May 1980, p. 8.
70. *Janata*, 16 May 1982, pp. 1–2; *HIE*, 10 October 1981, p. 4; Joshi, *Bhindranwale*, p. 5.
71. *T*, 11 May 1980, p. 16; 12 May 1980, p. 12.
72. *T*, 10 November 1980, p. 10.
73. *T*, 19 August 1980, p. 1.
74. *IT*, 15 October 1982, p. 30; 31 December 1982, p. 46; 31 May 1983, p. 41; *EPW*, 5 March 1983, p. 333; *FEER*, 15 November 1984, p. 106; S. Venkat Narayan, *NTR – A Biography* (New Delhi: Vikas, 1984).
75. *T*, 10 June 1980, p. 4; *IWI*, 27 December 1981, p. 24.
76. *T*, 8 October 1980, p. 4; 17 June 1980, pp. 1, 12; 2 September 1980, p. 8.
77. *HIE*, 2 May 1981, p. 4; *OHT*, 16 May 1981, p. 6; *T of I*, 13 April 1981.
78. *IT*, 30 November 1981, pp. 103–5. For Sikhs in North America, see the series by W. Una in the *Statesman*, 28 March to 7 April 1985.
79. *T*, 20 December 1980, p. 11.
80. *OHT*, 11 June 1981, p. 3; *Mainstream*, 18 August 1981, pp. 19–23.
81. *HIE*, 1 August 1981, p. 1.
82. *OHT*, 6 August 1981, p. 1; 17 September 1981, p. 4; *T*, 8 September 1981, p. 1.
83. *T*, 14 September 1981, p. 1; 15 September 1981, p. 1.
84. *T*, 21 September 1981, p. 1.
85. *T*, 24 December 1981, p. 9.
86. *T*, 6 November 1981, p. 7; 29 September 1981, p. 4.
87. *T*, 30 December 1981, p. 3; 31 December 1981, p. 3.

7 EXPLOSION

1. *Weekend Australian*, 3–4 November 1984, p. 1; *Sydney Morning Herald*, 3 November 1984, p. 17; telephone interview (RJ).
2. R. Jeffrey, 'Smell of decay in India's Army', in *Age*, 10 December 1984, p. 13.
3. *IWI*, 22 July 1984, p. 50; *Sikh Review*, August 1984, p. 38; *IT*, 15 November 1982, p. 44, estimated 15 per cent. Khushwant Singh in *FEER*, 12 February 1982, p. 34, had the proportion 'at least a tenth'.
4. *FEER*, 21 June 1984, pp. 15–16; *OHT*, 23 June 1984, p. 16; *IT*, 28 February 1985, p. 58.
5. McLeod, 'Caste'. p. 94n; C. Shackle, *The Sikhs* (London: Minority Rights Group, report no. 65, 1984) p. 9; *Age*, 9 November 1984, p. 10.
6. *IT*, 15 December 1984, p. 64.
7. J. de St Jorre, *The Nigerian Civil War* (London: Hodder & Stoughton, 1972) pp. 58–122.
8. *T*, 11 July 1984, p. 7; *IE* (Chandigarh) 7 July 1984, p. 1.
9. *T*, 17 July 1984.
10. V. D. Chopra, R. K. Mishra, Nirmal Singh, *Agony of Punjab* (New Delhi: Patriot Publishers, 1984) pp. 116, 199–214; *IT*, 15 March 1983, p. 67.

11. *IT*, 31 May 1982, p. 15.
12. *T*, 23 October 1981, p. 5; 5 November 1981, p. 5.
13. *IT*, 31 May 1982, p. 15.
14. *T*, 17 July 1984, p. 1, quoting Ashish Nandy.
15. *T*, 11 July 1984, pp. 1, 7; *Army Action*, pp. 24–5, lists five occasions on which the government is alleged to have aborted talks.
16. *HIE*, 9 June 1984, p. 1.
17. Nayar and Khushwant Singh, *Tragedy*, pp. 62–3.
18. Ibid, p. 65.
19. Ibid, pp. 65–6; *HIE*, 23 June 1984, p. 9 (H. S. Surjit); *OHT*, 24 February 1983, p. 7 (Sitanshu Das); *IT*, 15 December 1982, p. 9.
20. Nayar and Khushwant Singh, *Tragedy*, p. 66; *IT*, 15 November 1983, p. 21; 15 December 1982, p. 9; *Army Action*, p. 56 and *T of I*, Sunday Review, 28 October 1984, p. 1, for Shabeg Singh; *Statesman*, 1 April 1985, for Bhullar in the USA.
21. *IT*, 30 November 1982, p. 9; Nayar and Khushwant Singh, *Tragedy*, p. 63.
22. *OHT*, 27 January 1983, p. 1.
23. *IT*, 15 February 1983, p. 19.
24. *Janata*, 20 March 1983, p. 13.
25. *HIE*, 17 April 1982, p. 2.
26. *EPW*, 4 February 1984, p. 195.
27. *Mainstream*, 6 August 1983, p. 1.
28. *Hindu* (Coimbatore) 22 November 1983, p. 1.
29. *HIE*, 25 February 1984, p. 3; 3 March 1984, p. 3.
30. *HIE*, 19 May 1984, p. 4.
31. Rajni Kothari and Guri Deshingkar, *IWI*, 15 July 1984, p. 21.
32. Tandon, *Punjabi*, p. 42.
33. *HIE*, 17 April 1982, p. 2.
34. *IT*, 31 May 1982, p. 12.
35. *T of I Yearbook, 1983*, pp. 105–6.
36. Pettigrew, 'Growth', p. 50.
37. *OHT*, 6 May 1982, p. 1; *HIE*, 8 May 1982, p. 1. Other estimates suggested 560 members. *IT*, 31 May 1982, p. 13; *Sunday*, 11–17 March 1984, p. 15.
38. *Mainstream*, 22 May 1982, p. 5 (Narendra Sharma). *IT*, 31 May 1982, p. 11.
39. Amarindar Singh to Tavleen Singh, quoted in the *Sikh Review*, September 1984, p. 54.
40. *HIE*, 28 August 1982, p. 9 (K. K. Katyal); *OHT*, 5 July 1982, pp. 3, 11 (Jeevan Nair).
41. *Sikh Review*, September 1984, p. 54.
42. *OHT*, 12 August 1982, p. 3; *Mainstream*, 28 August 1982, p. 4.
43. *OHT*, 16 September 1982, p. 3.
44. *HIE*, 18 September 1982, p. 4.
45. *OHT*, 21 October 1982, p. 1; *IT*, 15 November 1982, p. 40.
46. *HIE*, 1 January 1983, p. 3; Tavleen Singh in *The Punjab Story* (New Delhi: Roli Books International, 1984) p. 50.
47. *HIE*, 5 March 1983, p. 3.
48. *HIE*, 19 March 1983, p. 3.

49. *OHT*, 7 April 1983, p. 3; 14 April 1983, p. 1.
50. *OHT*, 14 April 1983, p. 16; *HIE*, 16 April 1983, p. 4.
51. *Link*, 17 April 1983, p. 9. Compare the mood with that of Dublin in 1919–20, in M. Forester, *Michael Collins – The Lost Leader* (London: Sphere Books, 1972) pp. 128–9.
52. *HIE*, 16 and 23 April 1983, both p. 4; *OHT*, 21 April 1983, p. 1.
53. *HIE*, 7 May 1983, p. 3.
54. *OHT*, 5 May 1983, p. 1; 12 May 1983, p. 1.
55. *HIE*, 26 March 1983, p. 3; 7 May 1983, p. 3.
56. *HIE*, 25 June 1983, p. 4; 23 July 1983, p. 4; 1 October 1983, p. 3. *Link*, 16 October 1983, p. 16.
57. *T*, 31 October 1983, p. 10.
58. *T*, 11 November 1983, p. 1.
59. *HIE*, 25 February 1984, p. 3; *Sunday*, 4–10 March 1984, p. 31; Kumar *et al.*, *Punjab Crisis*, p. 88.
60. *IT*, 15 March 1984, p. 10; *OHT*, 24 March 1984, p. 1; *HIE*, 14 April 1984, p. 3; *T*, 16 April 1984, p. 1; *IT*, 15 May 1984, p. 30; *OHT*, 5 May 1984, p. 16; *HIE*, 19 May 1984, p. 4; 28 April 1984, p. 3.
61. *FEER*, May 1984, p. 33.
62. M. J. Akbar, *India: The Siege Within* (Harmondsworth: Penguin, 1985) p. 188. For Longowal, *T*, 15, 18 and 21 September 1978, pp. 7, 4 and 9 and 12 respectively; *Link*, 9 May 1978, p. 14; *HIE*, 4 June 1983, p. 9; *The Listener*, 21 June 1984, p. 9.
63. *EPW*, 2 June 1979, p. 931; *IT*, 16–30 June 1979, cover story, and 15 November 1979, p. 88; *Seminar*, no. 252 (August 1980); *OHT*, 7 April 1984, p. 10.
64. *IT*, 15 June 1984, p. 25.
65. *IT*, 15 December 1983, p. 26.
66. J. Pettigrew, 'Conflict escalation in the Punjab', in M. J. Aronoff (ed.) *Freedom and Constraint* (Amsterdam: Van Gorcum, 1976) p. 40.
67. Ibid, p. 39; *T*, 6 June 1979, p. 4.
68. *T*, 14 May 1979, p. 4; 9 May 1979, pp. 1, 10.
69. *T*, 8 June 1979, p. 8; 7 June 1979, p. 1; 26 April 1980, p. 6.
70. *T*, 14 May 1979, p. 4.
71. *T*, 16 April 1980, p. 1; 5 November 1980, p. 11.
72. *IT*, 15 July 1983, p. 10.
73. *OHT*, 4 February 1982, p. 10; 29 July 1982, p. 11.
74. *IT*, 15 July 1983, p. 11.
75. *Sunday*, 25–31 March 1984, p. 29.
76. *IT*, 15 May 1984, pp. 30–1; *Sunday*, 11–17 March 1984, pp. 14–15; *HIE*, 26 May 1984, p. 3; *Sunday*, 22–8 April 1984, p. 40; Kumar *et al.*, *Punjab Crisis*, pp. 78–9.
77. *IT*, 31 August 1984, p. 55.
78. *IT*, 31 August 1984, p. 50; *Caravan*, 2 August 1984, p. 27.
79. *OHT*, 22 October 1981, p. 12.
80. *T*, 30 September 1981, p. 1.
81. Gopal Singh, 'Socio-Economic Bases of Punjab Crisis', *EPW*, 7 January 1984, p. 47.

82. The woman who fell out with Bhindranwale and allegedly killed his guard, Sodhi, was said to be from an ex-Untouchable caste. Soon after, she herself was found brutally murdered. *IT*, 15 May 1984, p. 30; *Punjab Story*, p. 47.

83. F. Houtart, *Religion and Ideology in Sri Lanka* (Bangalore: TPI, 1974) pp. 347–53.

84. *OHT*, 1 January 1981, p. 10; *HIE*, 13 December 1980, pp. 3, 8; *IT*, 30 April 1982, p. 32; 31 August 1982, p. 15.

85. *Punjab Story*, p. 40.

86. E.g. *Caravan*, 2 August 1984, p. 27.

87. E.g. Sumanta Banerjee, *In the Wake of Naxalbari* (Calcutta: Subarnarekha, 1980) and Biplab Dasgupta, *The Naxalite Movement* (Bombay: Allied, 1974).

88. *Weekend Review*, 1–7 July 1984, p. 7 (Ashwini Kumar).

89. Joshi, *Bhindranwale*, p. 108; J. Pettigrew, 'Take Not Arms Against Thy Sovereign: The present Punjab Crisis and the Storming of the Golden Temple', *South Asia Research*, IV, 2 (November 1984) p. 111, quoting Major-General J. S. Bhullar and Bhindranwale.

90. *FEER*, 21 June 1984, p. 14.

91. *IE* (Chandigarh), 1 September 1984, p. 3.

92. *Sunday*, 11–17 March 1984, p. 13.

93. *IT*, 31 May 1982, p. 13.

94. *IE* (Chandigarh), 7 July 1984.

95. *HIE*, 23 June 1984, p. 3, reported 3038 arrests up to 12 June.

96. *OHT*, 24 February 1983, p. 3.

97. *T*, 19 April 1984, p. 1; *IT*, 15 June 1984, p. 24.

98. *IT*, 30 June 1984, p. 13.

99. *Punjab Story*, pp. 76–9; *Sunday Observer*, 10 June 1984, in *Sikh Review*, August 1984, p. 49.

100. *IT*, 30 June 1984, p. 16, quoting Jagjit Singh Aurora. See also Aurora's article in *Punjab Story*, pp. 90–104. A biting attack on Shabeg Singh by an old colleague is in *T of I*, Sunday Review, 28 October 1984, p. 1. *Army Action*, p. 56, says he was acquitted of wrongdoing in February 1984 but that the media suppressed the fact.

101. *HIE*, 23 June 1984, p. 3; *OHT*, 21 June 1984, p. 1; The government's White Paper put the number of deaths in all Punjab at 512; *T*, 11 July 1984, p. 12. For a vivid account of the assault, see Shekhar Gupta in *Punjab Story*, pp. 53–75.

102. Mohan Ram, *FEER*, 21 June 1984, p. 14.

103. *Surya*, quoted in *Sikh Review*, Supplement, September 1984, p. 6.

104. Interview with Tavleen Singh, of *Sunday*, quoted in *Sikh Review*, September 1984, p. 51.

105. *T*, 11 July 1984, p. 1; *IT*, 15 July 1984, p. 15; *IE*, (Chandigarh), 23 August 1984, for round-up and 14 September 1984.

8 WHAT'S HAPPENING TO INDIA? THE TEST FOR FEDERALISM

1. *IT*, 15 December 1984, pp. 22–3.
2. *The Times* (London) 14 March 1940, p. 8; S. P. Sen, *Dictionary of National Biography*, vol. IV (Calcutta: Institute of Historical Studies, 1974) p. 369.
3. For the constitution, G. Austin, *The Indian Constitution: Cornerstone of a Nation* (Bombay: OUP, 1976; first pub. 1966).
4. Sen (ed.) *Dictionary*, IV, pp. 267–8.
5. Bhagwan D. Dua, 'India: a Study in the Pathology of a Federal System', *JCCP*, XIX–XX (1981–2) p. 271; *T*, 7 August 1978, p. 4.
6. *EPW*, 3 November 1984, p. 1850.
7. *T*, 21 August 1978, p. 4; 24 July 1978, p. 4.
8. Asok Chanda, 'Institutional Base of Centre-State Relations', in B. L. Maheswari (ed.) *Centre-State Relations in the Seventies* (Calcutta: Minerva, 1973) p. 135.
9. K. K. George and I. S. Gulati, 'Centre-State Resource Transfers, 1951–84', *EPW*, 16 February 1985, p. 287. See also Gulati, 'Financial Relations', *Seminar*, no. 289 (September 1983) pp. 33–8, and Chandra Pal, *State Autonomy in Indian Federation* (New Delhi: Deep & Deep, 1984) p. 191.
10. George and Gulati, 'Centre-State', p. 290.
11. *HIE*, 22 September 1984, p. 9; *OHT*, 4 August 1984, p. 7; *EPW*, 12 February 1983, p. 203.
12. P. R. Brass, 'Pluralism, Regionalism and Decentralization Tendencies in Contemporary Indian Politics', in A. Jeyaratnam Wilson and D. Dalton (eds) *The States of South Asia* (London: Hurst, 1982) pp. 235–6.
13. George and Gulati, 'Centre-State', p. 294.
14. Ajit Kumar Singh, 'Regional Imbalances and National Integration', *Mainstream*, 6 August 1983, p. 18.
15. George and Gulati, 'Centre-State', p. 292.
16. *IT*, 28 February 1985, pp. 16–18, for the plight of defeated national politicians.
17. For Karnataka, J. Manor, 'Blurring the Lines between Parties and Social Bases', *EPW*, 15 September 1984, pp. 1623–32. For Andhra Pradesh, *IT*, 15 September 1984, p. 7. For Jammu and Kashmir, *IT*, 31 July 1984, p. 8. For Sikkim, *HIE*, 9 June 1984, p. 10.
18. *T of I*, 16 January 1980, p. 1; Dalip Singh, *Dynamics*, pp. 155–6.
19. *T of I*, 20 January 1980, p. 1 and 16 January 1980, p. 1.
20. Speech, 8 February 1947, in Austin, *Indian Constitution*, p. 190.
21. Pal, *State Autonomy*, p. 117; B. D. Dua, *Presidential Rule in India, 1950–74* (New Delhi: Chand, 1979).
22. Brass, 'Pluralism', p. 246.
23. Zareer Masani, *Indira Gandhi* (New York: Thomas Y. Cromwell, 1975) pp. 58–96.
24. Prem Shankar Jha, *India: a Political Economy of Stagnation* (New Delhi: OUP, 1980) p. 34.

25. W. Hangen, *After Nehru, Who?* (London: Rupert Hart-Davis, 1963) p. 282.
26. Dua, 'India: a Study', p. 262.
27. Sarhadi, *Punjabi Suba*, p. 377.
28. Nayar, *Minority*, p. 155; *IT*, 16–31 March 1980, p. 53.
29. M. Brecher, *Succession in India* (London: OUP, 1966) pp. 190–225; Hangen, *After*, p. 279.
30. Rajni Kothari, *Politics in India* (New Delhi: Orient Longman, 1970) p. 117.
31. W. H. Morris-Jones, 'India – More Questions than Answers', *Asian Survey*, XXIV, 8 (August 1984) p. 812.
32. Dua, 'India: a Study', pp. 266–7.
33. *IT*, 1–15 April 1981, p. 33 and 1–15 October 1980, p. 18.
34. *IT*, 28 February 1982, p. 29; *OHT*, 11 March 1982, pp. 3, 7; Dua, 'India: a Study', p. 275n.
35. *IT*, 25 February 1985, p. 50.
36. *HIE*, 15 January 1983, pp. 1, 3.
37. *Age* (Melbourne) 23 January 1985, p. 8, using a *New York Times* story by Christopher Wren.
38. Rasheeduddin Khan, 'The Regional Dimension', *Seminar*, no. 164 (April 1973) p. 37.
39. *FEER*, 7 June 1984, p. 27; *IT*, 31 May 1984, p. 11.
40. F. A. Presler, 'Studying India's Political Culture', *JCCP*, XXII, 3 (November 1984) p. 234.
41. K. D. McRae, 'Introduction', in McRae (ed.) *Consociational Democracy* (Toronto: McClelland & Stewart, 1974) p. 8.
42. *OHT*, 16 March 1985, p. 16.
43. Harsh Sethi, 'Groups in a New Politics of Transformation', *EPW*, 18 February 1984, p. 315. After arriving at 'reasons for hope' as a heading for this section, I discovered in this article that it had also been used to head a piece by Arun Shourie in the *Indian Express*, 15 August 1982.
44. Rajni Kothari, 'The Non-Party Political Process', *EPW*, 4 February 1984, p. 221.
45. Nikhil Chakravarty in *Holiday* (Dhaka) 15 and 29 March 1983, both p. 6.
46. *The Marxist*, April–June 1984, quoted in Harsh Sethi, 'The Immoral "Other": Debate between Party and Non-Party Groups', *EPW*, 23 February 1985, p. 378.
47. Sunderlal Bahuguna, *Walking with the Chipko Message* (Tehri Garhwal: Chipko Information Centre, 1983) p. 25. I am grateful to Tom Weber of Melbourne for literature on Chipko.
48. Interview in a Sunday edition of the *Deccan Herald* (Bangalore) in mid-1984. Precise date missing; clipping with Tom Weber.
49. *FEER*, 19 July 1984, pp. 78–9. *Kerala Sastra Sahithya Parishat: A People's Science Movement* (Trivandrum: KSSP, c. 1983) pp. 2–8; *EPW*, 12 March 1983, p. 372 and 22 September 1984, p. 1656.
50. Sethi, 'Groups', pp. 305–16; Kothari, 'Non-Party', p. 221.
51. Sethi, 'Groups', pp. 311–12; Kothari, 'Non-Party', p. 220.
52. Kothari, 'Non-Party', p. 220.
53. *IT*, 15 March 1984, p. 10; *OHT*, 7 April 1984, p. 7.

POSTSCRIPT: NOVEMBER 1985

1. The Memorandum's proposed solutions to the three substantial matters (sections 5, 7 and 9) had indeed been mooted for at least two years. No. 5 committed the Government of India to 'consider the formation' of laws to regulate *gurdwaras* throughout the entire country. No. 7 awarded the city of Chandigarh to Punjab from 26 January 1986 (Mrs Gandhi made a similar award in 1970) and referred other boundary problems to commissions. No. 9 sent the dispute over the shares of river water to a commission presided over by a Supreme Court judge. Four of the eleven sections (Nos 1, 3, 4 and 6) stemmed directly from the bloodletting of 1984. They promised compensation to the victims of riot and murder, extended judicial inquiries to cities other than New Delhi, promised efforts to 'rehabilitate' soldiers dismissed from the army after the mutinies of June 1984 and withdrew special courts and legislation in Punjab. The four remaining sections (Nos 2, 8, 10 and 11) simply affirmed good intentions: merit, rather than regional quotas, would be the criterion from army recruitment; the Anandpur Sahib Resolution was proclaimed to be 'entirely within the framework of the Indian Constitution'; the Prime Minister would write to all state Chief Ministers to emphasise the need to protect minorities; and 'the Central Goverment may take some steps for the promotion of the Punjabi Language'.
2. *T*, 26 July 1985, editorial. See also Pranay Gupte, *Vengeance* (New York: Norton, 1985) pp. 126–7.
3. *IT*, 15 September 1985, p. 10.
4. *OHT*, 14 September 1985, p. 6 (N. C. Menon).
5. The advertisements appeared in *The Tribune* and the Chandigarh edition of the *Indian Express* in September.
6. *OHT*, 14 September 1985, p. 1; *FEER*, 31 October 1985, p. 28.
7. *OHT*, 5 October 1985, p. 16.
8. *T*, 6 April 1977, p. 3.
9. *IT*, 15 October 1985, p. 13.
10. *HIE*, 12 October 1985, p. 14.
11. *IT*, 31 October 1985, p. 10, quoting Barnala.
12. *Who Are the Guilty?*, p. 11 and Annexure 4.
13. *OHT*, 5 October 1985, p. 7; Australian Broadcasting Corporation, 'Report from Asia', 15 September 1985; *IT*, 15 October 1985, pp. 46–8.
14. *FEER*, 11 July 1985, p. 18.
15. Mark Tully and Satish Jacob, *Amritsar: Mrs Gandhi's Last Battle* (London: Jonathan Cape, 1985), quoted in *OHT*, 2 November 1985, p. 7.
16. BBC World Service, 'South Asia Survey', 9 November 1985.
17. *HIE*, 10 August 1985, p. 6.
18. *SMH*, 21 October 1985, quoting the *New York Times*.
19. *Age*, 6 June 1985, p. 9, quoting the *Los Angeles Times*. *SMH*, 18 October 1985.
20. *Age*, 9 November 1985, p. 7.
21. *SMH*, 21 October 1985, quoting the *Sunday Telegraph*.
22. *The Truth*, no date, no place of publication, cyclostyled: 'Information

Bulletin of the Ad-Hoc Action Committee of Gurdwaras and Societies of Malaysia'.

23. *HIE*, 23 February 1985, p. 3.
24. *HIE*, 21 September 1985, p. 3.
25. *South*, October 1985, p. 19.

Select Bibliography

The sources on which this book is based are acknowledged in the notes. My aim here is to suggest to interested readers a number of books and articles that I have found stimulating and enjoyable or are particularly timely and up-to-date. The abbreviations are the same as those used in the notes.

INDIA SINCE 1947

Austin, G., *The Indian Constitution: Cornerstone of a Nation* (Bombay: OUP, 1976; first pub. 1966).

Barnett, M. R., *The Politics of Cultural Nationalism in South India* (PUP, 1976).

Brecher, M., *Nehru* (London: OUP, 1959).

——, *Succession in India* (London: OUP, 1966).

Breman, J., *Patronage and Exploitation. Changing Agrarian Relations in South Gujarat* (New Delhi: Manohar, 1979; first pub. 1974).

Chaudhuri, Pramit, *The Indian Economy: Poverty and Development* (New Delhi: Vikas, 1979).

Chopra, Pran, *Uncertain India. A Political Profile of Two Decades of Freedom* (Bombay: Asia Publishing House, 1968).

Dua, B. D., *Presidential Rule in India* (New Delhi: Chand, 1979).

——, 'India: a Study in the Pathology of a Federal System', *JCCP*, XIX–XX (1981–2) pp. 257–75.

Frankel, F. R., *India's Political Economy, 1947–77. The Gradual Revolution* (PUP, 1978).

Gopal, S., *Jawaharlal Nehru*, 3 vols (New Delhi: OUP, 1976–83).

Hangen, W., *After Nehru, Who?* (London: Hart-Davis, 1963).

Hardgrave, R. L., Jr., *India: Government and Politics in a Developing Nation* (New York: Harcourt, Brace, Jovanovich, 1986) 4th edn.

Hart, H. C., *Indira Gandhi's India: A Political System Reappraised* (Boulder, Colorado: Westview Press, 1976).

Harrison, S. S. *India: The Most Dangerous Decades* (PUP, 1960).

Jha, P. S., *India: A Political Economy of Stagnation* (New Delhi: OUP, 1980).

Kochanek, S. A., *Business and Politics in India* (Berkeley: UCP, 1974).

Kothari, Rajni., *Politics in India* (New Delhi: Orient Longman, 1970).

Lewis, Primila., *Reason Wounded: An Experience of India's Emergency* (New Delhi: Vikas, 1978).

Mayer, P. B., 'Congress (I), Emergency (I): Interpreting Indira Gandhi's India', *JCCP*, XXII, 2 (July 1984) pp. 128–50.

Morris-Jones, W. H., *Parliament in India* (Philadelphia: University of Pennsylvania Press, 1957).

——, 'India – More Questions than Answers', *Asian Survey*, XXIV, 8 (August 1984) pp. 809–16.

Masani, Zareer, *Indira Gandhi* (New York: Crowell, 1976).

Nayar, Kuldip, *India after Nehru* (New Delhi: Vikas, 1975).

Sen Gupta, Bhabani, *Communism in Indian Politics* (New York: Columbia UP, 1972).

ETHNICITY

Glazer, N. and Moynihan, D. P., *Ethnicity: Theory and Practice* (Cambridge, Massachusetts: Harvard UP, 1975).

Katzenstein, M. F., *Ethnicity and Equality: The Shiv Sena Party and Politics in Bombay* (Ithaca: Cornell UP, 1979).

Keyes, C. F. (ed.) *Ethnic Change* (Seattle: University of Washington Press, 1981).

Schermerhorn, R. A., *Ethnic Plurality in India* (Tucson: University of Arizona Press, 1978).

Weiner, M., *Sons of the Soil: Migration and Ethnic Conflict in India* (PUP, 1979).

—— and Katzenstein, M. F. (eds) *India's Preferential Politics: Migrants, the Middle Classes and Ethnic Equality* (Chicago: University of Chicago Press, 1981).

FACTION

Brass, P. R., *Factional Politics in an Indian State. The Congress Party in Uttar Pradesh* (Berkeley: UCP, 1965).

Hardiman, D., 'The Indian "Faction": a Political Theory Examined', in Ranajit Guha (ed.) *Subaltern Studies I* (New Delhi: OUP, 1982) pp. 198–231.

Hoffman, S. A., 'Faction Behaviour and Cultural Codes: India and Japan', *JAS*, XL, 2 (February 1981) pp. 231–54.

Rastogi, P. N., *The Nature and Dynamics of Factional Conflict* (New Delhi: South Asia Books, 1972).

EVENTS OF 1984

Army Action in Punjab. Prelude and Aftermath (New Delhi: Samata Era, 1984).

Chopra, V. D., Mishra, R. K., Nirmal Singh, *Agony of Punjab* (New Delhi: Patriot Publishers, 1984).
Delhi, 31 October to 4 November 1984. Report of the Citizens' Commission (New Delhi: Citizens' Commission, 1985).
Joshi, Chand, *Bhindranwale: Myth and Reality* (New Delhi: Vikas, 1984).
Kumar, Pramod; Sharma, Manmohan; Sood, Atul; and Handa, Ashwani, *Punjab Crisis: Context and Trends* (Chandigarh: Centre for Research in Rural and Industrial Development, 1984).
The Punjab Story (New Delhi: Roli Books, 1984).
Nayar, Kuldip and Khushwant Singh, *Tragedy of Punjab* (New Delhi: Vision, 1984).
Who Are the Guilty? (New Delhi: People's Union for Democratic Rights and People's Union for Civil Liberties, 1984).

PUNJAB HISTORY

Aggarwal, Subhash Chander, *Punjab: A Select Bibliography, including Haryana, 1939–1979* (Chandigarh: Arun Publications, 1980).
Aryan, K. C., *The Cultural Heritage of Punjab, 3000 B.C. to 1947 A.D.* (New Delhi: Rekha Prakashan, 1983).
Banerjee, Himadri, *Agrarian Society of the Punjab, 1849–1901* (New Delhi: Manohar, 1982).
Banga, Indu, *Agrarian System of the Sikhs* (New Delhi: Manohar, 1978).
Darling, M., *The Punjab Peasant in Prosperity and Debt*, introduction by Clive J. Dewey (New Delhi: Manohar, 1977; first pub. 1925).
Gustafson, W. E. and Jones, K. W., *Sources on Punjab History* (New Delhi: Manohar, 1975).
Harbans Singh and Barrier, N. G. (eds) *Punjab Past and Present: Essays in Honour of Dr Ganda Singh* (Patiala: Punjabi University, 1976).
Jones, K. W., *Arya Dharm: Hindu Consciousness in 19th-Century Punjab* (Berkeley: UCP, 1976).
——, '*Ham Hindu Nahin*: Arya–Sikh Relations, 1877–1905', *JAS*, XXXII, 3 (May 1973) pp. 457–75.
Keller, S. L., *Uprooting and Social Change. The Role of Refugees in Development* (New Delhi: Manohar, 1975).
Kessinger, T. G., *Vilyatpur 1848–1968: Social and Economic Change in a North Indian Village* (Berkeley: UCP, 1974).
Randhawa, M. S. (ed.) *Green Revolution: A Case Study of Punjab* (Delhi: Vikas, 1974).
——, *Out of the Ashes: An Account of the Rehabilitation of Refugees from West Pakistan in rural areas of East Punjab* (Chandigarh: Public Relations Department, Punjab, 1954).
Thorburn, S. S., *The Punjab in Peace and War* (Patiala: Languages Department, Punjab, 1970; first pub. 1883).
Trevaskis, H. K., *The Land of the Five Rivers* (Oxford: OUP, 1928).

PUNJAB SOCIETY

Aggarwal, P. C., *The Green Revolution and Rural Labour* (New Delhi: Shri Ram Centre, 1973).

Herschman, P., *Punjabi Kinship and Marriage* (New Delhi: Hindustan Publishing, 1981).

Ibbetson, D., *Panjab Castes* (Delhi: B.R. Publishing Corporation, 1974; first pub. in this form, 1916, but based on census report of 1881).

Izmirlian, H., Jr., *Structure and Strategy in Sikh Society: The Politics of Passion* (New Delhi: Manohar, 1979).

Juergensmeyer, M., 'Cultures of Deprivation: Three Case Studies in Punjab', *EPW*, Annual Number (February 1979) pp. 255–62.

Leaf, M. J., *Information and Behaviour in a Sikh Village: Social Organisation Reconsidered* (Berkeley: UCP, 1972).

Lloyd, Sarah, *An Indian Attachment* (London: Harvill Press, 1984).

Mamdani, Mahmood, *The Myth of Population Control. Family, Caste and Class in an Indian Village* (New York: Monthly Review Press, 1972).

Marenco, E. K., *The Transformation of Sikh Society* (Portland, Oregon: The Ha Pi Press, 1974).

Pradhan, M. C., *The Political System of the Jats of Northern India* (Bombay: OUP, 1966).

Saberwal, Satish, *Mobile Men: Limits to Social Change in Urban Punjab* (New Delhi: Vikas, 1976).

Wyon, J. B. and Gordon, J. E., *The Khanna Study: Population Problems in the Rural Punjab* (Cambridge, Massachusetts: Harvard UP, 1971).

PUNJAB POLITICS

Brass, P. R., *Language, Religion and Politics in North India* (CUP, 1974).

Ajit Singh Sarhadi, *Punjabi Suba: The Story of the Struggle* (Delhi: Kapur, 1970).

Dalip Singh, *Dynamics of Punjab Politics* (New Delhi: Macmillan, 1981).

Gulati, K. C., *The Akalis Past and Present* (New Delhi: Ashajanak, 1974).

Hari Singh, Master, *Agricultural Workers' Struggle in Punjab* (New Delhi: People's Publishing House, 1980).

Josh, Bhagwan, *Communist Movement in Punjab (1926–47)* (Delhi: Anupama Publications, 1979).

Mohinder Singh, *The Akali Movement* (Delhi: Macmillan, 1978).

Narang, A. S., *Storm over the Sutlej: The Akali Politics* (New Delhi: Gitanjali Publishing House, 1983).

Nayar, Baldev Raj, *Minority Politics in the Punjab* (PUP, 1966).

——, Baldev Raj, 'Punjab' in Myron Weiner (ed.) *State Politics in India* (PUP, 1968) pp. 433–502.

Wallace, P. and Chopra, Surendra (eds) *Political Dynamics of Punjab* (Amritsar: Guru Nanak Dev University, 1981).

PUNJAB MEMOIRS

Bhatia, Prem, *All My Yesterdays* (New Delhi: Hind Pocket Books, 1977).

Khosla, G. D., *The Murder of the Mahatma* (Bombay: Jaico, 1968).

Mehta, Ved, *Face to Face* (New Delhi: OUP, 1978; first pub. 1957).

Mohan Lal, Pandit, *Disintegration of Punjab* (Chandigarh: Sameer Prakashan, 1984).

Pavate, D. C., *My Days as Governor* (New Delhi: Vikas, 1974).

Tandon, Prakash, *Punjabi Century, 1857–1947* (New Delhi: Orient Paperbacks, 1961).

SIKHS

Barrier, N. G. (ed.) *The Sikhs and Their Literature* (New Delhi: Manohar, 1970).

Cole, W. O. and Piara Singh Sambhi, *The Sikhs: Their Religious Beliefs and Practices* (London: Routledge & Kegan Paul, 1978).

Grewal, J. S. and Bal, S. S., *Guru Gobind Singh (A Biographical Study)* (Chandigarh: Punjab University, Dept. of History, 1967).

Grewal, J. S. and Indu Banga (eds) *Maharaja Ranjit Singh and His Times* (Amritsar: Dept. of History, Guru Nanak Dev University, 1980).

Griffin, Lepel, *Ranjit Singh* (Delhi: Chand, 1967; first pub. c. 1890).

Harbans Singh, *The Heritage of the Sikhs* (New Delhi: Manohar, 1983).

Helweg, A. W., *Sikhs in England* (New Delhi: OUP, 1979).

Juergensmeyer, M. and Barrier, N. G. (eds) *Sikh Studies: Comparative Perspectives on a Changing Tradition* (Berkeley: Berkeley Religious Studies Series, 1979).

Khushwant Singh, *The Sikhs Today* (Bombay: Sangam Books, 1976) 5th edn.

——, *A History of the Sikhs* (PUP, 1966) 2 vols.

—— and Raghu Rai, *The Sikhs* (Varanasi: Lustre Press, 1984).

McLeod, W. H., *The Evolution of the Sikh Community: Five Essays* (Oxford: Clarendon, 1976).

——, (trans. and ed.) *Textual Sources for the Study of Sikhism* (Manchester: Manchester UP, 1984).

Pettigrew, J., *Robber Noblemen: A Study of the Political System of the Sikh Jats* (New Delhi: Ambika Publications, 1978).

——, 'Take Not Arms against Thy Sovereign: The Present Punjab Crisis and the Storming of the Golden Temple', *South Asia Research*, IV, 2 (November 1984) pp. 102–23.

Shackle, C., *The Sikhs* (London: Minority Rights Group, Report No. 65, 1984).

Sohan Singh Josh, *Tragedy of Komagata Maru* (New Delhi: People's Publishing House, 1975).

INDIA SINCE 1985

A narrative of events can be found in the essay on India which appears each year in the February number of the journal, *Asian Survey*. The *Asia Yearbook*, published annually by the *Far Eastern Economic Review* in Hong Kong, carries a similar update. To piece together a picture of the challenges facing India since 1985, a reader needs to appreciate the varied themes illustrated in the following selection.

Chakravarti, Uma and Haksar, Nandita (eds), *The Delhi Riots: Three Days in the Life of a Nation* (New Delhi: Lancer, 1987).

Engineer, A. A. (ed.), *Shah Bano Controversy* (New Delhi: Orient Longman, 1987).

Gopal, Sarvepalli (ed.), *Anatomy of a Confrontation: The Babri – Masjid – Ramjanambhumi Issue* (New Delhi: Viking, 1991/New York: Humanities–Zed, 1992).

Harkishan Singh Surjeet, *Deepening Punjab Crisis: a Democratic Solution* (New Delhi: Patriot Publishers, 1992).

Kohli, Atul, *Democracy and Discontent: India's Growing Crisis of Governability* (Cambridge and New York: Cambridge University Press, 1991).

Nugent, Nicholas, *Rajiv Gandhi: Son of a Dynasty* (London: BBC Books, 1990/New York: BBC–Parkwest, 1990).

Pandey, Gyanendra, *The Construction of Communalism in Colonial North India* (New Delhi: Oxford University Press, 1990/New York: Oxford University Press., 1991).

Rudolph, Lloyd I. and Rudolph, Susanne Hoeber, *In Pursuit of Lakshmi: The Political Economy of the Indian State* (Chicago: University of Chicago Press, 1987).

Sarkar, Sumit, *et al.*, *Khaki Shorts and Saffron Flags* (New Delhi: Orient Longman, 1993).

Shiva, Vandana, *The Violence of the Green Revolution: Third World Agriculture, Ecology and Politics* (Penang: Third World Network, 1991/New York: Humanities–Zed, 1991).

Tully, Mark, *No Full Stops in India* (London: BBC Books, 1991). Published in the USA as *The Defeat of a Congressman and Other Parables of Modern India* (New York: Knopf, 1992).

Tully, Mark and Jacob, Satish, *Amritsar: Mrs Gandhi's Last Battle* (London: Jonathan Cape, 1985).

Index

Abdali, Ahmad Shah 57
Abdullah, Farooq 21
Abdullah, Sheikh Mohammad 105
abortion 26
action groups xliii, 201–5
Advani, L. K. xxvii–xxx
advertising 78
Afghanistan xxxv, xli–xlii, 150
Afghans 59–60
Air India 206, 211
Akal Takht xxxiv
Akali Dal xxxii, xxxv–xxxvi, 10, 19, 33, 60, 69, 74–7, 90, 92, 94, 106, 108, 111, 114–15, 118, 121, 127–8, 130–2, 136-7, 141, 146, 153, 155–6, 160–2, 164, 168–9, 173–4, 176–7, 179, 185–6, 190, 198, 206–10, 212; blocks roads, 1983, 165–6; coalition, 1977–80, 86, 125–6; changes character, 110, 119; Congress and, 99, 113; factions in, 143; founded, 65; opposes 'emergency', 116; Second World War and, 68; SGPC elections and, 139; talks with centre, 153-9; youth wing, 175
Akbar, Emperor 52–4
Akbar, M. J. 168
Akhand Kirtani Jatha 175
Alexander the Great 36, 50, 95
Alexander, Dr P. C. 154
All-India Anna Dravida Munnetra Kazhagam (AIADMK) 197
All-India Sikh Students' Federation (AISSF) 14, 139, 144, 162, 175, 178; banned, 180
Amarindar Singh xxxvi, 42, 163, 181, 210
Amarjit Kaur 175
Amethi 17
Amrik Singh 139, 141, 144, 175; arrested, 162–3
Amritsar xxxv, 9–10, 36, 41, 46–7, 53, 57, 64–5, 69, 73, 85, 109, 129, 132, 138, 141, 143–5, 150, 161–4, 167–8, 172, 180–1; procession in, 1956, 106–7
'Analyst' 136, 186
Anandpur Sahib 77, 91, 126–9
Anandpur Sahib Resolution 144, 158, 164–5, 169
Andhra Pradesh 7–8, 19–22, 104, 142, 156, 189, 191, 196, 200; elections, 1982 and 1985, 8
Anglo-Indians xxxii
Anjiah, T. 196
Arabic 102
Ardas 40, 56
Arjan, Guru 53–4, 73, 134
arms *see* weapons
army xxxii, 30, 38, 41, 93, 133, 181, 195; deployed in Punjab, 174, 180; mutiny in, 1984, 148–9; Sikhs in, 62–3, 66, 148–9
Aroras 48
Arun Singh 42
Arya Samaj 89
Aryans 36
Asian Games 152, 154–6, 158, 164
Assam 7, 22, 156, 187, 209
assassinations: notable Indian xxx, 183
Atwal, Avtar Singh 166–7, 170–1, 174
Aurora, Jagjit Singh 116, 148, 210
Australia xxxix, 1, 63, 120, 122, 184, 190–1
Ayodhya xxi, xxiii, xxvii–xxx, xli–xlii, xlv

Babari Masjid (mosque) xxi, xxvii; destruction of, xxix-xxx
Babbar Khalsa 175, 178–9, 211
Babur, Emperor 51
Badal, Parkash Singh xxxiii-xxxiv, 92, 94, 114, 117, 119, 125–7, 131–2, 138–40, 145, 159, 164, 173, 183, 186, 210; ancestral lands, 161; background, 118; burns constitution,

243